The Savage Years

Tales From the 20th Century

Rupert Colley

Rupert Colley

Rupert Colley was born one Christmas Day and grew up in Devon. A history graduate, he worked as a librarian in London before starting 'History In An Hour' – a series of non-fiction history ebooks that can be read in just sixty minutes, acquired by Harper Collins in 2011. Now a full time writer, speaker and the author of historical novels, he lives in Waltham Forest, London with his wife, two children and dog.

Titles by Rupert Colley:

Fiction:
My Brother the Enemy
The Black Maria
This Time Tomorrow
The Torn Flag
The White Venus
The Woman on the Train
The Unforgiving Sea

History In An Hour series:
1914: History In An Hour
Black History: History In An Hour
D-Day: History In An Hour
Hitler: History In An Hour
Mussolini: History In An Hour
Nazi Germany: History In An Hour
Stalin: History In An Hour
The Afghan Wars: History In An Hour
The Cold War: History In An Hour
The Russian Revolution: History In An Hour
The Siege of Leningrad: History In An Hour
World War One: History In An Hour
World War Two: History In An Hour

History of the World Cup
The Savage Years: Tales From the 20th Century

The Savage Years:
Tales From the 20th Century

Rupert Colley

Historyinanhour.com
Rupertcolley.com

Contents

Introduction   1

1   21 January 1924, the Death of Vladimir Lenin   3
2   23 January 1930, the Birth of Tanya Savicheva, young victim   8
    of the Leningrad Siege
3   27 January, Holocaust Memorial Day, the 'Jews Out' Board   12
    Game
4   29 January 1928, the Death of Douglas Haig   15
5   30 January 1933, Hitler Appointed Chancellor   20
6   30 January 1945, the Sinking of the *Wilhelm Gustloff*, the   25
    Worst Maritime Disaster In History
7   2 February 1943, the Germans Surrender at the Battle of   31
    Stalingrad
8   13 February 1945, the Bombing of Dresden   37
9   21 February 1965, the Assassination of Malcolm X   44
10 23 February 1930, the Making of a Nazi Martyr, Horst   50
    Wessel
11 27 February 1881, the Death of the Cleverest General, Sir   54
    George Pomeroy Colley
12 27 February 1933, the Reichstag Fire   58
13 8 March 1655, John Casor Becomes the First Legally-   63
    Recognised Slave
14 15 March 1938, the Execution of Nikolai Bukharin   66
15 21 March 1960, the Sharpeville Massacre   73
16 10 April 1971, Ping Pong Diplomacy During the Cold War   76
17 22 April 1915, Fritz Haber and the First Successful Gas   79
    Attack
18 30 April 1945, the Death of Adolf Hitler   84
19 1 May 1945, the Suicide of Joseph Goebbels, the Not-So-   89
    Great German novelist
20 2 May 1957, the Death of Joseph McCarthy   93

21   3 May 1975, the Death of Dmitri Bystrolyotov, Stalin's   97
Romeo Spy

22   6 May 1937, the Hindenburg Disaster   100

23   9 May 1946, the Abdication of Italy's Victor Emmanuel III   104

24   10 May 1857, the Start of the Indian Mutiny   109

25   10 May 1941, Rudolph Hess Arrives in Scotland   114

26   24 May 1941, the Sinking of HMS *Hood*   119

27   4 June 1937, the Death of Ekaterina Dzhugashvili, Stalin's   123
Mother

28   16 June 1953, the Start of the East German Uprising   125

29   16 June 1958, the Execution of Imre Nagy   129

30   18 June 1974, the Death of Georgy Zhukov   135

31   20 June 1756, the Black Hole of Calcutta   139

32   22 June 1940, France Surrenders   144

33   22 June 1941, Hitler Launches Operation Barbarossa,   151
Germany's Invasion of Russia

34   28 June 1914, the Assassination of Archduke Franz   156
Ferdinand

35   30 June 1934, the Night of the Long Knives   162

36   1 July 1916, the First Day of the Battle of the Somme   166

37   4 August 1944, the Betrayal of Anne Frank   170

38   9 August 1942, the Greatest Performance: The Leningrad   176
Symphony

39   19 August 1969, the East German Athlete Who Made a   181
Dash for Freedom

40   20 August 1968, the USSR Invades Czechoslovakia   188

41   21 August 1940, the Assassination of Leon Trotsky   193

42   30 August 1918, Fanny Kaplan Tries to Kill Lenin   198

43   31 August 1939, World War Two's First Death   202

44   18 September 1931, the Suicide of Geli Raubal, Hitler's   205
Niece

45   12 October 1915, the Execution of British Nurse, Edith   210
Cavell

46   15 October 1946, the Suicide of Hermann Goring   214

47   20 October 1952, the Start of the Mau Mau Uprising   220

48   23 October 1956, the Start of the Hungarian Revolution   224

49   27 October 1962, the Cuban Missile Crisis   230

50	30 October 1979, the Death of Rachele Mussolini	236
51	8 November 1939, Georg Elser Almost Assassinates Hitler	243
52	9 November 1970, the Death of Charles de Gaulle	248
53	10 November 1918, the Abdication of Kaiser Wilhelm II	254
54	19 November 1863, Abraham Lincoln Delivers His Gettysburg Address	259
55	22 November 2011, the Death of Svetlana Alliluyeva, Stalin's Daughter	263
56	Winston Churchill, born 30 November 1874, and the First World War	268
57	7 December 1941, Pearl Harbor, the Day of Infamy	274
58	23 December 1953, the Execution of Lavrenty Beria	280
59	23 December 1948, the Execution of Hideki Tojo	284
60	30 December 1916, the Assassination of Grigory Rasputin	287
	Selected Bibliography	295
	Other Works by Rupert Colley	299
	Images and Disclaimers	303
	Index	305

Introduction

In 2009, I wrote a short book on the Second World War. Intended for the beginner, the idea was to provide a basic outline of the war without the reader having to invest a huge amount of time and effort. I called it *World War Two In An Hour*. Then, having written it, I decided I needed a website. Launched in December 2009, History In An Hour was born.

Over the years, as well as writing more titles for the series, published by Harper Collins in the UK, I wrote some 200 articles for the website. Sixty of these articles form this collection. I've updated and expanded most, if not all, of them. The suicide of Hitler's niece, World War Two's first victim, the killing of Rasputin, the assassinations of Malcolm X and Franz Ferdinand, the Battle of the Somme, the betrayal of Anne Frank and the woman who almost killed Lenin – these are just some of the articles within this book.

Despite the subtitle, *Tales From the 20th Century*, there are, in fact, five articles from before and one, the death in 2011 of Stalin's daughter, from after. But calling it *Tales Mostly From the 20th Century* wouldn't have had the same ring.

I may, one day, gather and update another sixty articles and produce a volume two.

But until then, if it happens at all, I hope you enjoy volume one…

Rupert Colley

1.
21 January 1924,
The Death of Vladimir Lenin

On 21 January 1924, Vladimir Lenin, the leader of the Russian Bolshevik Revolution, died aged only 53.

Today I shot at Lenin

Five and a half years previously, on 30 August 1918, Lenin survived an assassination attempt. His would-be killer, 28-year-old Fanny Kaplan, a Socialist Revolutionary, shot at him three times, hitting Lenin twice – in the jaw and the neck. Interrogated by the Cheka, the state's secret police, Kaplan said, 'Today I shot at Lenin. I did it on my own. I will not say from whom I obtained my revolver. I will give no details.' She was executed on 3 September. Lenin survived but was weakened by his injuries which, less than six years later, contributed to his early death.

One of the bullets fired into Lenin by Kaplan was only removed in April 1922. The effect of his wounds, together with the strains of revolution, civil war, uprisings and forging a new country, took its toll on Lenin. His workload as head of state was enormous and in latter years he suffered increasingly from fatigue and headaches. He suffered his first stroke in May 1922 which temporarily deprived him of speech and impeded his movement. Six months later he returned to work, albeit on a lighter schedule.

Vladimir Lenin, 1918. German Federal Archives.

Lenin's Testament

A second stroke in December 1922 obliged Lenin to retire from politics to his dacha in the village of Gorki, six miles south of Moscow, and where Joseph Stalin became a frequent visitor. Recuperating, Lenin had to learn to write with his left hand.

While convalescing from his second stroke, Lenin wrote his 'Testament', in which he proposed changes to the structure of the party's Central Committee and commented on its individual members, including Leon Trotsky and Nikolai Bukharin. Of Trotsky, for example, Lenin describes him as *'distinguished not only by outstanding ability. He is personally perhaps the most capable man in the present C.C., but he has displayed excessive self-assurance and shown excessive preoccupation with the purely administrative side of the work.'*

But his most severe criticism was reserved for Stalin whom he had in April 1922 appointed as the party's General Secretary. Lenin was regretting his haste, questioning the amount of authority placed in Stalin's hands: *'I suggest the comrades think about a way of removing Stalin from that post and appointing*

4

another man in his stead who in all other respects differs from Comrade Stalin in having only one advantage, namely, that of being more tolerant, more loyal, more polite, and more considerate to the comrades, less capricious, etc.'

Lenin with Joseph Stalin, 1922.

Entrusted to his wife, Nadezhda Krupskaya, Lenin's Testament was due to be read out at the Twelfth Party Congress in April 1923 but, fatefully, Krupskaya kept it secret in the hope that her husband would recover. He did not.

Poison

A third stroke in March 1923 left Lenin bedridden and took away for good his ability to speak. Such was the pain experienced by Lenin during his final months, that he begged Stalin to obtain a dose of potassium cyanide to put him out of his misery. He specifically asked Stalin, probably because he knew that only Stalin, a man so devoid of any humanity, would be strong enough to do it. But even Stalin baulked at the thought of it and couldn't bring himself to administer the fatal dose: 'I do not have the strength to carry out Ilyich's (Lenin) request and I have to decline this mission, however humane and necessary it might be'.

Despite his apparent squeamishness, it was not beyond Stalin's reach to have poisoned his former mentor, especially as his own position was at risk following Lenin's damning indictment of him. Poisoning was one of Stalin's favourite methods of dealing with his opponents and the suspicion has always remained that he may have had a hand in Lenin's demise. As Bukharin once said of Stalin, 'Koba (Stalin's revolutionary nickname) is capable of anything'. Indeed, during his final hours, Lenin suffered a number of violent seizures. Seizures are not associated with strokes – but they are with poison.

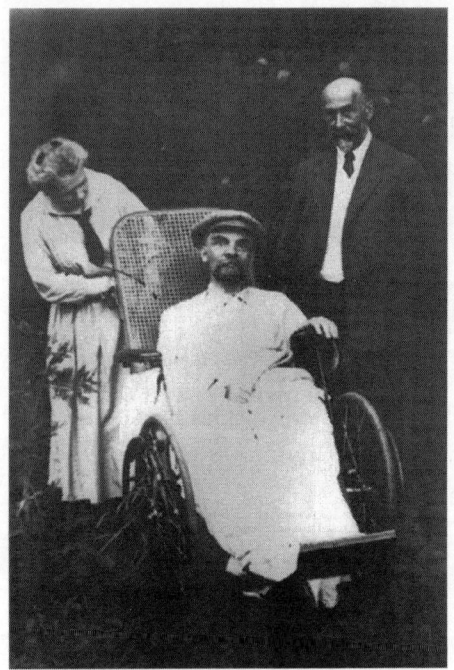

Last known photograph of Vladimir Lenin, 15 May 1923.

Lenin's Funeral

Following Lenin's death on 21 January 1924, Stalin led the funeral arrangements, ensuring he maintained a high profile, acting as the lead pallbearer and chief mourner. Lenin lay in state for four days in Moscow's House of Unions, during which time almost a million mourners paid their respects.

Trotsky, Stalin's rival for power, who was recovering from illness near the Black Sea, missed the funeral – having been told the wrong date by the scheming Stalin.

The Cult of Lenin

Following his death, Lenin's brain was removed and kept in formaldehyde for two years before being sliced into 30,963 wafer-thin slices to be studied and examined in minute detail to work out how the brain of a genius worked. Despite Nadezhda Krupskaya's objections, Lenin's corpse was embalmed and placed in a wooden mausoleum in Moscow's Red Square. In October 1930, he was placed in the marble and granite mausoleum that for 60 years became the 'mecca' of communism and where it still remains to this day.

Stalin instigated an era of deferential religious-like worship for the Great Leader of the Revolution in which Lenin's image was seen everywhere and his memory held in reverential terms. In every town, statues were erected; his word was taken as gospel and unquestioned – the cult of Lenin had begun. Lenin himself would not have approved of this hero worship, once stating, 'Wherever you look, they are writing about me. I consider this un-Marxist emphasis on the individual extremely harmful.'

But through his devotion to Lenin, Stalin was able to establish himself as Lenin's pupil, the successor of Lenin's great vision. To question Stalin was to doubt Lenin's wisdom and thereby question the legitimacy of the revolution, an act of heresy not tolerated by the regime. Through Lenin, Stalin gained the initiative.

The era of Vladimir Lenin was at an end; the era of Joseph Stalin was about to begin. It was to last almost thirty years.

2.
23 January 1930,
The Birth of Tanya Savicheva,
young victim of the Leningrad Siege

Tanya Savicheva died near her hometown of Leningrad on 1 July 1944, aged only 14. But who was Tanya Savicheva? The name in Russia is what Anne Frank is to the West – a young innocent victim of World War Two, who left behind a small but lasting legacy.

But whereas Anne's legacy is a diary carefully kept over a period of two years, Tanya's was little more than a few scribbled lines over six sheets of notepaper.

Leningrad Siege

Leningrad (modern-day St Petersburg) was in the midst of a devastating 900-day blockade that lasted from September 1941 until January 1944. The German army had laid siege to the city, bombarded it and cut off all supplies in its attempt to 'wipe it off the map', as Hitler had ordered.

The Savicheva family had all answered the call to help bolster the city's defences. Tanya, only 11 years old, helped dig anti-tank trenches. On 12 September 1941, the largest food warehouse, the Badayev, was destroyed, bombed with German incendiaries. Three thousand tons of flour burned, thousands of tons of grain went up in smoke, meat frazzled, butter melted, sugar turned molten and seeped into the cellars. 'The streets that night ran with melted chocolate,' said one witness, 'and the air was rich and sticky with the smell of burning sugar.' The situation, already severe, became critical.

Tanya Savicheva, c1936

The Road of Life

As winter approached, Lake Ladoga, to the east of the city, froze. From December 1941, supplies of foodstuffs, fuel and medicine came through by convoys of trucks, a hazardous journey over thin ice and through enemy bombardment. But what was brought in on this 'Road of Life', although vital, was only ever a fraction of what was needed.

Within the city, as that first winter progressed, whatever could be eaten had been consumed – pets, livestock, birds and vermin. And whatever could be burnt had been used for firewood. Tanya had kept a thick diary but this, as with every other book in the household, had been used for fuel – except for a slim notebook.

The youngest of five children, Tanya Savicheva's father had died when she was six. Tanya, her mother and her siblings, in common with every citizen of Leningrad during the siege, suffered terribly from hunger and cold. One winter's day, Tanya's sister, Nina, 12 years older, failed to return. The family assumed that like so many hundreds of others, she had succumbed and died. In fact, Nina had been evacuated out of the city across Lake Ladoga at a moment's notice. She returned to the city only after the war.

Savichevs died

One by one, the remaining members of Tanya's family died, and it was recording of each death that constituted the notebook.

The first entry recorded the death of Tanya's sister, Zhenya, who died at midday on 28 December 1941. Others were to follow until the sixth and final death, that of Tanya's mother, on 13 May 1942. A neighbour described the tragic figure of this young girl, Tanya:

'When Tanya lost everyone, she became deranged with grief. She would clutch at a small house plant, which had only a few withered leaves left, and was virtually dead. Somehow, it seemed to remind Tanya of her family. She would stand by her stove, swaying from side to side, holding it close to her, in a terrible trance. She was trying to bring it back to life.'

Tanya herself was eventually evacuated out of the city in August 1942, along with about 150 other children, to a village called Shatki. But whilst most of the others recovered and lived, Tanya, already too ill, died of tuberculosis on 1 July 1944.

Her notebook was presented as evidence of Nazi terror at the post-war Nuremberg Trials, and today is on display at the History Museum in St Petersburg.

The text of Tanya's notebook reads as follows:

Zhenya died on Dec. 28th at 12:00 P.M. 1941
Grandma died on Jan. 25th 3:00 P.M. 1942
Leka died on March 5th at 5:00 A.M. 1942
Uncle Vasya died on Apr. 13th at 2:00 after midnight 1942
Uncle Lesha on May 10th at 4:00 P.M. 1942
Mother on May 13th at 7:30 A.M. 1942
Savichevs died.
Everyone died.
Only Tanya is left.

Pages from Tanya Savicheva's notebook.

3.
27 January, Holocaust Memorial Day:
The 'Jews Out' Board Game

The Wiener Library in London has on display a macabre board game intended to be a bit of fun for your average family living in 1930s Nazi Germany. It is called *Juden Raus!* 'Jews Out!' – with an exclamation mark. The object of the Jews Out board game is to force the Jews beyond the medieval walls and out the city. The first player to rid the city of six Jews wins the game.

The game comes with a dice, a 50×60 cm board and a number of figurines. The board has thirteen circles representing various Jewish-owned shops and businesses. Each player adopts one of six red figurines with a pointy hat and a belt around its waist, representing the German police force, and the idea is to land on the Jewish business and eject the Jew. The Jew is represented by 32 hat-shaped counters, the same shape as the hats Jews were compelled to wear during the Middle Ages. Each Jew is depicted with a vile, contorted face.

The rules explain that the Jews Out board game is an 'extraordinarily amusing and up-to-date family game'. On the board are written three bits of text: *Display skill in the dice game, so that you collect many Jews! / When you succeed in driving out 6 Jews, you will be winner beyond all question!* And at the bottom right, a 'typical' Jewish family on the move accompanied by the text, *Off to Palestine!*

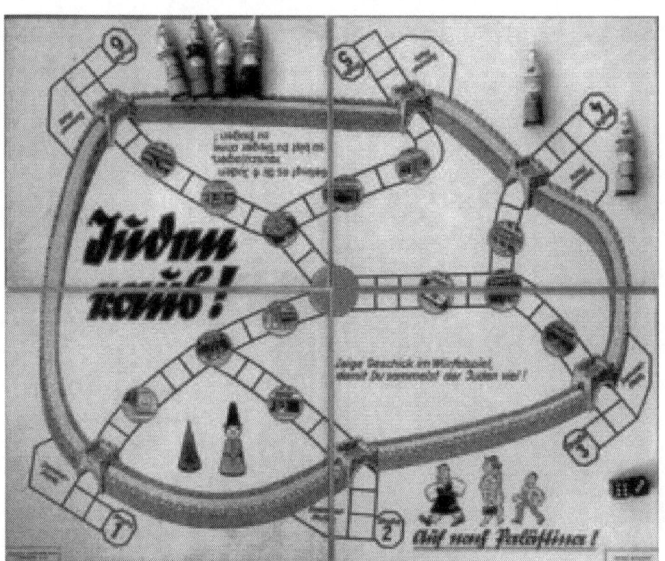

The 'Jews Out!' board game. Photographed by the author.

As well as the copy at the Wiener library, the only other copy of the game known to have survived intact is on display at New York's Museum of Jewish Heritage.

Trivial

This vile little game was produced by a Dresden-based company called Günther & Co. in 1936 and was not actually sanctioned by the Nazi party; it was purely a commercial venture, hoping to capitalize on the anti-Semitic hysteria sweeping through Germany at the time. The game never received official Nazi approval. Indeed, Heinrich Himmler's SS thoroughly disapproved of the game, criticizing it for trivializing their work: 'We do not slave ourselves away with the solution of the Jewish question, to relieve toy manufacturers of their worries about a big seller or to entertain children with an amusing little game.'

The Wiener Library

Named after its founder, Alfred Wiener, the Wiener Library is, to use their words, *'one of the world's leading and most extensive archives on the Holocaust and*

Nazi era. Formed in 1933, the Library's unique collection of over one million items includes published and unpublished works, press cuttings, photographs and eyewitness testimony'.

4.
29 January 1928,
The Death of Douglas Haig

Douglas Haig, Britain's First World War commander-in-chief from December 1915 to the end of the war, is remembered as the archetypal 'donkey' leading 'lions' to their death by the thousands. But, a century on, is this a fair judgment?

Born in Edinburgh, 19 June 1861, Douglas Haig was the eleventh son of a wealthy whiskey distiller. An expert horseman, he once represented England at polo. In 1898, he joined the forces of Lord Kitchener in the Sudan and, the following year, he served under Sir John French in Kitchener's army during the Second Boer War.

During the first year of the First World War, Haig served as a deputy to John French, the commander-in-chief of the British Expeditionary Force. Haig's actions at the Battle of Mons and the First Battle of Ypres earned him praise while, conversely, John French's fortunes plummeted following the Battle of Loos. Haig contributed to the drive to have the mood-swinging French removed and, in turn, in December 1915, was appointed by Prime Minister Herbert Asquith as French's replacement.

Cavalry man

A Presbyterian and firmly believing that God was on his side and therefore his decisions had to be right, Haig insisted on full frontal attacks, convinced that victory would come by military might alone. Still a cavalry man at heart, he believed the machine gun to be a 'much overrated weapon'. It is one of the criticisms levelled at Haig – that he was adverse to new technology. The evidence is contradictory. Almost a decade after the war, Haig still believed in the use of cavalry: *'I believe that the value of the horse and the opportunity for the horse in the future are likely to be as great as ever. Aeroplanes and tanks are only accessories to the men and the horse, and I feel sure that as time goes on you will find just as much use for the horse – the well-bred horse – as you have ever done in the past.'*

Douglas Haig, c1913. Library of Congress.

But Douglas Haig did back the introduction of the new 'landship', as the prototype tank was originally known. On 15 September 1916, during the Battle of the Somme, Haig ordered these new weapons onto the battlefield. Although many broke down, Haig was impressed enough to order a thousand more.

Butcher Haig?

Haig has often been criticized of being profligate of men's lives. His tenure as c-in-c saw the horrendous losses at the Battle of the Somme (July-November 1916) and the Third Battle of Ypres, otherwise known as

Passchendaele, (July-November 1917). One private wrote, 'Haig's nickname was the butcher. He'd think nothing of sending thousands of men to certain death. The utter waste and disregard for human life and human suffering by the so-called educated classes who ran the country. What a wicked waste of life. I'd hate to be in their shoes when they face their Maker.'

Douglas Haig as painted by Sir William Orpen, 1917.

David Lloyd George, prime minister of a coalition government from December 1916, had questioned the point of launching another costly offensive at Passchendaele but Haig had got the backing of the Conservatives within the coalition and so got his way. But Haig was often under pressure of his French allies to act, bringing forward, for example, the Somme offensive by six weeks to help take the pressure off the French at the long slug that was the Battle of Verdun. The question remains however would the extra six weeks to prepare made a difference? – the answer is probably not.

Historian, Basil Henry Liddell Hart, who fought during the war, described Haig as 'not merely immoral but criminal'. Yet the very nature of warfare during 1914-1918 meant that offence was no match against deeply entrenched defence. Haig was not alone – generals on all sides puzzled over this uncomfortable truth.

While Douglas Haig is remembered for the losses at the Somme and Passchendaele, it is often forgotten that from August 1918, he oversaw Britain's advance during what became known as the Hundred Days Offensive, the Allies' great push, in partnership with the overall Allied commander, the French c-in-c, Ferdinand Foch. The offensive ultimately led to victory and the surrender of the Germans on 11 November.

A land fit for heroes

Despite having a personal rapport with the king, George V, Haig never enjoyed the confidence of Lloyd George, who was openly critical of Haig's cavalier attitude with his men's lives. Lloyd George, in his *War Memoirs*, published in 1936, accused Haig of being 'second rate'. 'When he had to fight battles in quagmires he had never seen and over an area extending to a hundred miles which he never did or could personally inspect, he was lost.'

But by then Haig was dead and unable to defend himself.

It was Lloyd George, who during the election campaign of 1918, had promised a land 'fit for heroes to live in'. But it was Haig who did much to help veterans. In 1921, Haig was one of the founders of the Royal British Legion, becoming its first president, a post he held until his death, and helped introduce the poppy of remembrance into Britain. He championed the rights of ex-servicemen and refused all state honours until the government improved their pensions, which duly came in August 1919. (Only then did Haig accept an earldom).

On 29 January 1928, Douglas Haig died from a heart attack brought on, according to his widow, by the strain of wartime command. He was 66.

Haig's reticence certainly didn't help his own cause – prone to long silences and often coming across as callous. One journalist at the time described him as 'shy as a schoolgirl'. But at war's end, Haig was hailed as a hero, and his death saw much public grief, especially in his hometown of Edinburgh, and London, where up to a million people turned out to pay their respects.

Beastly attitudes

Haig's only son, Dawyck Haig, who was imprisoned in Colditz during the

Second World War and who died in 2009, was a staunch defender of his father. In an interview to the BBC in June 2006, the eve of the 90th anniversary of the first day of the Somme, he said, 'He was not a brutish man, he was a very kind, wonderful man and by God, I miss him... I believe it has now turned full circle and people appreciate his contribution. But it saddens me my three sisters have not survived to see it. They died suffering from the beastly attitudes of the public towards our father.'

The Douglas Haig statue, Whitehall, London.
Photographed by the author.

In 1937, a bronze statue of Douglas Haig, the Earl Haig Memorial, was unveiled on London's Whitehall. Designed by sculptor, Alfred Frank Hardiman, and eight years in the making, it won many plaudits and prizes but unfortunately, the stance of the horse is that of one in the process of urinating.

5.
30 January 1933,
Hitler appointed Chancellor

On 30 January 1933, Adolf Hitler was appointed Chancellor of Germany. The supposed one thousand year Reich had started, although it would be another nineteen months before Hitler achieved absolute power.

1932 Germany saw the rise of the Nazi party into a prominent political force. The Weimar government had failed its people and, following the worldwide depression, Germany was in economic ruin, people's livelihoods shattered and the nation still burdened with the humiliation of the post-First World War Treaty of Versailles. Many Germans, fearful of Communists and Jews, looked for an alternative and that alternative seemed to lay in Adolf Hitler and the Nazi Party.

Elections

In the July 1932 Reichstag elections, the Nazi party gained almost 40 per cent of the vote making it the most powerful party in Germany. There was a slight dip in the elections four months later but the party still had enough electoral clout that Hitler, as dictated by the Weimar constitution, should have been appointed chancellor.

Hitler and President Paul von Hindenburg, 1 May 1933.
German Federal Archives.

But the Weimar president, the 85-year-old Paul von Hindenburg, was reluctant to appoint the former corporal: 'That man a chancellor?' he exclaimed, 'I'll make him a postmaster and he can lick stamps with my head on them.'

Franz von Papen, Hindenburg's former chancellor, who believed the Nazis were already a spent force after the dip in the Nazi vote in November 1932, decided to work with Hitler (or rather his objective was to manipulate the Nazi leader). Hitler would become chancellor and Papen would serve as his vice chancellor.

Justice to everyone

But the real power, Papen persuaded the aging president, would be himself. Hitler, Papen argued, needed to be contained and this would be far easier with Hitler working inside the government than agitating from outside. 'In two months,' said Papen, 'we'll have pushed Hitler into a corner where he can squeal to his heart's content.'

Reluctantly, Hindenburg agreed.

Adolf Hitler, 1933. German Federal Archives.

And so on 30 January 1933, Hitler was appointed Chancellor within a coalition government. At around noon, Hitler took his oath: '*I will employ my strength for the welfare of the German people, protect the Constitution and laws of the German people, conscientiously discharge the duties imposed on me, and conduct my affairs of office impartially and with justice to everyone*'. Yes, Hitler promised to respect the German constitution with justice for all.

He had done it – Hitler had achieved what he had striven for since 1923 following the failed attempt to seize power by force, the Munich *Putsch* – power through legitimate means.

The new Reich has been born

That evening Hitler looked out from his balcony at the Chancellery. Below him filed passed thousands of torch-bearing Nazis, singing the Nazi anthem, the *Horst Wessel* song (so named after a martyr of the Nazi cause). This was their moment of triumph, the day of national exultation; the Nazi era had begun and their mood was jubilant. That evening, an ecstatic Joseph Goebbels wrote his in diary, '*It is almost like a dream – a fairy tale. The new*

Reich has been born. Fourteen years of work have been crowned with victory. The German revolution has begun!'

Not everyone however was delighted by the turn of events. Hindenburg's old wartime partner, Erich Ludendorff, who had been at Hitler's side during the Munich *Putsch*, wrote to the president: *'By appointing Hitler Chancellor of the Reich you have handed over our sacred German Fatherland to one of the greatest demagogues of all time. I prophesy to you this evil man will plunge our Reich into the abyss and will inflict immeasurable woe on our nation. Future generations will curse you in your grave for this action.'*

Franz von Papen, 1936. German Federal Archives.

Meanwhile, Papen was to soon realise the folly of his intrigue – it was he, not Hitler, who was pushed into a corner and became an inconsequential figure. He was fortunate to survive Hitler's murderous purge, the Night of the Long Knives, in which close associates of Papen's, including his speechwriter, were shot. In 1934, he was shunted off to serve as German ambassador first in Vienna then later, during the war, in Turkey.

He lived to the age of 89, dying in Germany on 2 May 1969.

The Road to Ruin

But for Hitler in January 1933, the road to absolute power had only just begun. The fortuitous (or not) Reichstag Fire, a month later, followed by the Enabling Act in March 1933 which, despite his oath, allowed Hitler to dispense with the German constitution, augmented his power. But it was the death of President Hindenburg, in August 1934, that allowed Hitler to establish his dictatorial rule. The road to ruin lay ahead.

6.
30 January 1945,
The Sinking of the *Wilhelm Gustloff*,
the Worst Maritime Disaster In History

30 January 1945 – nine hours after leaving port and seventy minutes after being hit, the huge liner, the *Wilhelm Gustloff*, slipped under the waves and sunk. A small fleet of ships and boats arrived on the scene and managed to pluck a few survivors from the icy Baltic waters and rescued many of those on the lifeboats. Over a thousand were rescued but… an estimated 9,343 people died, half of them children – six times the 1,517 that died on the *Titanic* in 1912.

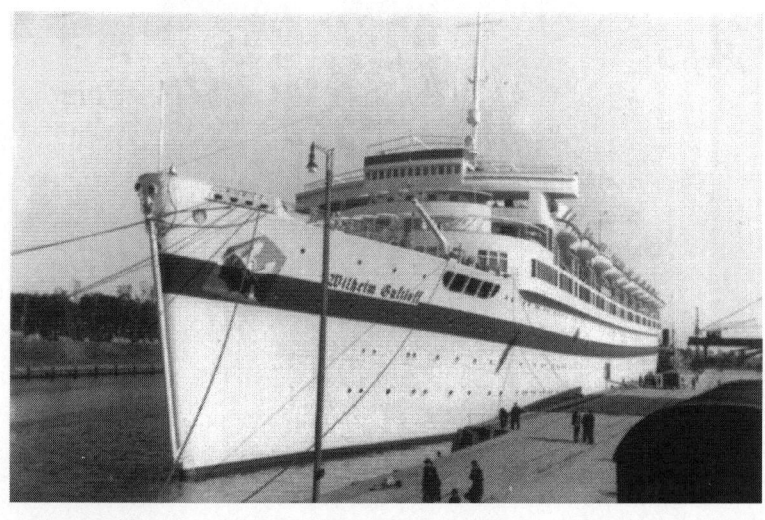

The sinking of the *Wilhelm Gustloff* remains the biggest maritime disaster in history.

We have all heard of the *Titanic*. A century after that fateful night, the disaster remains within our global consciousness. Even before James Cameron's epic 1998 film, we knew of the iceberg, the 'women and children first', and the band that played on.

But how many of us have even heard of the *Wilhelm Gustloff*?

The Luxury Liner

The ship was named after the assassinated leader of the Swiss Nazi Party (yes, Switzerland in the 1930s had its own Nazi Party), murdered in his own home in February 1936.

Wilhelm Gustloff.

The ship, the *Wilhelm Gustloff*, weighing 25,000 tons and almost 700 feet in length, was an impressive sight, and could carry almost 2,000 passengers and crew. Launched in 1937, it began its life as a luxury cruise liner for the German workers of Hitler's Third Reich, and, until the outbreak of the Second World War, had sailed over fifty cruises.

Wartime

For the first year of the war the *Wilhelm Gustloff* served as a hospital ship before being held in dock in the port of Gotenhafen on the Baltic coast (modern-day Gdynia) where, until early 1945, it served as barracks for U-boat trainees.

Hitler had launched Operation Barbarossa, the invasion of the Soviet Union, in June 1941 and German forces had fought all the way to within sight of Moscow. But then the tide of war turned against the Nazis, and Stalin launched his own counterattack.

By October 1944, the Soviet Union's Red Army had fought the Germans out of the Soviet Union and broken through into East Prussia.

The Red Army Approaches

With the apocalyptic Red Army bearing down on them, the German civilians of East Prussia, desperate to get away, fled to the Baltic ports hoping to be evacuated out. Many of those caught in the maelstrom of the Soviet advance were murdered and raped.

The *Wilhelm Gustloff*, along with any other serviceable ship in the area, was pressed into service to aid the evacuation of German civilians. With forty-eight hours notice before departure, the scenes in frozen Gotenhafen were of panic as people, frantic for a place, fought on the dock and surged aboard the ship.

Evacuation

By the time it left, on 30 January, 10,582 people (40 per cent of whom were children) had crammed onto a ship designed for less than 2,000. Of the three designated military escorts, two broke down, leaving only one torpedo boat to accompany the huge liner. The ship had four captains who argued over the best course to take – shallow or deep waters, a straight line for speed or zig-zags to help avoid detection. Poor visibility, heavy snow and freezing temperatures further hampered progress.

When the captains were informed of a German minesweeper convoy coming towards them, they decided, after much argument, to switch on the navigation lights to avoid colliding into the convoy, but by doing so the ship also became visible to a Soviet submarine lurking nearby.

Hit

The submarine fired three torpedoes, each hitting its target. The ensuing scenes of panic cannot be imagined. Most of the lifeboats had frozen onto their davits, leaving only a few that could be put into use. As the ship listed to one side, many people were trapped below decks, others crushed in the stairways, while many fell into the freezing waters. Children drowned in lifejackets too big. People fought and clubbed each other to get onto the few available lifeboats, while many jumped to their deaths.

It was, coincidentally, the birthdate of Wilhelm Gustloff, born 30 January 1895. The day the ship sunk would have been his fiftieth birthday. It was also the twelfth anniversary of Hitler coming to power.

The sinking of the *Wilhelm Gustloff* on 30 January 1945 remains the greatest maritime disaster to ever have taken place. But why, when the tragic story of the *Titanic* is so known to us, does the *Wilhelm Gustloff* remain a forgotten catastrophe?

To help answer this, I quote from David F. Krawczyk, who has put together an excellent website, wilhelmgustloff.com, devoted to the subject. Below I paraphrase some of his observations:

1. The disaster occurred during wartime
Many view wartime disasters as less 'tragic' than those occurring during peacetime.

2. The victims were on the 'losing' side
Although the passengers were predominately civilian, they were German, and post-war sympathy for Germany was not overly forthcoming.

3. German war-guilt has repressed the disaster
A nation's war guilt and repression of memory has served to push the *Wilhelm Gustloff* into obscurity, although German writer and Nobel Prize winner, Gunter Grass, wrote of the disaster and the preceding assassination of Gustloff in his 2002 novel, *Crabwalk*.

4. Russian retribution for Nazi occupation

When the Nazis broke their pact with Stalin and invaded Soviet Russia in 1941, their tactics were often brutal. Hitler himself made it clear that this was a war different from that waged in the West, calling it a 'war of extermination'. When the tide eventually turned against Germany and the Soviets were marching towards Berlin, the Red Army showed no mercy – and exacted horrific revenge. Since the Soviets were in control of the Bay of Danzig both near the end of the war and for many years after, the Polish civilians were not allowed to mourn the loss of life on a German ship.

5. World sentiment regarding Nazi atrocities

As the world learned more about Nazi war crimes and systematic genocide, subdued global reaction to a disaster on this scale was perhaps understandable. Under other circumstances, 4,000 innocent children dying in a single disaster would certainly be mourned by almost anyone in a 'friendly' or 'enemy' nation.

6. The ship was named after a prominent Nazi leader

Wilhelm Gustloff was leader of the Nazi Party in Switzerland. David Krawczyk, on his site, wonders if the profile of the ship might have been higher if it had been named after a city or non-Nazi figure.

7. Demise of so many refugees (mostly women and children)

For months, the disaster remained largely unreported both inside and outside Germany. Inside the imploding Germany, Hitler wanted to suppress awareness about the death of so many. The Western Allies avoided it too; it would not have made for a popular news story where one of its allies had caused a disaster that had claimed the lives of so many women and children.

8. There is no American connection or Hollywood profile

Since comparisons are inevitable, we can see how the Titanic profile was raised even higher worldwide with an Academy-Award winning movie from Hollywood. Unlike the *Titanic*, the *Wilhelm Gustloff* was not sailing towards America, nor did it have any American passengers on its decks.

9. There were no rich victims on board

In another comparison to the *Titanic*, none of the *Wilhelm*

Gustloff passengers on the fateful voyage were rich or of society's elite. They were simply refugees trying to escape a terrible situation.

7.
2 February 1943,
The Germans Surrender at the Battle of Stalingrad

On 2 February 1943, in what is considered *the* turning point of the Second World War in Europe, the final remnants of the German Sixth Army surrendered at the Battle of Stalingrad, perhaps the bloodiest, fiercest battle ever fought.

Stalin's City

The city, originally called Tsaritsyn, was renamed Stalingrad, Stalin's city, in April 1925, in recognition of Joseph Stalin's leading role in saving the city from the counterrevolutionary 'Whites' during the Russian Civil War. (The fact that Leon Trotsky was more instrumental in saving Tsaritsyn was quietly forgotten). Considered important because of its supply of oil, the symbolic significance of Stalingrad, bearing the name of the Soviet leader, soon outweighed its strategic importance.

Not One Step Back
The Germans started their attack on Stalingrad, Operation Blue, on 28 June 1942. Led by the Sixth Army, Germany's largest wartime army commanded by General Friedrich Paulus, the Germans were fully expecting a total victory as they pushed the Soviet forces back.

Friedrich Paulus, June 1942. German Federal Archives.

The swift German advance alarmed Stalin so much, he issued his infamous 'Not One Step Back' directive of 28 July, ordering execution for the slightest sign of defeatism. Behind the Soviet frontlines roamed a second Soviet line ready to shoot any retreating 'cowards' or 'traitors of the Motherland'. As Georgy Zhukov, one of Stalin's top generals, said, 'In the Red Army it takes a very brave man to be a coward'.

By 23 August, the German advance had reached the outskirts of Stalingrad and, with 600 planes, unleashed a devastating aerial bombardment. Entering the city, the Germans, along with their Axis comrades, comprising of Italians, Romanians and Hungarians, fought the Soviets street for street, house for house, sometimes room for room. This, as the Germans called it, was rat warfare, where a strategic stronghold changed sides so many times people lost count, where the front lines were so close one could throw back a grenade before it exploded, where snipers took their toll on the enemy, and where a soldier's life expectancy was three days – if lucky.

Stalin charged Zhukov to defend the city and formulate a plan to repulse the invader. (It's worth noting here the difference between Stalin and Hitler as military leaders. After a series of blunders earlier in the war, Stalin, although he always like to take the credit, learnt to defer and listen to the experts, men like Zhukov. Hitler however always insisted he knew best and only canvassed the opinion of others if they agreed with him.)

On 19 November 1942, the Soviet Red Army launched Zhukov's meticulously-planned counteroffensive, attacking and sweeping in from two separate directions, a pincer movement. Within four days, the two-pronged Soviet attack had met in the middle and had totally encircled the beleaguered German forces. Their objective was achieved so quickly that the Soviet film crews missed the moment, and battalions of soldiers had to re-enact the essential scenes for the benefit of the cameras.

German soldiers on the streets of Stalingrad, October 1942.
German Federal Archives.

The Soviets squeezed the 250,000 Germans and their Axis comrades tighter and tighter. As the feared Russian winter set in and temperatures dropped to the minus forties, starvation, frostbite, disease and suicide decimated the Germans. Medical facilities were, at best, crude.

Unshakeable confidence

On Christmas Day 1942, with the temperature at –25 degrees Fahrenheit, Paulus received a message from Hitler: *'You should enter the New Year with the unshakeable confidence that I and the whole of the German* Wehrmacht *will do everything in our power to relieve the defenders of Stalingrad.'*

Whether Paulus and his staff believed it and took any comfort from Hitler's promise is doubtful. Either way reinforcements, although sent, were easily repulsed and the already hideous conditions only got worse. As one German officer put it, Stalingrad had become a 'mass grave of the *Wehrmacht*'. Even the cats and dogs had fled the city. But the Germans refused, at this point, to surrender for fear they'd be executed by the Russians.

A few German planes did manage to land within the city and were able to get troops out amidst scenes of panic, with hundreds of men fighting for the few remaining places whilst being shot at by the Soviets. (On one of the last flights out, Paulus sent his wedding ring back to his wife. He hadn't seen her since mid-1942 and would never see her again. She died in 1949).

Hitler continued to dictate strategy from far away in East Prussia with no sense of the reality on the ground, and sacking generals whose opinion differed from his. As one general recalled, 'The Fuhrer used to move his hands in big sweeps over the map – "Push here, push there". It was all vague and regardless of practical difficulties.'

Hermann Goring, his chief of the Luftwaffe, the German air force, promised Hitler that his planes could drop 500 tons of supplies each day into Stalingrad. But with Soviet anti-aircraft guns and poor weather against them, only a fraction, perhaps up to ten per cent, got through. The starving Germans resorted to eating rats and raw horseflesh. One German infantryman wrote in his diary, 'The horses have already been eaten. I would eat a cat; they say its meat is tasty. The soldiers look like corpses or lunatics. They no longer take cover from Russian shells; they haven't the strength to walk, run away and hide'. Frozen German corpses were piled up and used as sandbags.

Surrender

On 24 January, Paulus requested permission to surrender: *'Troops without ammunition or food. Effective command no longer possible. 18,000 wounded without any supplies or dressings or drugs. Further defence senseless. Collapse inevitable. Army requests immediate permission to surrender in order to save lives of remaining troops.'*

Hitler refused, saying it was the Sixth Army's historic duty to stand firm to the 'last man'.

The same day, Goring, equally as ignorant as his boss of the true situation, waxed lyrical: 'A thousand years hence Germans will speak of this battle with reverence and awe, and will remember that in spite of everything Germany's ultimate victory was decided there.'

By 26 January 1943, however, the Sixth Army was trapped within two small pockets of the city. Despite the hopeless situation, Hitler still forbade surrender. On the 30th, the tenth anniversary of his coming to power, Hitler promoted Paulus to the rank of field marshal on account that no German field marshal had ever surrendered. The following day, however, Paulus did.

Hitler, 1,000 miles away, was furious. Paulus, he shouted, '*could have freed himself from all sorrow and ascended into eternity and national immortality, but he prefers to go to Moscow ... What is life? Life is the Nation. The individual must die anyway ... What hurts me most, personally, is that I still promoted him to field marshal. I wanted to give him this final satisfaction. That's the last field marshal I shall appoint in this war.*'

As a Catholic, however, 'honourable' suicide was not an option for Paulus. Later, during captivity, he explained 'I [had] no intention of shooting myself for this Bohemian corporal' (referring to Hitler's highest army rank during the First World War).

A demoralised German soldier surrenders at Stalingrad, January 1943.
German Federal Archives.

Two days after Paulus' surrender, on 2 February 1943, the remnants of his stricken army also surrendered; the Battle of Stalingrad was lost.

Over a million soldiers on all sides had died in the city; over 90,000 Axis troops were taken prisoner of war, including, much to Stalin's delight, 22 German generals, many later paraded through the streets of Moscow. Up to half the prisoners died on the marches to the Soviet prisoner-of-war camps, and most of the other half died in captivity; only about 6,000 returned home on their eventual release in 1955; about six per cent of those captured during the battle of Stalingrad.

The Captive Field-Marshal

Friedrich Paulus was the Soviet Union's highest-ranking capture of the war. Later, during 1943, the Germans offered a swap – Paulus for Yakov Dzhugashvili, Stalin's son. (Stalin's real name was Dzhugashvili). Yakov had been serving as a lieutenant in the Red Army artillery when, on 16 July 1941, within a month of the Nazi invasion of the Soviet Union, he was captured by the Germans and taken prisoner. Stalin considered all prisoners as traitors to the motherland and those that surrendered he demonised as 'malicious deserters'. 'There are no prisoners of war,' he once said, 'only traitors to their homeland'. So, in response to the German offer, Paulus for his son, Stalin refused.

Following the failed assassination attempt on Hitler on 20 July 1944, Paulus, still a prisoner-of-war, became a leading opponent of Hitler's Germany, even going so far as to join the German anti-Nazi organization, the 'National Committee for a Free Germany'. Based in the Soviet Union, it called on Germans to desert Hitler for the sake of Germany's future and survival.

Post-war, Paulus appeared as a witness for the prosecution at the Nuremberg Trials. After ten years of captivity, he was released in 1953, and settled in the East German city of Dresden, where he died 1 February 1957, aged 66.

8.
13 February 1945,
The Bombing of Dresden

From about 10 pm on the night of 13 February 1945 until noon the following day, the East German city of Dresden was the subject of one the most intense bombing raids of the Second World War. Several German cities were targeted throughout the war but it is the bombing of Dresden, and its utter destruction, that came to symbolise the work of the RAF's Bomber Command and its commander, Sir Arthur Harris.

Florence of the Elbe

Germany's seventh largest city, 100 miles southeast of Berlin, Dresden was known as the 'Florence of the Elbe', such was its architectural splendour, its large collections of art and quaint timbered buildings. In February 1945, the city's population had been temporarily inflated by a huge influx of German refugees, perhaps up to 350,000, fleeing the Soviet advance sixty miles away to the east.

With only minimal anti-aircraft guns, few German troops, and limited war-related industry, Dresden was still deemed a legitimate target – for Arthur 'Bomber' Harris's intention was not so much military but 'moral bombing', to demoralise the civilian population and thereby shorten the war (despite evidence during the Blitz that instead of demoralising civilians, bombing only hardened resolve). The strategic objective of bombing Dresden and other cities in eastern Germany was, as agreed at the Anglo-

American Yalta Conference, to help alleviate the pressures on Soviet forces advancing into Germany on the Eastern Front.

Dresden, c1900. Library of Congress.

The Allied commanders studied aerial photographs of German cities and specifically targeted areas of heavy residential populations. His aim, said Harris, was to make the 'rubble bounce'.

Thus, on Tuesday, 13 February 1945, two waves of RAF Lancaster bombers, numbering 773 in total, attacked Dresden. The following morning, 527 bombers of the USAAF (US air force) attacked with the objective of hitting the fire fighters tackling the inferno caused by the RAF the previous evening and causing even greater chaos. Of all these aircraft, only eight were shot down.

Devastation

2,640 tons of bombs were dropped on Dresden, two thirds of which were incendiary bombs. A firestorm erupted in an area eight miles square reaching temperatures of 1,500 degrees centigrade engulfing the narrow, medieval streets. Ninety per cent of buildings within the city centre were destroyed, including over twenty hospitals. Smoke rose up to 15,000 feet.

Dresden had been obliterated.

The Allies knew that a bomb shelter or a cellar would only provide protection for about three hours before becoming unbearably hot and full of carbon monoxide, and so forcing the civilians back outside. Thus a second wave of bombs was dropped precisely three hours after the first batch – again to maximise the number of casualties. Many bombs were adapted so that they would explode hours after falling – the idea to cause maximum casualties against civilians who were trying to remove the devices. Air bombs were dropped with the intention of blowing off roof tiles, allowing incendiary bombs to fall unimpeded into the interior of buildings, and to blow out windows to allow greater ventilation to stoke the flames.

The RAF's Bomber Command bombing Dresden, February 1945.

People died from the lack of oxygen as the firestorm sucked the air out of the atmosphere. One witness described seeing people suddenly falling dead as if shot but, as she found later, they were dropping dead from the lack of oxygen. Many unfortunates jumped into a huge water tank hoping to escape the suffocating heat, only to find the water inside was boiling. 'Human beings were thrown to the ground or flung alive into the flames by winds which exceeded 150 mph,' wrote one witness.

The Dresden zookeeper wrote, 'The elephants gave spine-chilling screams. The baby cow elephant was lying in the narrow barrier-moat on her back, her legs up in the sky. She had suffered severe stomach injuries and could not move. A 90 cwt. cow elephant had been flung clear across the barrier moat and the fence by some terrific blast wave, and stood there trembling. I had no choice but to leave these animals to their fate.'

One witness described the city as a 'sea of flames'. Another described 'the hot wind of the firestorm (which) threw people back into the burning houses they were trying to escape from.' A labour camp inmate, a British soldier called Victor Gregg, incarcerated nearby, described the scene: 'As the incendiaries fell, the phosphorus clung to the bodies of those below, turning them into human torches. The screaming of those who were being burned alive was added to the cries of those not yet hit'.

But not all witnesses were horrified: one Jewish inmate of a German labour camp watched the sky burn bright over the city of Dresden: 'We were in heaven,' he wrote later. 'To all of us, it was absolute salvation. This was how we knew that the end (of the war) was near.'

Slaughterhouse-Five

The American novelist Kurt Vonnegut, who died in 2007, was a prisoner-of-war near Dresden, having been captured in December 1944 during the Battle of the Bulge. In the days following the raid on the city, Vonnegut and his fellow PoWs were put to work collecting bodies for burial while German civilians swore and threw stones at them. Eventually, wrote Vonnegut, 'there were too many corpses to bury. So instead the Germans sent in troops with flamethrowers. All these civilians' remains were burned to ashes.' Vonnegut's experiences in Dresden formed the backdrop of much of his work, including his most famous novel, *Slaughterhouse-Five*.

For the sake of increasing the terror

Estimates to how many died varied with the Nazis exaggerating the figure for propaganda purposes, but it is now accepted that some 25,000 lost their lives in this single raid.

During the blitz, Germany's bombardment of the UK, some 60,000 civilians lost their lives. The Allied bombing of Germany caused eight times that number of deaths. For every ton of bombs dropped by the Germans during the war, the Allies dropped 300.

Dresden destroyed, autumn 1945. Deutsche Fotothek

Although initially enthusiastic about the bombing raids, Winston Churchill tried to distance himself and, following Dresden, questioned Harris's methods of *'bombing German cities simply for the sake of increasing the terror ... The destruction of Dresden remains a serious query against the conduct of Allied bombing ... I feel the need for more precise concentration upon military objectives.'* Harris responded angrily that the attacks had been necessary in order to hasten the German surrender and diminish further allied casualties.

In 1956, Dresden was twinned with Coventry, a city that was heavily bombed several times during the early years of the war, most notably on 14 November 1940, at the height of the Blitz.

Bomber Harris

In his memoirs, *Bomber Offensive*, published 1947, Arthur Harris wrote, 'the attack on Dresden was at the time considered a military necessity by much more important people than myself.' In a televised interview from 1977, never broadcast and only rediscovered in 2013, Harris said: 'If I had to have the same time again I would do the same again, but I hope I wouldn't have to … The bombers kept over a million fit Germans out of the German army… Manning the anti-aircraft defences; making the ammunition, and doing urgent repairs, especially tradesmen.'

Sir Arthur Harris, 1944. Imperial War Museums.

One story has it that one evening, during the war, Harris was driving home when he was pulled up by a policeman on a motorbike. 'Sir, you're driving much too fast, you might kill someone.' To which, Harris replied, 'It's my business to kill people – Germans.' On realising who he was talking to, the policeman apologised and gave Harris a fast escort home.

Finally recognised

But whatever the morality of Bomber Command's work, its pilots faced a dangerous task: 55,573 British, Australian, New Zealand, Canadian and other Commonwealth pilots and crewmen lost their lives and 8,403 were wounded, a sixty per cent causality rate, far higher than most other forms of armed service during the war.

Post-war, those who fought with Bomber Command and survived were dismayed and insulted to find that their efforts were not to be recognised with a campaign medal. In June 2012, seven decades on, a Bomber Command memorial was unveiled in London's Green Park. Initially, Dresden objected to the memorial but an inscription commemorating all the lives lost during the bombing raids eased their concerns.

Bomber Command Memorial, Green Park, London.
Photographed by the author.

In December 2012, British Prime Minister, David Cameron, acknowledged that the veterans of Bomber Command had 'been treated inconsistently with those who served in Fighter Command'.

9.
21 February 1965,
The Assassination of Malcolm X

Delivering the eulogy for Malcolm X, Ossie Davis, a social activist, said of his fallen friend, 'We will know him then for what he was and is – a Prince – our own black shining Prince! – who didn't hesitate to die, because he loved us so'.

Malcolm X was born Malcolm Little on 19 May 1925, the fourth of eight children. The family lived in Omaha in Nebraska where Malcolm's father, a Baptist minister, Earl Little, was a prominent member of the local branch of the Universal Negro Improvement Association and an ardent supporter of Marcus Garvey. He was, according to Malcolm's autobiography, a 'big, six-foot-four, very black man. He had only one eye'. Rev Little's prominence brought the unwanted attention of the local Ku Klux Klan. Such was the level of harassment, the family moved to the town of East Lansing in the state of Michigan. It was 1929; Malcolm was four years old. There, unfortunately, the harassment was, if anything, worse. Soon after moving into their new home, the house was set on fire. Malcolm later recalled, bitterly, how fire fighters arrived on the scene but, on seeing that it was the home of a black family, refused to help.

Malcolm X, 1964. Library of Congress.

In 1931, Malcolm's father died in mysterious circumstances, run over by a streetcar. Although it was never proved, the suspicion remained that he had been killed by members of the Ku Klux Klan. The police recorded the death as suicide, thereby annulling Earl Little's life insurance.

Malcolm Little

Left poverty-stricken, Malcolm's mother, 'looked like a white woman … and her accent did not sound like a Negro's', struggled to make ends meet for her large family. The pressure took its toll and in 1937, six years after her husband's death, she was committed to an asylum. The children were farmed out to various foster parents and homes. Malcolm went to school where a teacher, Mr Ostrowski, asked the vulnerable Malcolm what he wanted to be. Malcolm answered, a lawyer. The teacher scoffed, 'You've got to be realistic about being a nigger. A lawyer – that's no realistic goal for a nigger.' Instead, Mr Ostrowski recommended Malcolm become a carpenter – 'You're good with your hands – making things'. Disillusioned, Malcolm dropped out of school at the age of 15 and went to Boston to live with his older half-sister, Ella.

Detroit Red

From Boston, Malcolm moved to the Harlem district of New York City where he got a job as a shoeshine boy. Nicknamed 'Detroit Red' for the reddish tint in his hair, he drifted into a life of petty crime, involving robbery and drug selling. He lived well off the proceeds but in 1946, following a failed robbery, Malcolm was sentenced to ten years imprisonment. Whilst incarcerated he spent much of his time reading in the prison library, obtaining the education he felt was lacking in his life. He converted to Islam and became a member of the Nation of Islam, or the Black Muslims. Founded by Elijah Muhammad, the self-proclaimed Messenger of Allah, the Black Muslims rejected Christianity as a white man's religion and preached separation of the races.

Malcolm X

Having served six years, Malcolm was released from prison in 1952. He moved to Chicago and founded (or took over – sources differ on this point) the Nation's newspaper, *Muhammad Speaks*, which espoused racially controversial views about the natural superiority of blacks. Malcolm, having shed his 'slave name', advocated black separatism and the use of violence, if necessary, to achieve it. Airtime on national television brought him immediate fame, or notoriety. His preaching drew new converts and his charismatic style appealed to much of America's black youth.

Malcolm X and Martin Luther King, Jr.

Describing himself as the 'angriest black man in America', Malcolm rejected Martin Luther King's non-confrontational approach and mocked King's March on Washington (August 1963). Achieving integration through non-violence and, as Malcolm saw it, long-term suffering, would not progress the African American's place in society. America's blacks, he said, were in the midst of a revolution and there was 'no such thing as a non-violent revolution'. 'I am for violence if non-violence means we continue postponing a solution to the American black man's problem – just to avoid violence. I don't go for non-violence if it also means a delayed solution. To me a delayed solution is a non-solution.' Instead, Malcolm preached independence, black power and black consciousness, a message that had widespread appeal. The Civil Rights Movement had, in Malcolm's view, 'begged the white man for freedom', and begging for freedom did not, he continued, set you free. 'The price of freedom is death'.

Malcolm X meeting Martin Luther King, Jr, 26 March 1964. Library of Congress.

El-Hajj Malik El-Shabazz

Elijah Muhammad, impressed by Malcolm's undoubted abilities, named him his second-in-command. Although the two men argued over the direction of the organization, Malcolm saw Muhammad as a mentor and a spiritual guide, and perhaps even a father-figure. But Muhammad's private life failed to match his public persona as a man beyond reproach. Malcolm was left feeling betrayed when he learnt that Muhammad had fathered six children with different women. Their relationship deteriorated further when, following the assassination of President Kennedy in 1963, Malcolm said it was a case of 'chickens coming to roost'. Malcolm was ordered to observe a 90-day period of silence. Refusing to comply, in March 1964 Malcolm left the Nation of Islam and founded his own Islamic group, the Muslim Mosque, Inc. In 1965 he formed the secular group, the Organization of Afro-American Unity.

Malcolm embarked on a tour of Africa and the Middle East, paid a pilgrimage to Mecca, and, having changed his name to El-Hajj Malik El-Shabazz, converted to the Sunni branch of Islam. He returned to the US a more moderate man: 'I recognize that anger can blind a man', he later said.

The Assassination of Malcolm X

Having left the Nation of Islam, Malcolm X received numerous death threats. In 1964, Elijah Muhammad said that 'hypocrites like Malcolm should have their heads cut off'. Indeed, an edition of *Muhammad Speaks* that year featured a cartoon of Malcolm X's decapitated head. On 14 February 1965, Malcolm's family home in New York was firebombed. He firmly believed that those responsible were members of the Nation of Islam.

A week later, on 21 February, as he was about to deliver a lecture at the Audubon Ballroom in Harlem, Malcolm was shot fifteen times and killed. He was three months short of his fortieth birthday. Three of Elijah Muhammad's followers were later found guilty of the murder. The last of the three, Talmadge Hayer, having served 45 years in jail and having been refused parole sixteen times, was released from prison in 2010.

Elijah Muhammad, on hearing of Malcolm's death, said, 'Malcolm X got just what he preached... We knew such ignorant, foolish teachings would bring him to his own end'.

In 1958, Malcolm had married Betty Shabazz, who, like Malcolm, called herself 'X'. They were to have six daughters, the youngest two, twins, born after Malcolm's assassination. On 1 June 1997, Betty's home was set on fire by her 12-year-old grandson, Malcolm Shabazz. Three weeks later, she died of her injuries. Shabazz, who spent four years in a juvenile detention centre, immediately expressed his remorse. Shabazz himself was murdered in Mexico City on 9 May 2013. He was 28.

Malcolm's *Autobiography of Malcolm X*, dictated to Alex Haley, author of the phenomenally bestselling *Roots*, and written over two years, was published soon after his death, and remains a cult hit.

10.
23 February 1930,
The Making of a Nazi Martyr, Horst Wessel

During the Nazi era, the *Horst Wessel Song* became a national 'hymn' sung at all official and solemn Nazi occasions alongside *Deutschlandlied*, the German national anthem. Named after the young man who penned its lyric, Horst Wessel died on 23 February 1930 from a gunshot wound sustained five weeks earlier.

Brownshirt

The son of a Lutheran minister, Horst Wessel was born on 9 October 1907 in the German city of Bielefeld. Much to his mother's displeasure, he dropped his law studies and became an active member of the Brownshirts, a paramilitary wing of the Nazis. His fanatical devotion to the Nazi cause soon attracted the admiring attention of the future propaganda minister, Joseph Goebbels who, in 1928, sent Wessel to Vienna to learn the subtle art of Nazi leadership and tactics.

On returning to Germany, Wessel relished the street brawls with the rival communists. (At this stage, the Nazis, although a powerful force in Germany, were not yet in power.) In one concerted assault, Wessel organised an attack on a regional communist headquarter in Berlin.

Horst Wessel, 1930. German Federal Archives.

Shot

On 14 January 1930, Wessel got into an argument with his landlady Elisabeth Salm, whose late husband was a communist. The finer details are lost in the mists of time – but it centred round his rent and Wessel's female guest: either he was refusing to pay an increased rent demand or refusing point blank to pay it at all, or that the young woman, Erna Jänicke, a former prostitute, was staying in Wessel's flat for free. Either way, his manner was abusive, and the aggrieved landlady stomped to a local bar filled with communists and complained to whoever listened about her troublesome tenant.

The communists had been looking out for Wessel for some time and had resorted to pasting up 'wanted' posters in eastern Berlin. Now, thanks to Mrs Salm, they knew where he lived. A group of men promptly went round to Wessel's flat to administer a 'good proletarian hiding'. But Wessel, on opening the door, was shot in the mouth. The perpetrators tried to disguise the political nature of the shooting by claiming that Wessel was a pimp and had been shot over a disagreement about Jänicke. Ali Höhler, the man who shot Wessel, escaped to Prague but returned to Berlin within weeks where he was arrested and, along with his accomplices, sentenced to prison. On coming to power, in January 1933, the Nazis had him shot.

But he is happy

Seriously wounded, Wessel was taken to a hospital. Goebbels visited frequently and waxed lyrical about the 'young leader' in his diary. When first told of the shooting, Goebbels 'trembled with fear', and 'felt as if the walls were collapsing around me. It was unbelievable'. On visiting Wessel, Goebbels wrote, *'A bullet in the head has done terrible damage to this heroic lad. His face is distorted. I hardly recognize him. But he is happy … His young, bright smile overcomes the blood and wounds. He still believes [in the Nazi cause].'*

Five weeks after the shooting, on 23 February 1930, Horst Wessel died. He was 22. On hearing of the death, Goebbels eulogised, *'One day in a German Germany, workers and students will march together singing his song. He will be with them. He wrote it in a moment of ecstasy, of inspiration. The song flowed from him, born of life and bearing witness to that life … In ten years, children will sing it in the schools, workers in the factories, soldiers on the march. His song makes him immortal.'*

The Nazi Martyr

Horst Wessel's funeral, March 1930. German Federal Archives.

The song Goebbels refers to was a lyric that Wessel had written, designed to be sung to a traditional German marching song. Called *Raise the Flag*, Goebbels had the song played at Wessel's funeral, an elaborate affair attended by some 30,000 Nazis. The martyrdom of Wessel had begun. His grave became a shrine; streets and ships were named after him, and his life the subject of numerous films, books and plays. One particularly gruesome tribute wrote, 'How high Horst Wessel towers over Jesus'.

Raise the Flag, now commonly known as the *Horst Wessel Song*, became a Nazi anthem to be played alongside the national anthem, for example, the night Hitler was appointed German Chancellor and, seven years later, at the signing ceremony following France's defeat to Germany in June 1940. Horst Wessel had become a true martyr to the Nazi cause.

11.
27 February 1881,
The Death of the Cleverest General,
Sir George Pomeroy Colley

When I was a child my parents had on their bookshelves an old red-bound nineteenth century tome called *The Life of Sir George Pomeroy Colley* by one W. F. Butler, published 1899.

Sir George Pomeroy Colley was a Victorian general who met his death on 27 February 1881, whilst fighting the Boers in South Africa.

(The author of the book, William Francis Butler, was the husband to the famous military painter, Lady Elizabeth Butler).

The title fascinated me because here was a book about a man that shared my family name, and an important one at that (he had to be important to have had a book written about him). I always assumed we were related because we were both Colleys. And, to add to the excitement, he was a 'Sir'. Perhaps some great-great-grandfather.

To this day I still don't know. It might be just a coincidence of name but then why would my father have this book on his shelves rather than a more famous Victorian general?

Colley was an all-round clever man and well thought of. He passed through his military school with the highest ever-recorded marks, was fluent in various languages and was a dab hand with the paintbrush. But like many a British general of the time, he underestimated his enemy – and that proved his undoing.

Sir George Pomeroy Colley, c1870s

The First Boer War

In 1877 the British had annexed the South African state of the Transvaal, and two years later made it a crown colony. The Boers naturally resented this, and in December 1880 revolted. At the time there were only 1,700 British troops dotted around the Transvaal in small, isolated garrisons. Colley, recently appointed governor in neighbouring Natal, was ordered to deal with the situation.

The Boers, fully expecting the arrival of the British, set up camp on the Natal / Transvaal border at a pass called Laing's Neck, the only practical route into the Transvaal from Natal. Sure enough, Colley, leading a convoy of over 1,000 troops, duly appeared.

On 28 January 1881, the British attacked the Boers at Laing's Neck and were thoroughly repulsed. That was the first defeat. Whilst Colley awaited reinforcements, another skirmish resulted in another bloody nose, heavy losses and a second defeat. Within two weeks Colley had lost two battles and a third of his men. And the Boers, it has to be remembered, were not trained soldiers, but simply farmhands who happened to be excellent shots. But things were about to get a whole lot worse for Sir George and his professionally trained army.

Majuba Hill

Colley decided to make use of a flat-topped hill called Majuba Hill overlooking the valley. If he could occupy the hill it would put the Boers, down in the pass, at a disadvantage.

Thus, in the late hours of 26 February, Colley led 500 of his men, each with three day's worth of rations, on a march up the hill. Silently, most silently, they climbed. Four o'clock the following morning they reached the summit, found it unoccupied and felt so jubilant they started yelling down and jeering at the Boers far below.

Colley too was pleased. The hill provided a commanding position – 'We could stay here forever,' he said.

Colley's assistant suggested that perhaps they should dig some entrenchments. Colley, over brimming with new-found confidence, refused. There was no way the Boers could climb up this hill with his men on top. Satisfied that his position was secure, and tired after the long trek, Colley went off to his tent for a well-earned snooze.

But the Boers did climb the hill – not the seasoned older men, but the younger boys, 200 of them. By midday they had reached the summit and crackshots that they were, the boys quickly decimated the British troops. Over half of Colley's men fell, killed or wounded; others, in panic, fled back down the hill.

Poor Sir G. Colley killed

Colley was last seen emerging from his tent brandishing a pistol. A bullet hit him right through the forehead and there, on Majuba Hill, he fell. He was 45.

A bunch of untrained boys barely out of school had finished off a professional force double its size and with it, one of Britain's most-thought of generals. 'Poor Sir G. Colley killed,' as Queen Victoria wrote in her diary.

Sir George Pomeroy Colley on the day of his death, 27 February 1881.
The Illustrated London News, 14 May 1881

And thus the First Boer War (or South African War) ended in defeat after just three battles over the course of three months. The British government recognised Boer independence and all was well for almost two decades before war erupted again, with the second, much longer Boer War of 1899 to 1902.

A colleague of mine, on an occasion I cocked up at work, said, 'Good God, Colley, no wonder we lost Majuba!'

W. F. Butler's book is still there in my parental home, and I still don't know whether I'm related to Sir General George Pomeroy Colley.

Somehow I rather hope not.

12.
27 February 1933,
The Reichstag Fire

9 p.m. 27 February 1933, Berlin's Reichstag building was set ablaze. By the time fire-fighters had arrived, the parliament building was already gutted. But the Reichstag Fire provided Hitler with a perfect excuse...

A communist outrage

Only four weeks earlier, Adolf Hitler had been appointed German Chancellor. On hearing the news of the fire at the Reichstag, Hitler and Joseph Goebbels were rushed (at 60 mph) to the site and there were met by a sweaty and overexcited Hermann Goring, who declared, 'This is a communist outrage! One of the communist culprits has been arrested. Every Communist official must be shot where he is found. Every Communist deputy must this very night be strung up.' Hitler agreed and saw the fire as a 'God-given signal' to impose his rule over the German people. Hitler, with his eyes 'almost bulging out of his head', and his entourage embarked on a brief tour of the building, inspecting the damage for themselves. About to enter a smoke-filled lobby, a policeman barred their way. 'The candelabra may crash at any moment, Herr Chancellor,' said the policeman with his arm outstretched.

The 'Communist culprit' was 24-year-old Marinus van der Lubbe, an unemployed Dutch bricklayer, found half naked on the premises, having used his shirt to start the fire.

Marinus van der Lubbe, 27 February 1933.
Dutch National Archives.

Van der Lubbe readily confessed to the crime, stating, 'I considered arson a suitable method. I did not wish to harm private people but something belonging to the system itself. I decided on the Reichstag.' But he denied any involvement with the communists.

For the protection of the people and state

The following day, 85-year-old Paul von Hindenburg, the increasingly senile German president, accepted Hitler's request for a decree suspending all political and civil liberties as a 'temporary' measure for the 'protection of the people and state'.

The communists, according to Hitler, were attempting a putsch, a revolt, and thousands of known communists were arrested, tortured and either murdered or placed in the newly-opened concentration camps, such as Dachau, near Munich, for 'protective custody'.

A bloody liar

So was the Reichstag fire the work of communists, as Hitler claimed? Although once associated with the Communist Party, van der Lubbe insisted he acted alone. But many, at the time and since, felt this unlikely. Van der Lubbe was, apparently, of limited intelligence and in his desire for attention had, more than once, persuaded the German press that he would swim the English Channel. With photographers and reporters poised, he coated himself in grease, swam out a few yards, only to return declaring unfavourable currents. On another occasion van der Lubbe, following a strike at his workplace, offered to accept responsibility and take any reprimand as long as no one else was punished. It was obvious however to his employers that van der Lubbe had no or little involvement in stirring up the workers.

The Reichstag on fire, 27 February 1933. German Federal Archives.

Rumours persisted even at the time that the Nazis were implicated in starting the Reichstag Fire, if not the government, then the party. When the head of the Berlin SA, Karl Ernst, was asked of his involvement, he replied, 'If I said yes, I'd be a bloody fool, if I said no I'd be a bloody liar'. It was rumoured that an underground passage ran all the way from Goring's residence in Berlin to the Reichstag.

In the post-war Nuremberg trials, witnesses testified hearing Goring boast about setting the Reichstag on fire but Goring, who was to kill himself on 15 October 1946, the night before he was due to be executed, steadfastly denied any involvement.

But historians do now believe that Marinus van der Lubbe did indeed manage to set such a large building ablaze with just his shirt and a few matches.

The Reichstag Fire helped Hitler consolidate his power. The temporary suspension of liberties was never revoked and any active opposition to the Nazis was stifled. When, the following month, the last parliamentary elections took place, only Hitler, it was claimed, could save Germany from the Jews and communists. The SA intimidated all other parties into silence and the Nazis polled 44 per cent of the vote, not enough for a majority but enough to squash any future political resistance.

The Enabling Act, passed in late March 1933, effectively did away with the constitution altogether. There would be no more elections nor a constitution to keep Hitler in check.

Van der Lubbe on trial

Van der Lubbe and four others were put on trial, including Ernst Torgler, chairman of the German Communist Party and Georgi Dimitrov, a Bulgarian communist who, in 1949 became Bulgaria's prime minister. Tried by the German High Court, van der Lubbe was found guilty but Torgler and companions were acquitted for the lack of evidence.

Hitler was furious with the acquittals and decreed that future cases of treason should be facilitated, not by the High Court, but by the People's Court, where a guilty verdict was virtually a forgone conclusion.

On 10 January 1934, three days short of his twenty-fifth birthday, Marinus van der Lubbe was guillotined.

Seventy-four years later, in January 2008, the German state overturned the verdict against van der Lubbe and officially pardoned him.

13.
8 March 1655,
John Casor Becomes the
First Legally-Recognised Slave

On 8 March 1655, John Casor of Virginia became the first person to be legally declared a slave for life.

Indentured servants

The administrators of Virginia, Britain's first North American colony, offered land to any of their colonists who could import more colonists. There were many who were willing to make the trip, but who lacked the money for their passage. So Virginia introduced the concept of 'indentured servants' – those who gave their labour for free in return for their benefactor having paid their passage over. By the time most indentured servants had completed their term of service, they had learnt a skill that would earn them a living.

One such example and one of Virginia's original indentured servants, arriving in 1619, was an African named Anthony Johnson who worked on a tobacco farm owned by one Edward Bennett. On Good Friday 1622, local Tidewater Indians attacked Bennett's plantation, killing 52 of its 57 residents. Johnson was one of the five survivors.

In 1623, Johnson married fellow servant, Mary. Having worked out his period of indenture and obtained his freedom, Johnson and his wife bought a plot of 250 acres and employed five black and white indentured servants of their own, one being an African by the name of John Casor. Once Casor had completed his term of seven years, he requested his freedom, a request that Johnson turned down. Against his better judgement, however, Johnson was persuaded by his family to allow Casor to work for a white colonist neighbour called Robert Parker.

Anthony Johnson

Johnson v Parker

But Johnson had a change of mind and decided not to let the matter rest. In 1654, he took the case to the County Court of Northampton County, Virginia, claiming that Parker had taken his 'negro servant' and declaring that, by rights, 'Thee had ye Negro for his life.' On first hearing, the court disagreed and Casor was allowed to remain with Parker. But, on appeal, on 8 March 1655, the Court changed its mind and found in Johnson's favour, demanding that Parker return Casor to his original owner and pay damages. The court's declaration reads as follows:

This daye Anthony Johnson negro made his complaint to the court against mr. Robert Parker and declared that hee deteyneth his servant John Casor negro under the pretence that said negro was a free man. The court seriously consideringe and maturely weighing the premisses, doe fynde that the saide Mr. Robert Parker most unjustly keepeth the said Negro from Anthony Johnson his master ... It is therefore the Judgement of the Court and ordered That the said John Casor Negro forthwith returne unto the service of the said master Anthony Johnson, And that Mr. Robert Parker make payment of all charges in the suit.'

Lifelong slave

John Casor was duly returned to Johnson and, as a result, became the first man in the North American colonies to be legally classed as a lifelong slave as a result of a civil suit, and, consequently, made Johnson the first legally recognised slave holder in American history, setting the precedent for lifelong slavery. Casor did indeed remain in Johnson's service until his death. There had been an earlier case – in 1640, an African indentured servant called John Punch was also made a lifelong slave, predating Casor, but this was as a result of a punishment imposed by the courts. Punch, also a resident of Virginia, had tried to escape to Maryland. Caught, tried and found guilty, Punch was sentenced to life in servitude.

Meanwhile, Anthony Johnson died in 1670 and his 300 acres of land passed, not to his children, but by court ruling, to a white colonist. The courts declared that 'as a black man, Anthony Johnson was not a citizen of the colony.'

14.

15 March 1938,
The Execution of Nikolai Bukharin

On 15 March 1938, Nikolai Bukharin, one of the leading members of the post-Russian Revolution politburo, was executed on the orders of his one-time friend Joseph Stalin.

Born in Moscow on 9 October 1888 to two primary school teachers, the 17-year-old Bukharin joined the workers' cause during the Russian Revolution of 1905 and, the following year, became a member of the Bolshevik Party. Like many of his radical colleagues, he was arrested at regular intervals to the point that, in 1910, he fled into exile. At various times he lived in Vienna, Zurich, London, Stockholm, Copenhagen and Krakow, the latter where he met Bolshevik leader, Vladimir Lenin, and began working for the party newspaper, *Pravda*, 'Truth'. In 1916, he moved to New York where he met up with another leading revolutionary, Leon Trotsky.

Favourite of the whole party

Following the February Revolution of 1917 and the overthrow of the tsar, Nicholas II, Bukharin returned to Moscow and was elected to the party's central committee. Bukharin clashed with Lenin on the latter's decision to surrender to Germany, thus ending Russia's involvement in the First World War, believing that the Bolsheviks could transform the conflict into a pan-European communist revolution. Lenin got his way, and the Treaty of

Brest-Litovsky was duly signed in March 1918.

Nikolai Bukharin

Bukharin was a thinker and produced several theoretical tracts, works that didn't always meet with Lenin's full approval. In Lenin's Testament, in which he passed judgement on various members of his Central Committee, Lenin wrote that Bukharin was *'rightly considered the favourite of the whole Party,'* but *'his theoretical views can be classified as fully Marxist only with the great reserve, for there is something scholastic about him.'* (Lenin's Testament was particularly damning of Joseph Stalin but, following Lenin's death on 21 January 1924, was quietly suppressed).

Not a man, but a devil

In 1924, Bukharin was appointed a full member of the Politburo. It was here, during the immediate post-Lenin years, that Bukharin became an unwitting pawn in Stalin's deadly power games. Bukharin had opposed collectivization and believed agriculture was best served by encouraging the richer peasants, the *kulaks*, to produce more. In this he was supported by Stalin – but only in order for Stalin to marginalise then remove those he saw as threats, men such as Trotsky, Lev Kamenev and Grigory Zinoviev. Kamenev and Zinoviev soon caved in to Stalin. Trotsky, who did not, was exiled, first within the Soviet Union, then to Turkey and ultimately to Mexico where, in August 1940, he was killed by a Stalinist agent. Having defeated his opponents, Stalin then took their ideas and advocated rapid collectivization and the liquidation of the *kulaks*, criticizing Bukharin for holding opposite views.

Bukharin realised what Stalin was doing: *'He [Stalin] is an unprincipled intriguer who subordinates everything to his appetite for power. At any given moment he will change his theories in order to get rid of someone.'*

During a visit to Paris in February 1936, where, on Stalin's orders, he was retrieving the archives of Marx and Engels, Bukharin visited an exiled Menshevik and there, momentarily free from the all-seeing eyes of the Soviet state, talked of his boss: 'If anyone can talk better than him, that person is doomed, Stalin won't let him live. Stalin is a little evil man; no, not a man, but a devil.'

Downfall

Bukharin's downfall was rapid – Stalin removed anyone who showed support for Bukharin and, in 1929, expelled Bukharin from the Politburo. Bukharin, realising the danger he was in, renounced his views. In 1934, speaking at a party congress, he said meekly: *'The members of the Communist Party ought to stand together to make the ideals of Comrade Stalin come true.'* Stalin seemingly forgave him and appointed Bukharin editor of *Izvestia* and asked him to oversee the text for the new Soviet Constitution. But it was all part of the cat-and-mouse games Stalin revelled in.

Meanwhile, Bukharin's old comrades, Kamenev and Zinoviev, were put on show trial, accused of ludicrous crimes, and, in 1936, executed. Bukharin was not sorry, crowing that he was 'glad' they had been shot like 'dogs'. It would not be long until it was his turn.

Bukharin was a competent cartoonist and pictured is a cartoon he did of the man that would one day order his execution.

It is impossible to live

In February 1937, the arrest duly came. He responded by going on hunger strike. Stalin criticized him: 'How dare you give us an ultimatum. Who are you to challenge the Central Committee?' Bukharin responded, 'With such accusations hanging over me, it is impossible to live', to which Stalin accused him of blackmail.

During his year of incarceration, awaiting trial within the feared walls of Lubyanka Prison in Moscow, Bukharin wrote. And he wrote a lot – some 1,400 pages, including 200 poems and even a novel, *How It All Began*. Remarkable – given his circumstances, not just of imprisonment but knowing his life would soon end by an executioner's bullet. The novel, a semi-autobiographical work, known in Russia as 'the prison novel', was left unfinished; indeed it ends mid-sentence.

Bukharin was accused, amongst many obviously false accusations, of planning to assassinate Stalin and of being a Trotskyite. (Soon, the word 'Bukharinite' came into common usage. To be labelled as such was almost as damning as being labelled a Trotskyite).

Bukharin only confessed when his interrogators used a favourite tack and threatened to bring in his wife and family. Later, however, he retracted his confession. Ultimately, his confession, or lack of it, was immaterial – the result was a forgone conclusion. 'The monstrousness of my crime is immeasurable,' he said on the final day of his trial; 'Everybody perceives the wise leadership of the country that is ensured by Stalin.' The state prosecutor assigned to preside over his trial, Andrey Vyshinsky, dismissed Bukharin as a 'hybrid: half fox, half pig'.

Nikolai Bukharin, 1920s. NNDB.

A newspaper article, published 7 March 1938, stated: 'The pretensions of the garrulous, hypocritically vile murderer Bukharin to look as an "ideologist" lost in theoretical blunders are hopeless. He will not succeed in separating himself from the gang of his accomplices. He will not succeed in averting full responsibility for the chain of monstrous crimes. He will not wash his academic hands. These hands are stained with blood. These are the hands of a murderer.' Its author, Mikhail Koltsov, was to have his turn... shot by the NKVD on 2 February 1940.

Letters of a condemned man

Meanwhile, Bukharin, in prison and awaiting his fate, wrote thirty-four desperate letters to Stalin. Not one was answered. In one he promises that if released he would 'wage a mortal war against Trotsky', even offering up his wife as a hostage for six months as an 'added insurance'. In another letter, he asks of Stalin, 'Koba, why do you need me to die?' ('Koba' being a revolutionary nickname used by Stalin in his younger days. The letter was found hidden in Stalin's desk following Stalin's death 15 years later.)

In his last letter to Stalin, Bukharin writes pathetically, '[I] have learned to cherish and love you wisely.' He begs Stalin to allow him to die by poison not by a bullet: 'I implore you beforehand, I entreat you ... let me have a cup of morphine.' Not only did Stalin ignore this request, but Bukharin was forced to sit and watch as others were shot before him.

In the same letter, Bukharin maintains his innocence, writing, *'My heart boils over when I think that you might believe that I am guilty of these crimes ... Standing on the edge of a precipice, from which there is no return, I tell you on my word of honour, as I await my death, that I am innocent of those crimes to which I admitted.'*

It did him little good – Nikolai Bukharin was executed 15 March 1938, aged 49, a victim of the system he helped create.

Anna Larina's Great Ordeal

Bukharin had married three times. All three wives ended up in a gulag. He married his third wife, Anna Larina, in January 1934, and as newly-weds they lived for a while in the Kremlin apartment where Nadezhda Alliluyeva, Stalin's second wife, had committed suicide in November 1932.

Soon after his arrest, Bukharin wrote a letter to Anna, in which he warned: 'You are the person closest, dearest to me, only you... I beg you to use all your strength and spirit to help yourself and the family *endure* this terrible phase... A great ordeal awaits you. I beg you, my dearest, muster all your strength, tighten all the strings of your heart, but don't allow them to break.' Yet, even in this darkest hour, Bukharin still can't quite let go of political rhetoric: 'Remember that the great cause of the USSR lives on, and this is the most important thing. Personal fates are transitory and wretched by comparison.' But Anna herself had been arrested. She received the letter fifty-four years later, in 1992. One can only imagine the impact – reading such a desperate letter written over a half a century before.

Following Bukharin's arrest, Anna Larina spent 18 months in a cell, ankle-deep in water, during which time she learned from another prisoner, via the tapping on her cell wall, that her husband had been executed. She served a further eighteen years in a gulag and was only released in 1959. She spent years trying to clear Bukharin's name which, in 1988, fifty years after his execution, she finally managed to achieve. She wrote *This I Cannot Forget*, published 1993, about Bukharin and their life together. She died in 1996 – five years after the collapse of the Soviet Union.

15.
21 March 1960,
The Sharpeville Massacre

The Sharpeville Massacre of 21 March 1960, which left 69 unarmed black South Africans dead and more than 180 injured, drew the world's attention to the evil of the apartheid system practiced within South Africa.

Pass Laws

The protest at Sharpeville, a black township about forty miles south of Johannesburg, was part of a campaign against the so-called Pass Laws. This law required South Africa's black population to carry around at all times an identity book which contained pertinent information about themselves, such as name, address, employer details and even their tax code. Those caught without the books were liable to immediate arrest.

The demonstrations against the Pass Laws were organised and led by the PAC (Pan-Africanist Congress), an offshoot of the ANC (African National Congress). The march on Sharpeville was to be the first in a series of non-violent actions due to take place over a five-day period. Participants on the march were to present themselves at the police station at Sharpeville without their pass books and demand to be arrested. If enough blacks were arrested and kept from going to work, the country's economy would collapse. That, at least, was the theory according to Robert Sobukwe, leader of PAC.

Sobukwe fully informed the police beforehand of the Sharpeville demonstration, emphasising the non-violent intention of the marchers.

Down with the passes

And so on the morning of 21 March 1960, a Monday, 5 to 7,000 people (cited numbers vary) converged on the police station at Sharpeville. Many, according to witnesses, were cajoled by PAC members who threatened to burn their passes unless they joined the march. Nonetheless, most joined the demonstration willingly and the march was good-natured, with the unarmed marchers singing songs, dancing and chanting 'Down with the passes'.

Three hundred police officers with loaded guns were waiting for them at the Sharpeville police station, many being reinforcements especially drafted in, some sitting on top of armoured cars.

They must learn their lessons

The Sharpeville Massacre, 21 March 1960. Ian Berry.

At about 1.15, a policeman was knocked down and the crowd surged. The police later claimed that the demonstrators had started throwing stones at them but none of the journalists present, of whom there were many, could confirm this. The police opened fire straight into the mass of people in front of them – there was no warning, no announcement, no warning shots. Across a field, people ran for their lives. 'Some of the children', wrote one journalist, 'hardly as tall as the grass, were leaping like rabbits. Some of them were shot. Still the shooting went on … One of the policemen was swinging his sten gun around in a wide arc from his hip as though he was panning a movie camera.' The shooting lasted no more than two minutes, but armed with sub-machine guns, the police killed sixty-nine. Most of the victims, it was later revealed, were found to have been shot in the back. One police officer infamously said, 'If they do these things, they must learn their lessons the hard way.'

Unlawful Organizations

The Sharpeville Massacre prompted the ANC leaders to call on black people to make a public display of burning the hated pass books. The outbreak of demonstrations caused further violence and the government reacted by declaring a state of emergency. Meetings of more than ten persons were prohibited, and 18,000 arrests were made including leaders of the ANC and PAC. Both organisations were initially banned, then outlawed altogether with the introduction on 7 April of the Unlawful Organizations Act.

When, six months later, victims filed claims against the government, the president, H. F. Verwoerd, responded by rushing through the Indemnity Act which rendered all police officers immune from prosecution for their part in the Sharpeville Massacre or subsequent demonstrations.

Thirty-six years later, on 10 December 1996, following the end of the apartheid era, the new South African president, Nelson Mandela, signed the new national constitution into law – the venue he chose was Sharpeville.

16.
10 April 1971,
Ping Pong Diplomacy During the Cold War

On 10 April 1971, the simple game of table tennis marked the beginning of a thaw in the diplomatic freeze that had existed between the US and China for over 20 years. The occasion became known as ping-pong diplomacy.

The US ping-pong team was in Nagoya, Japan, for the 31st World Table Tennis Championships, and following a team practice 19-year-old Californian student, Glenn Cowan, accidentally got on the Chinese team bus. The Chinese players didn't know what to do. Zhuang Zedong, a Chinese player and three times world champion, later said, 'We were all tense. Our team had been advised not to speak to Americans, not to shake their hands, and not to exchange gifts with them.' Nonetheless, Zedong nervously approached the American.

The ping heard round the world

Talking through an interpreter, the two men found a rapport. Zedong gave the American a silk gown by way of a present, and invited the American team to play a friendly championship in China. This seemingly innocuous invitation has to be seen in the context of the time – no American had stepped on Chinese soil since Chairman Mao had come to power 22 years earlier in 1949. *Time* magazine called it 'The ping heard round the world.'

By the time they had got off the bus the Chinese team and their

American passenger were surrounded by press. Within hours, Zedong's informal invitation had been endorsed by Mao and been made official. Mao later said, 'Zhuang Zedong is not only good at ping-pong, he is good at diplomacy too.'

Mao Zedong, portrait painted by Zhang Zhenshi.

Thus, on 10 April 1971 nine US players, four officials, two spouses and five US journalists crossed a bridge from Hong Kong onto Chinese soil.

Friendship First Competition Second

Under the slogan 'Friendship First Competition Second', the Chinese men's team won 5-3, and the women's team 5-4; the Chinese politely refraining from inflicting a white-wash on the Americans. Glenn Cowan, with this American long hair and red hair band, was clearly the crowd's favourite.

In between matches, the US team, followed every step by a scrum of media, was treated to a sightseeing tour which took in the Great Wall, the Summer Palace and frequent banquets, whilst everywhere they went they were bombarded with images of Mao and loudspeakers condemning American imperialism.

At one such banquet, at the Great Hall of the People on 14 April, Chinese premier, Chou En-lai, said, 'You have opened a new chapter in the relations of the American and Chinese people... I am confident that this beginning of our friendship will certainly meet with majority support of our two peoples'. He also invited more American journalists to visit China, provided, he added, they do not 'all come at once'.

Nixon in China

From this 'ping-pong diplomacy' great advances were made – China was admitted into the UN; America, on the day Chou En-lai made his speech, ended a 21-year trade embargo on China, and, two months later in July 1971, Secretary of State Henry Kissinger's secret visit to China paved the way for President Nixon's official visit in February 1972, where, amongst handshakes, toasts and photo-opportunities, Mao and Nixon found a meeting of minds.

Chairman Mao meeting US President Nixon, 29 February 1972.
US National Archives.

17.
22 April 1915,
Fritz Haber and the First Successful Gas Attack

On 22 April 1915, during the Second Battle of Ypres, French and Algerian soldiers, fighting together, noticed a strange yellow-grey-coloured cloud floating across no man's land in their direction. As it descended over them, many collapsed, coughing and wheezing, gasping for air, frothing at the mouth. Men nearby watched as their colleagues fell to the ground in agony yet there were no gunshots to be heard and they appeared not to be visibly wounded in any way. Seized by panic, they bolted, throwing away their rifles, and even their tunics so that they might run faster, leaving a hole some four miles wide. But the Germans, wary of stepping into the cloud of poison gas protected only by their crude gasmasks, felt unable to exploit the opportunity. This, with 400 tones of chlorine gas, was the world's first successful chemical weapon attack, resulting in 6,000 casualties, mostly from asphyxia.

This new terrible weapon was inhumane, cried the Allied generals, only to be using it themselves within five months. Britain's first use of chlorine gas, at the Battle of Loos in September 1915, was not a great success. Sir John French and the British commanders had banned the use of the word 'gas', believing it too provocative a word; instead they called it the 'accessory', a vague euphemism if ever there was one. Having waited for a favourable wind, they released the gas from cylinders. But the wind turned and the gas ended up causing greater causalities among the British than it did the Germans.

Detail from John Singer Sargent's 'Gassed', 1919.
Google Arts Project.

Arthur Empey, an American fighting with the British, described a gas attack: 'German gas is heavier than air and soon fills the trenches and dugouts, where it has been known to lurk for two or three days, until the air is purified by means of large chemical sprayers. A company man on our right was too slow in getting on his helmet; he sank to the ground, clutching at his throat, and after a few spasmodic twistings, went West (died). It was horrible to see him die, but we were powerless to help him. In the corner of a traverse, a little, muddy cur dog, one of the company's pets, was lying dead, with his two paws over his nose. It's the animals that suffer the most, the horses, mules, cattle, dogs, cats, and rats, they having no helmets to save them.'

Fritz Haber

The pioneer of poison gas was a German called Fritz Haber, a Jew who, conscious of the anti-Semitism already prevalent in *fin-de-siècle* Germany, had, in 1893, converted to Christianity. Haber had developed the means to convert nitrogen in a way that it could be used to produce cheap and effective fertilizer, which greatly improved and revolutionized agricultural efficiency. As one historian put it, 'It has been claimed that as many as two out of five humans on the planet today owe their existence to the discoveries made by [this] one brilliant German chemist.' His work won Haber the Nobel Prize for Chemistry in 1918.

Fritz Haber, 1919. The Nobel Foundation.

The use of poisonous gas in war was prohibited by the 1899 Hague Convention yet as soon as the First World War broke out Fritz Haber and his team worked on developing gas as a weapon. Haber, as a Jew, was determined to prove his devotion and loyalty to Germany. 'During peace time,' Haber once said, 'a scientist belongs to the World, but during war time he belongs to his country'. Killing enemy troops with gas was, according to Haber, no worse than blowing their heads off with artillery. For his work, Haber was personally made an honorary captain by Kaiser Wilhelm II.

Clara Immerwahr

The successful use of chlorine gas at Ypres in April 1915 was, for the

Germans, and Haber in particular, an occasion for celebration. But not so for Haber's wife, Clara. Clara Immerwahr, who herself had been a successful chemist, had been appalled by her husband's work, which she saw as a perversion of science. On 2 May, at their Berlin home, Haber hosted a party. While he and his friends toasted his success, Clara took her husband's service revolver, went into their garden and shot herself in the heart. She died the following morning in the arms of her 13-year-old son, Hermann.

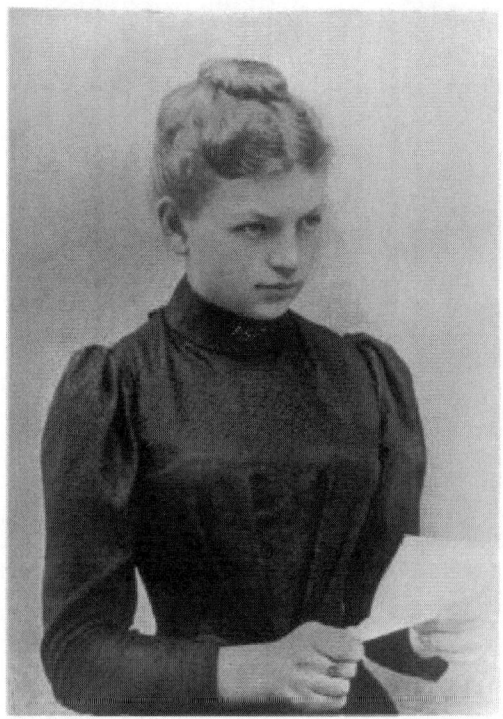

Clara Immerwahr, c1890.

Despite the setback of his wife's suicide, Haber was buoyed by his success with chlorine at Ypres but conscious of its limitations. He developed a new, more effective gas, called phosgene, which omitted a smell akin to hay. Its first use, on the Eastern front, in January 1916, proved successful. Those inflicted often showed no immediate ill effects but then would succumb, violently, some 48 hours later.

In 1917, the Germans introduced mustard gas, so named because of its odour, which could penetrate clothing and be absorbed through skin. Gas had become a common feature by the end of the war and although it was effective at incapacitating troops and causing long-term illness, gas accounted for only three per cent of fatalities.

Post-war

Following the war, Fritz Haber continued his work. But, despite his Christian conversion, and despite his efforts on behalf of Germany's war efforts, he was still a Jew, and hence felt very vulnerable once, in 1933, Hitler had come to power. On seeing many of his Jewish colleagues harassed, mistreated and dismissed, Haber resigned. He emigrated to England in 1933 but, after only four months, decided to start afresh in Palestine. Stopping off in Basel in Switzerland, Haber, aged 65, died of a heart attack on 29 January 1934.

His son, Hermann, later emigrated to the US where, apparently ashamed by his father's work, he committed suicide in 1946.

Zyklon B

But the most tragic irony was that in his agricultural research, Haber helped develop pesticide gases, which included a cyanide-based pesticide called Zyklon B; indeed one of his assistants was credited as the official inventor of Zyklon B. Zyklon B was the main component used by the Nazis in their death camps. Among the six million killed in the gas chambers during the Holocaust were several members of Fritz Haber's extended family, including several of his nieces and nephews.

18.
30 April 1945,
The Death of Adolf Hitler

In January 1945, with the Soviet Red Army bearing down on Germany, Hitler left his HQ in East Prussia and moved back to Berlin and into the Reich Chancellery. A month later, he went underground into the Chancellery's air-raid shelter, a cavern of dimly-lit rooms made of solid, high-quality concrete.

Hitler's Health

During his last few months, Hitler's health deteriorated rapidly. In February 1945, after so many years of shouting and screaming, he had to have an operation on his vocal chords which obliged him to stay silent for a whole week.

Despite the implorations of his staff, Hitler refused to leave Berlin, and finally, realising the war was truly lost, he decided to end his life. Shuffling around with a stoop, Hitler looked much older than his fifty-six years. A new pain in his eye required daily doses of cocaine drops, and, perhaps from the onset of Parkinson's disease, his left hand shook constantly. His eyesight had become so poor he had to have his documents written in extra-large print on specially-made 'Fuhrer' typewriters.

Adolf Hitler, 1938. German Federal Archive.

He ate poorly – devouring large portions of cake. He'd fallen out with many of his senior colleagues – in particular Hermann Goring and Heinrich Himmler, both of whom he accused of treachery and ordered to be arrested on sight and court-martialled. Joseph Goebbels, however, remained loyal to the last, broadcasting to the nation, demanding greater effort and sacrifice against the enemy.

Hitler the General

In his final days Hitler ordered a scorched-earth policy throughout eastern Germany and the destruction of anything that could be of use to the Soviets. What happened to the German citizen was not of Hitler's concern – as far as he was concerned, they had proved themselves unworthy of him.

From within the bunker, Hitler continued to dictate operations but his grip on reality had deserted him. He refused to listen to the glum reports from the front and ordered a constant stream of counterattacks deploying non-existent troops and refusing the troops that did exist room to retreat and re-group.

On his 56th (and last) birthday on 20 April 1945, a group of nineteen or so Hitler Youth boys lined-up in the Chancellery garden for Hitler to inspect and decorate with Iron Crosses. Lined-up from the eldest to the youngest, Hitler, with his shaking left hand behind his back, shook hands with each child, pinching the cheek of the last, the youngest child, a 12-year-old boy called Alfred Czech. 'The Führer shook my hand,' said Mr Czech decades later, 'then he pinched my left cheek. He told me, "Keep it up!" I certainly had the feeling that I had done something remarkable.' Hitler delivered a short speech and thanked them for their bravery before shuffling back into the bunker. It was to be Hitler's last appearance in public.

Eva Braun, June 1942. German Federal Archive.

Hitler and Eva

A week later, just past midnight on 29 April, in a ten-minute ceremony,

Hitler married his long-term partner, Eva Braun. Twenty-three years his junior, the German people knew nothing of her. Her presence, although not a secret amongst the Nazi hierarchy, was not something Hitler wished publicized lest it should diminish the adoration of Germany's women. Goebbels and Martin Bormann stood as witnesses as a hastily-found registrar nervously asked the couple whether they were of pure Aryan descent and free of hereditary diseases.

That night, following the subdued and rather surreal marital celebrations, Hitler dictated his last political testament and private will to his secretary, where, in the former, he drew-up the make-up of the government following his death. The admiral, Karl Donitz, was named as his successor, not as 'Fuhrer' but as president, and Goebbels as Chancellor.

Fighting to his last breath against Bolshevism

On 29 April, Hitler made preparations for his death. 200 litres of benzene were delivered into the bunker. Hitler insisted that his body be burnt, not wanting his corpse to finish up in Soviet hands like an 'exhibit in a cabinet of curiosities'. He also ordered the testing of the newly-arrived batch of cyanide capsules. The chosen victim was Hitler's much-loved Alsatian dog, Blondi.

On 30 April, with the Soviets only 300 metres away, Goebbels tried one last time to convince the Fuhrer to leave Berlin but Hitler had already made it plain a week earlier, bellowing at his generals, 'If you gentlemen think I'm going to leave Berlin you are very much mistaken. I'd rather blow my brains out'.

Near four o'clock on the 30th, after a round of farewells, Hitler and his wife of forty hours retired to his study. Hitler wore upon his tunic, his Iron Cross (First Class) and his Wounded Badge of the First World War. His entourage waited anxiously outside. A shot was heard. Hitler had shot himself through the right temple. Braun was also dead. She had swallowed the cyanide. The pistol Hitler had used was the same one that his niece, Geli Raubal, had used when she committed suicide almost 14 years before. Hitler's body, collapsing over the table, overturned a vase, the water it contained drenching Eva's top.

U.S. Army newspaper Stars and Stripes *announcing Hitler's death, May 1945.*

The bodies, covered in blankets, were carried out into the Chancellery garden. There, with artillery exploding around them and neighbouring buildings ablaze, Hitler's wishes were honoured – the benzene was poured on the corpses and set alight. With the bodies blazing, the entourage gave one final Hitler salute before scampering back into the bunker.

The official announcement, the following day, stated that 'Hitler had fallen at his command post fighting to his last breath against Bolshevism and for Germany'.

Hitler had come to power as German Chancellor, aged 43, in January 1933. But with his death, the Third Reich, which was meant to last a thousand years, had come to an end after just twelve.

19.
1 May 1945,
The Suicide of Joseph Goebbels,
the Not-So-Great German novelist

In 1923, the future Nazi minister for propaganda, Joseph Goebbels, wrote a novel. Eighty years later, a carbon copy bearing the author's corrections and amendments, came up for auction in Connecticut. 158 pages long, *Michael Voormann: A Man's Fate in the Pages of a Diary* was written as a diary and is both autobiographical and a tribute to Goebbels' friend, Richard Flisges, to whom the novel is dedicated.

Goebbels and the First World War

One imagines there's a degree of envy here – born on 29 October 1897, Joseph Goebbels was old enough to fight in the First World War but was rejected due to his clubfoot. (Throughout his life he had to wear a special shoe to compensate his shorter leg.) After the war, he sometimes liked to pretend that his disability was in fact a war wound. In his novel, Michael, in common with Flisges, sees active service on the Eastern Front during the Great War; Michael's war record a reflection of Goebbels' wishful thinking.

Michael returns to a democratic Germany, seeking revolution and answers, but not sure where to find it. Michael is a socialist and a Christian, attempting to write a play about Jesus (as indeed Goebbels had) in which he describes Jesus as one of the greatest men to have lived.

Joseph Goebbels photographed by Heinrich Hoffman.
German Federal Archive.

Goebbels in Love

While at college, Michael falls in love with a Hertha Holk (based on Goebbels' first love, Anka Stalherm, a woman with an 'extraordinary passionate mouth', whom Goebbels met in 1918 at Heidelberg University, from where he would receive a doctorate in literature). After their split, Michael finds works in the mines and just as things are coming together for him, is killed in a mining accident – a fate that had befallen Flisges in July 1923.

One recent review of *Michael* describes its characters as 'never rising above their basic two-dimensionality; they are cardboard cut-outs whose greatest glory is to become sounding boards for the author's lugubrious philosophizing'.

Goebbels' parents had hoped he'd become a priest (as did Stalin's mother of her son). But Joseph dreamt of being a writer and wrote numerous plays, poems and articles but *Michael* was his only novel. His literary aspirations however fell well short of his expectations – *Michael* was eventually published in 1929 by the Nazi's own publishing house, Eher-Verlag, but merely on the back of Goebbels' growing status within the party. Back in the early twenties, unable to make a living as a writer, Goebbels was forced to find employment, working on the stock exchange and as a bank clerk, both of which he loathed.

Both great and simple

Goebbels joined the Nazi Party in 1922, seduced, as many were, by the charisma of its leader, Adolf Hitler. But for a couple of years, Goebbels sided with the more socialist side of the party, a division that momentarily threatened to split the movement. 'I no longer fully believe in Hitler,' Goebbels confided to his diary. Hitler went on the offensive and through a mixture of bullying and charm, healed the rift. Goebbels was left reeling and utterly in awe of Hitler. From then on, he devoted his life to his leader and remained loyal to the last. 'Adolf Hitler, I love you because you are both great and simple at the same time. What one calls a genius.'

In 1926, just four years after joining the party, Goebbels was made Gauleiter of Berlin and, in 1929, appointed the party's propaganda minister where he edited a weekly newspaper called *Der Angriff* (The Assault). In 1933, following Hitler's assumption of power, he became the Reich Minister for Public Enlightenment and Propaganda.

Goebbels married Magda Ritschel on 19 December 1931, with Hitler as a witness. They were to have six children, all of whose names began with an H in honour of Hitler.

Following Hitler's suicide on 30 April 1945, Goebbels succeeded him as chancellor, a post he was to retain for a single day. With the Red Army bearing down on Berlin and defeat inevitable, Goebbels and his wife couldn't bear the thought of their children living in a post-Hitler world. Thus, on 1 May, they drugged up their children, aged four to twelve, on morphine, then, with the help of a doctor, crushed ampules of cyanide into their mouths. The girls had ribbons tied in their hair. A couple of hours later, Magda and Goebbels walked out into the Reich Chancellery garden. Goebbels shot his wife and then himself.

Joseph and Magda Goebbels and children, including Magda's son from her first marriage, 1944. German Federal Archive.

In 1987, *Michael* was issued for the first time in English, published by Amok Press.

20.
2 May 1957,
The Death of the Great Communist Witch Hunter, Joseph McCarthy

Aggressive, intimidating, and unfazed by the truth, Joe McCarthy single-handedly whipped 1950s USA into a frenzy of anti-communist fear and paranoia.

It was near the beginning of the Cold War: the Soviet Union had surged ahead of America in the arms race, Chairman Mao had not long come to power in China, and Americans everywhere feared the presence of 'Reds Under the Beds' within their own communities. In stepped Joseph McCarthy to shock the nation with a sensational announcement that confirmed their worst fears.

McCarthy exposes the Reds

It was the evening of 9 February 1950, at a Republican Women's Club meeting in West Virginia, when 41-year-old McCarthy declared that he had in his hand a list of 205 names of State Department employees known to be members of the American Communist Party. (A month later, McCarthy had reduced the figure to fifty-seven.) These informants, said McCarthy, were passing on information to the Soviet Union 'The reason why we find ourselves in a position of impotency,' he continued, 'is not because the enemy has sent men to invade our shores, but rather because of the traitorous actions of those who have had all the benefits that the wealthiest nation on earth has had to offer – the finest homes, the finest college educations, and the finest jobs in Government we can give.'

Joseph McCarthy, 1954. Library of Congress.

And so began the era of the communist witch-hunts. The eruption of the Korean War four months later with the communist North invading the democratic South Korea, merely confirmed the aggressiveness of global communism.

McCarthy's rise

A Republican, Joseph McCarthy slandered his opponents on his way up the political pole, accusing them in turn of senility, financial irregularity, draft-dodging, and war profiteering. But when his own political career came under threat with claims that he had lied about his role during the war, McCarthy played on American's fear of communism, and overnight became the most talked about politician in America.

One of McCarthy's victims was a 66-year-old judge called Edgar Werner. Writing in 1951, Werner's son described the effect of McCarthyism on his father: 'McCarthy not only drove my father to his grave but turned long-standing friends against our whole family. It was amazing how one man could wreck the reputation of another man so loved and honoured in his community.'

Red Hollywood

Hollywood, already under suspicion, became the next target of McCarthy's intense scrutiny. From the struggling novice to the stars, actors were interrogated. Those who confessed could wipe the slate clean by repenting and providing names of others. One screenwriter named 162 Hollywood actors, writers or directors who were communist, ex-commie, or at least sympathetic to the socialist cause. Many were purged, not to work again for years. Others fled abroad rather than face their turn in the McCarthy spotlight.

The studios, desperate to claw back the trust of the American people, turned out a series of propagandist films, *I Married a Communist*, or *I Was A communist for the FBI* (which won the 1951 Oscar for Best Documentary).

Next in McCarthy's glare came the universities, the 'reducators' of the impressionable American youth. Libraries were targeted and 30,000 anti-American titles banned from the shelves.

Joe and Ike

Republican presidential candidate, Dwight 'Ike' Eisenhower, disliked McCarthy but needed his support to win the 1952 election. McCarthy had the gall to accuse George C. Marshall, originator of the post-Second World War Marshall Plan, of having communist leanings and being 'part of a conspiracy so immense, an infamy so black, as to dwarf any in the history of man'. Eisenhower planned to defend Marshall but, concerned at losing McCarthy's support at such a vital time, failed to do so.

Once in power Eisenhower still felt reluctant to pull in the increasing excesses of McCarthyism, which by now were targeting members of Eisenhower's administration. 'Attacking him,' said one purged victim, 'is regarded as a certain method of committing suicide.'

In 1953, a young New York couple, the Rosenbergs, were executed for passing atomic secrets to the Soviets. Although McCarthy was not involved in the case, it intensified still further the paranoia of mid-50s America.

McCarthyism was rampant.

McCarthy takes on the US Army

In 1954 McCarthy decided to take on the US Army, right up to the Secretary of the Army, Robert Stevens. The army, according to McCarthy, was full of 'dangerous spies'. The Republican Party tried to stop their renegade senator but too late – the subsequent investigations based on McCarthy's allegations were televised throughout a 36-day hearing.

The nation watched aghast as McCarthy thumped the table, shouted, heckled and bullied his way through the hearing, with little regard for etiquette or procedure and failing to back up his wild claims with any substantial evidence.

As one observer noted in 1954, 'The line between investigating and persecuting is a very fine one and the junior Senator from Wisconsin has stepped over it repeatedly.'

Fall from grace

This time he had gone too far. The media, for so long in awe of McCarthy, attacked him for his 'degrading travesty of the democratic process'. The Republican Party finally brought his misadventures to an end and in December 1954 stripped him of office, asking of McCarthy on live television: 'You have done enough. Have you no sense of decency, sir, at long last? Have you left no sense of decency?'

McCarthy faded into obscurity. 'McCarthyism,' quipped Eisenhower, 'was now McCarthywasm'.

Already an alcoholic, McCarthy drank himself into hospital and on 2 May 1957, aged only 48, died of an inflammation of the liver.

21.
3 May 1975,
The Death of Dmitri Bystrolyotov,
Stalin's Romeo Spy

Charming, dashing and aristocratic, Dmitri Bystrolyotov's life reads like a far-fetched spy thriller. Addicted to danger, Bystrolyotov seduced French, British and German women procuring for Joseph Stalin vital information in the years leading up to war, including, amazingly, Hitler's plans for rearmament. He was, without question, Stalin's most daring and successful spy.

But then, in 1938, at the height of Stalin's purges, Bystrolyotov was arrested by the Soviet secret police, the NKVD. Tortured and crippled, and made to 'confess' to fantastical charges, he was sentenced to 20 years hard labour. Incarcerated and broken, Bystrolyotov felt the full force of the corrupt regime he had served so loyally for so long. But always one to take risks, Bystrolyotov recorded his experience within the gulags. With the help of contacts he smuggled out, page by page, his damning first-hand account of Stalin's labour camps.

The name is Bystrolyotov, Dmitri Bystrolyotov

Dmitri Bystrolyotov is a well-known name in Russia, an action hero for today reclaimed from the myths of yesteryear. Hailed on TV and film, subject of books and documentaries, Bystrolyotov is to Russia what James Bond is to the West but with one slight difference – Bystrolyotov was real.

Dmitri Bystrolyotov.

Born 4 January 1901, Bystrolyotov's belief in the Soviet cause was total. As a teenager, he watched from the sidelines as the Russian Revolution of 1917 unfurled, then spent half a decade cruising round Central Europe, looking for direction. He didn't find it – it found him; Soviet Foreign Intelligence in Czechoslovakia recruited the 25-year-old drifter who just happened to be a polyglot. Furnished with a series of false passports and different IDs, Bystrolyotov used his flair for languages to good effect in the capital cities of Europe – London, Paris and Berlin.

But it wasn't his main tool in his box of tricks – that was in his good looks; his Clark Gable moustache, his perfect centre parting, the raised eyebrow. And armed with his looks, he seduced many an unsuspecting female into bed and into loosening their tongues. On his very own wedding night, Bystrolyotov abandoned his bride, Iolanta, in order to seduce a potentially-useful female source.

The wonderful garden

He soon recruited Iolanta into his game, persuading her to sleep with an informant. She did so; doing so for the 'greater good', for Stalin; and then very probably hating herself for it – for she left Bystrolyotov. He told her why he played such a dangerous game – he was, he said, 'swimming across a stormy river, risking his own life and drowning those who happen to be in his way'. She retorted that this 'wonderful garden' was nothing more than an illusion.

Bystrolyotov returned to the Soviet Union in 1937, at the very time Stalin's Great Purge was decimating the country like a virus. If Bystrolyotov thought his loyal and impressive contribution to the cause would provide him with immunity, he was very much mistaken. Stalin bore a deep distrust of foreigners, especially capitalist ones, and anyone who had been tainted by such foreigners. Bystrolyotov's wife and mother, both labelled as 'enemies of the people' took their own lives.

He served seventeen years in the gulag during which time he met and married his second wife, before being released as part of the post-Stalin amnesty. Dmitri Bystrolyotov died 3 May 1975, aged 74.

22.
6 May 1937,
The Hindenburg Disaster

On 6 May 1937, a tragedy took place that, caught on film, haunted the American consciousness for decades.

Hindenburg Disaster, 6 May 1937. Dutch National Archives.

Built in Germany in 1935 the 800-foot long Zeppelin airship, the *Hindenburg*, was considered the height of sophisticated travel. It may only have travelled at 80 mph yet it still provided the fastest means of crossing the Atlantic – twice as fast as the speediest ship. It was akin to being on a luxury liner and had already made dozens of journeys across the Atlantic from Germany to Brazil or America and back. Of course, it wasn't cheap – a one-way ticket across the Atlantic cost about US$400 (about US$7,000 / £4,500 in 2015).

With the Nazi swastika on its fins, it was named after the last president of the Weimar Republic, Paul von Hindenburg, who had appointed Hitler as chancellor in January 1933 and who died in August 1934. Goebbels had, apparently, wanted the airship to be named the *Adolf Hitler* but the owner of the Zeppelin Company, Hugo Eckener, a known anti-Nazi, refused.

But before it became a transatlantic airship, the *Hindenburg* began its life as a tool of the Nazi propaganda ministry, run by Goebbels. In March 1936, ahead of a German plebiscite to rally support ratifying the re-occupation of the Rhineland, the *Hindenburg* was used to drop propaganda leaflets while blaring out loud patriotic music and slogans from huge loudspeakers, and broadcasting political speeches from a temporary on-board radio studio. (The plebiscite returned a 99.8 per cent vote in favour). On 1 August 1936, the *Hindenburg* made a special appearance flying above the Olympic Stadium during the opening ceremony of the Berlin Olympics trailing an Olympic flag in its wake.

The *Hindenburg*'s last journey

On its 63rd and last, fateful journey, the *Hindenburg* had departed from Frankfurt on 3 May 1937 and was due to land at Lakehurst, New Jersey, at six on the morning of 6 May. But poor weather had delayed its landing by about twelve hours. The captain, Max Pruss, kept his passengers entertained by flying over New York City. The *Hindenburg* had a capacity for about 70 passengers but on this trip there were only 36 passengers plus 61 crew – 97 people altogether.

At 7.25 p.m. the *Hindenburg* was trying to land by docking onto a 270-foot high mooring mast, from where it could be winched down to the ground. The flight was the first North Transatlantic trip of the year and TV and radio crews had gathered to record its arrival. Radio reporter, Herbert Morrison, was describing the events when inexplicably the airship exploded into flames. The tail of the ship was soon engulfed but the *Hindenburg* remained level for a few more seconds before the tail began to drop. As the ship tilted, passengers and crew and bits of furniture were thrown against the walls; one passenger remembered being hurled 15 to 20 feet against a dining room wall and being pinned there by several others.

The *Hindenburg* continued to lurch as the flames spread at almost 50 feet per second. Many on board were able to jump for their lives. 'Oh, the humanity,' wailed Morrison, a phrase that entered the lexicon of American culture. Within just 37 seconds the *Hindenburg* had been utterly destroyed. 'Approaching Lakehurst,' reported British Pathé News in a bit of poetic reportage, 'the *Hindenburg* appeared a conquering giant of the skies. But she proved a puny plaything in the mighty grip of fate. It almost seemed as if fate had set the stage for the horrible tragedy. A graceful craft sailing serenely to her doom.'

Oh, the humanity

Of the 97 people on board 35 died: 13 passengers and 22 crew, plus one ground crew member. But 62 did survive by jumping at the right time and running to safety. It wasn't the first or worst airship disaster but the *Hindenburg* tragedy effectively brought the brief age of the airship to an abrupt end. Despite many theories, the exact cause of the fire remains a mystery but is generally believed to have been caused by an electrostatic discharge – in simpler terms, a spark that ignited leaking hydrogen.

Morrison's radio commentary was married up to the film footage and flashed across the world. The two mediums ran at slightly different speeds so Morrison's voice had to be speeded up to match the film, adding to its emotional intensity.

Here is Morrison's commentary:

It's burst into flames! It burst into flames, and it's falling, it's crashing! Watch it! Watch it! Get out of the way! Get out of the way! Get this, Charlie; get this, Charlie! It's fire… and it's crashing! It's crashing terrible! Oh, my! Get out of the way, please! It's burning and bursting into flames and the… and it's falling on the mooring mast. And all the folks agree that this is terrible; this is the one of the worst catastrophes in the world. Its flames… Crashing, oh! Four- or five-hundred feet into the sky and it… it's a terrific crash, ladies and gentlemen. It's smoke, and it's in flames now; and the frame is crashing to the ground, not quite to the mooring mast. Oh, the humanity! And all the passengers screaming around here. I told you; it—I can't even talk to people, their friends are out there! Ah! It's… it… it's a… ah! I… I can't talk, ladies and gentlemen.

Honest: it's just laying there, mass of smoking wreckage. Ah! And everybody can hardly breathe and talk and the screaming. Lady, I… I… I'm sorry. Honest: I… I can hardly breathe. I… I'm going to step inside, where I cannot see it. Charlie, that's terrible. Ah, ah… I can't. Listen, folks; I… I'm going to have to stop for a minute because I've lost my voice. This is the worst thing I've ever witnessed.'

23.
9 May 1946,
The Abdication of Italy's Victor Emmanuel III

On 29 July 1900, the king of Italy, Umberto I, was assassinated. The throne passed to his 30-year-old son, who, as Victor Emmanuel III, would reign until 1946, a period which saw both world wars and the rise and fall of Benito Mussolini's fascists.

Born in Naples on 11 November 1869, the future king was so short, the German kaiser, Wilhelm II, nicknamed him the dwarf, and, in private, Mussolini called him the 'little sardine'. He ruled over an Italy that had been in existence as a unified nation only since 1871. Despite unification, Italy was a deeply-fragmented society, steeped in poverty and corruption, and ruled over by a succession of weak coalition governments. But, as a figurehead king, Victor Emmanuel III chose to ignore the affairs of state, preferring instead to focus on his vast collection of coins.

Italy's War

With the outbreak of war in July 1914, Italy initially adopted a position of neutrality despite having been in alliance, the Triple Alliance, with Germany and the Austrian-Hungarian Empire since 1882. Victor Emmanuel favoured participation in the war, partly as a means of enhancing Italy's reputation on the international stage. Italy duly entered the war in May 1915, not as allies of Germany and Austria-Hungary, but on the side of the Triple Entente allies – France, Russia and Great Britain.

King Victor Emmanuel III, 1915. World's Work.

Mussolini

After 1918, Victor Emmanuel again retired to the sidelines as Italy struggled to cope with the post-war instabilities of demobilization, unemployment and inflation. Socialists, communists, anarchists and the newly-formed fascists fought on the streets and on the farms in a vicious cycle of ever-increasing violence.

In October 1922, with the country on the verge of civil war, the rising star of Italy's right, Benito Mussolini, led the fascist March on Rome, demanding to form a new government. At first, Victor Emmanuel resisted but then, fearing outright anarchy, bowed to Mussolini's persistence.

The murder of a leading socialist politician and outspoken critic of the fascists, Giacomo Matteotti, in June 1924 almost caused Mussolini's downfall. Many suspected Mussolini's involvement and demanded that the king remove Mussolini from power. Ignoring the national outcry, Victor Emmanuel, more fearful of a socialist takeover, threw his support behind the fascists. Mussolini survived.

For the next 18 years, Victor Emmanuel watched without undue concern as Mussolini ruled the country. Following Italy's successful invasions of Ethiopia (1935-36) and Albania (1939), Victor Emmanuel was made emperor of the former and the king of the latter. (On hearing of Italy's victory in Ethiopia, the king wept with joy.) Having never visited either, he renounced both titles in 1943.

Victor Emmanuel III, 1936 postcard.

World War Two

Victor Emmanuel opposed Italy's entry into the Second World War but was unable to prevent Mussolini from declaring war on France and Great Britain in June 1940. Three years later, on 24 July 1943, with Italy staring defeat in the face, the Italian Fascist Grand Council voted 19 to 8 (with three abstentions) in favour of a resolution to have Mussolini removed from power.

Benito Mussolini, May 1930. German Federal Archives.

The following day, Mussolini kept his fortnightly meeting with the king, believing that the vote the previous evening was neither constitutional nor binding. He was much mistaken. Almost apologetically, Victor Emmanuel III dismissed the 59-year-old dictator: 'My dear Duce, it's no longer any good. Italy has gone to bits... The soldiers don't want to fight any more... At this moment you are the most hated man in Italy.'

With Mussolini now arrested and held in captivity, Victor Emmanuel signed the armistice with the Allies on 8 September. A month later, having fled to the town of Brindisi, he declared war on Italy's former allies, Germany.

Princess Mafalda

The king's daughter, Princess Mafalda, married a prominent Nazi. When her husband fell out with the Nazi regime, they were arrested and Mafalda was interned in Buchenwald concentration camp, where she died on 27 August 1944.

Republic

On 9 May 1946, a year following the end of the war in Europe and after 46 years on the throne, Victor Emmanuel was forced to abdicate and leave Italy. He moved to Egypt. He named his son as his successor, Umberto II, three weeks ahead of a national referendum to decide on whether Italy should maintain its monarchy. On 2 June, the nation voted 54.3 per cent in favour of becoming a republic. After 85 years, the Kingdom of Italy was no more.

Victor Emmanuel III died in exile in Egypt on 28 December 1947, aged 78. His son, Umberto II, king for five weeks, died in Switzerland in 1983. (Benito Mussolini, meanwhile, was executed by Italian partisans on 28 April 1945).

24.
10 May 1857,
The Start of the Indian Mutiny

On 10 May 1857, the Indian Mutiny, as it became known, erupted in the town of Meerut in northern India. Discontent among the native Indian soldiers, the sepoys, had been simmering for months if not decades but the violence, when it came, took the British completely by surprise.

By 1857, the East India Company, the monolithic, monopolising commercial company that conducted trade in India and had become the *de facto* rulers of the country on behalf of the British government, ruled two thirds of India. The remaining third was overseen by Indian princes who paid tribute to the British. That the East India Company could maintain its authority was down to the might of its huge army, consisting of 45,000 Europeans and 230,000 Indian sepoys. While most sepoys were glad and even proud to serve in the army, their loyalty to it always took second place to their religion.

Religious sensibilities

Sepoys of all faiths were concerned for their respective faiths. The prospect of being made to serve overseas, for example, alarmed Hindu sepoys as travelling over water was a compromise of caste. (Similar grievances led to a much smaller rebellion, the Vellore Mutiny, in 1806).

A sepoy from the Bengal Native Infantry, 1819. Painting by Paul Chater.

Their fears were not without foundation – there was among the British an evangelical element keen on converting the Indian masses to Christianity and to persuade them to turn their backs on the 'monsters of lust, injustice, wickedness and cruelty', to use William Wilberforce (1759-1833)'s phrase. In the early nineteenth century, the British had outlawed various religious traditions, including the practice of *suttee* – the Hindu tradition by which a widow immolated herself on her husband's funeral pyre. General Sir Charles Napier, the Commander-in-Chief in India from 1849 to 1851, led the charge against *suttee*, saying, 'When men burn women alive we hang them'. Spreading their influence, the British built Christian schools and snatched orphaned Indian children to be brought up as Christians. (A Western education, the British believed, would eventually lead to greater responsibility and equip the Indian for eventual self-rule.)

The British were also rapidly developing Indian infrastructure on Western lines – expanding the network of railways and roads. The Hindus, in adhering to their caste system, could not tolerate such an imposition on their tradition – Hindus of differing castes could not share the same road, let alone the same train. The British, they assumed, were trying to destroy the caste system.

Unrest

The first symptom of unrest came in January 1857, when the recently-opened telegraph office in Barrackpore was burned down as a protest against the march of Westernized progress. Two months later, on 29 March 1857, a 29-year-old sepoy called Mangal Pandey, stoned with opium and brandishing a sword and a musket, urged his fellow sepoys to rebel. He wounded two officers by sword before turning the gun on himself, attempting to pull the trigger with his toe. He fired but managed only to wound himself. He was hanged for his efforts and was soon to become a martyr to the rebels' cause.

Mangal Pandey.

The Rifle

But it was something rather mundane that sparked the Indian Mutiny of 1857. The sepoys had been issued with a new Enfield rifle. In order to use the rifle, the soldier had to bite off the end of a lubricated cartridge before inserting the powder into the weapon. The problem was that the grease used to seal the cartridge was made from animal fat – both cow, a sacred beast to Hindus, and pork, an insult to the Muslim soldiers. The East India Company made amends by substituting the forbidden fats with that of sheep or, instead, beeswax. Too late. The sepoys saw it as another example of a deliberate ploy to undermine their respective religions and to convert them, through this perfidious route, to Christianity. The fact this was not the case did nothing to squash the rumour.

Revolt was in the air. One British officer wrote, on 5 May, 'I can hear the moaning of the hurricane. But I can't say how, when or where it will break forth'.

On the evening of 9 May, 85 Indian dissenters in Meerut, 40 miles from Delhi, who had been court-martialled for refusing to touch the new cartridges, were marched onto a parade ground, stripped of their uniforms, shackled with fetters and thrown into jail to serve sentences from five to ten years. Yet these were not recalcitrant men seething with anger but loyal subjects of the Company's army who obeyed every order but simply could not defile their religion.

When, that evening, Lieutenant Hugh Gough (later a general and recipient of the Victoria Cross) was warned by a sepoy of the impending mutiny in Meerut, he rushed to tell his senior officers only to have his concerns brushed aside.

Mutiny

On the late afternoon of the following day, 10 May, as the British residents prepared to go to evening song, the Indian comrades of the imprisoned sepoys broke open the jail and together they revolted, dragging the British out and hacking them to death. The violence was swift and intense; civilians joining the sepoys in an orgy of killing and arson.

None who came within sight of the enraged horde were spared – the sick, the pregnant and the very young were among the victims. Two particular atrocities inflamed the passions of the British – Mrs Chambers, a pregnant woman whose unborn baby was ripped from her womb, and Mrs Dawson, recovering from smallpox, who was burnt to death. Fifty or more were left dead. Come late evening, the rebels took to their horses and made for Delhi forty miles away.

A bungalow at Meerut under attack, 10 May 1857.
Illustrated London News.

Put the English to death

Upon arriving in the capital, the rebels sought to restore the old Mughal Empire and have the 82-year-old Bahadur Shah II as their figurehead. Bahadur Shah had had to suffer a demotion in title, the British stripping him of the title emperor and proclaiming him 'merely' the King of Delhi. Having been pensioned off by the British, he was content to wile away his remaining years writing poetry and painting, and believing he could, when the desire took him, turn himself into a gnat. When the rebels made their demands, he reluctantly gave them his support and issued a proclamation declaring a holy war and urging his 'subjects' to rise up and 'put the English to death'.

It would take two years and two months before the British were able to proclaim: 'War is at an end; [the] rebellion is put down.'

*The name 'Indian Mutiny', as it was taught to generations of British schoolchildren, has a very Eurocentric ring to it; Indians prefer to call it the First War of Independence or the First Nationalist Uprising.

25.
10 May 1941,
Rudolph Hess Arrives in Scotland

On 10 May 1941, occurred one of the most bizarre incidences of the Second World War – the appearance in Scotland of top-ranking Nazi, Rudolph Hess.

Hitler and Rudolph Hess

Hess was one of the original members of the Nazi Party, joining in 1920. Three years later he was involved in the failed Munich *Putsch* and, for his part, was imprisoned alongside his leader, Adolf Hitler. Devoted to Hitler, Hess acted as scribe as Hitler dictated his biographical *Mein Kampf.* Upon their release, Hess became Hitler's private secretary and in 1933 was promoted to deputy leader of the Nazi Party. In 1939 Hess was appointed second-in-line to Hitler as Head of State, second only to Hermann Goring.

Hess's Flight to Scotland

Although a fervent and ideological Nazi, Hess felt that, as fellow Anglo-Saxons, Britain and Germany should not be at war with one another. Thus, on 10 May 1941, he took it upon himself to fly single-handedly in a Messerschmitt the one thousand miles from Augsberg in Germany to Scotland with the express purpose of negotiating a peace between the two nations. Stocked-up with money, a gun, camera, maps, twenty-eight medications and various homeopathic remedies, Hess took off. Around 11 pm, after a five-hour flight, Hess jettisoned his plane and parachuted out, landing awkwardly and breaking his ankle. He had landed on Floors Farm, near the village of Eaglesham in Renfrewshire, eight miles south of Glasgow.

Rudolph Hess, 1933. German Federal Archives.

A 45-year-old ploughman, named David McLean, who had heard the crashing of the plane, rushed out, armed with a pitchfork, to find Hess who initially identified himself as Captain Albert Horn. Prodding the German with his pitchfork, McLean escorted the hobbling Hess back to his cottage where McLean's mother offered Hess a cup of tea (Hess refused, asking only for water). In a TV interview, Mr McLean, with his mother, described his strange encounter with the Nazi apparition from the skies. 'He was a gentleman,' she says, and 'after all he was somebody's son'.

The Duke of Hamilton

Upon being officially arrested, Hess demanded to see the Duke of Hamilton, whom he had previously met and whom he misguidedly believed had some influence within the British government, but was adamant he did not want to see Churchill, whom he held responsible for waging war on Germany. Churchill, on his part, had no intention of seeing Hess and ordered his internment, rather melodramatically, in the Tower of London (the Tower's last political prisoner). Then, until the end of the war, Hess was kept in various military prisons and hospitals, whilst observed, interrogated and analysed. On one occasion, Hess tried to commit suicide by throwing himself down a set of prison stairs but managed only to break his leg.

Hitler, on hearing of Hess's treachery, stripped his old comrade of all positions and responsibility, and ordered him shot should he ever step foot back in Germany. To the German public, the Nazi Party explained away Hess's defection as being a result of his 'mental illness'.

British Intelligence, backed up by medical opinion, had come to much the same conclusion – that Hess was mentally ill. The German was deeply depressed, had attempted suicide and was convinced he was about to be murdered.

Hess Stands Trial at Nuremberg

In 1946, Hess was sent back to Germany to stand trial at Nuremberg, irritating his co-defendants by continually fidgeting, rocking and laughing inappropriately. He was found guilty of various lesser charges, including conspiring against the peace, but crucially not of war crimes, which carried the death penalty. Instead, Hess was sentenced to life imprisonment within Spandau prison in Berlin. (Although in West Berlin, Spandau was jointly-managed by all four allied powers – Britain, the US, France and the Soviet Union).

Rudolph Hess in prison, 1945. US Holocaust Memorial Museum.

Hess in Spandau

From 1966, following the release of other Nuremberg-sentenced Nazis, including, most famously, Albert Speer, Hess became Spandau's sole inmate. His mental health had deteriorated still further and the three Western powers petitioned his release on humanitarian grounds. The Soviets however were determined that Hess should remain behind bars to the end of his life.

Finally, in 1987, during Mikhail Gorbachev's tenure as Soviet leader, the Soviet Union relented and agreed to Hess's release. He'd been a prisoner at Spandau for 41 years, 21 of them entirely by himself in a prison designed for 600 inmates. But on 17 August 1987, Hess, aged 93, was found dead. He'd hung himself in the prison summerhouse with an electric cord. Spandau prison was then destroyed to prevent it becoming a shrine to Neo-Nazis.

Alternative Theories about Rudolph Hess

The story of Rudolph Hess's flight to Scotland and his subsequent imprisonment does not end there. Conspiracy theories abound to this day. One such theory argues that Hitler approved of Hess's mission; wanting to make peace with Britain to allow him a free hand in the coming invasion of the Soviet Union (launched a month later in June 1941). Another theory postulates that Hess's plane was shot down and Hess killed (or shot soon after) and that it was a double that appeared in the Nuremberg dock and spent 41 years in Spandau.

Even his death raises questions – aged 93, Hess needed constant care and help – he was reportedly unable to tie his own shoelaces or lift his arms – let alone hang himself, and that, on the eve of his release, he was murdered on the orders of British Intelligence to prevent embarrassing revelations coming to light.

26.
24 May 1941,
The Sinking of HMS *Hood*

On 24 May 1941 two mighty ships engaged in battle – the respective pride of the German and British navies: the *Bismarck* and HMS *Hood*.

It started six days before when, on the evening of Sunday 18 May 1941, the *Bismarck*, accompanied by the *Prinz Eugene*, set sail from the Polish port of Gdynia. It was the *Bismarck's* first mission.

There had never been a warship like her

Named after the 19th century German chancellor, Otto von Bismarck, the *Bismarck* had been launched just two years earlier, in February 1939, by the chancellor's great granddaughter. The ship was an impressive sight – one sixth of a mile long and 120 feet wide. British writer and broadcaster, Ludovic Kennedy (1909-2009), wrote of the *Bismarck*: 'There had never been a warship like her… No German saw her without pride, no neutral or enemy without admiration.'

The mission set for the *Bismarck* and the *Prinz Eugene* was to head for the Atlantic and cause as much damage and disruption as possible to the British convoys shipping vital supplies across the Atlantic into Britain. On board the *Bismarck* were two of Hitler's most senior and able seamen – its captain, 45-year-old Ernst Lindemann, referred to by his crew as 'our father', and Fleet Commander, 51-year-old Admiral Gunther Lutjens.

From Poland, the two ships passed Norway where their presence was picked up by the British. British aircraft and ships, keeping a safe distance, monitored their progress as the German ships skirted north of Iceland and then south down the Denmark Straits between Iceland and Greenland.

It was here, in the Denmark Straits, that the British fleet, led by HMS *Hood* and *Prince of Wales*, was ordered to intercept.

The embodiment of British sea-power

Built in 1916, the *Hood* was, according to Kennedy, 'the embodiment of British sea-power and the British Empire between the wars.' But the *Hood* had been built at a time, during the First World War, when enemy shells came in low and hit the sides of a ship near the water line. But in 1941 shells were more likely to arch across the sky and fall onto the upper decks. The decks of the *Hood* had never been reinforced and therein lay its weak spot. The 'embodiment of British sea-power' had been built for a different war.

Painting by J.C. Schmitz-Westerholt capturing the moment of the Hood*'s sinking. In the foreground is the HMS* Prince of Wales.

The Battle of Denmark Straits

In the early hours of 24 May, the opposing fleets with their imposing ships engaged. Thirteen miles apart the ships fired one-ton shells that, travelling at 1,600 miles per hour, took almost a minute to reach their intended target. The noise, which could be heard in Iceland, was horrendous.

The battle lasted merely twenty minutes and both the *Bismarck* and the *Prince of Wales* took direct hits, but it was the fate of the *Hood* that stunned the world. A shell from the *Bismarck* hit the *Hood* on its vulnerable upper deck, tore through the ship and penetrated its ammunition room, causing an almighty explosion.

The ship sliced into two, its front end dramatically lifting out of the water. A huge fireball rocketed into the sky, followed by plumes of dense black smoke, with pieces of molten metal shooting like so many white stars, as one German sailor described it.

Within five minutes, the HMS *Hood*, pride of the Royal Navy, had sunk. It was no more. Of its crew of 1,421 men, all were killed – except for three.

The crew of the *Bismarck* was jubilant. For this they would be the toast of Germany. The *Prince of Wales* was also struggling, having been hit seven times. The German crew wanted to give chase and finish her off but Lindemann, as captain, not wanting to expose the *Bismarck* unnecessarily, erred on the side of caution and resisted the temptation.

Also, of greater concern for Lindemann, the *Bismarck* had been hit by a shell that failed to explode but had caused damage to her fuel tanks. Serious damage.

Leaking oil at an alarming rate, Lindemann knew he had to get her back to safety. He decided on Saint-Nazaire, northern France, a distance of 1,700 miles, a journey of some four days.

The *Prinz Eugene* and the *Bismarck* parted ways. The joy of the *Bismarck* crew had evaporated. Now there was nothing but concern – could they escape the British, could they make it all the way to France? The ship was limping – the fuel leak had forced the captain to greatly reduce speed. France seemed a long way away.

Sink the *Bismarck*

Meanwhile, in Britain, a nation reeled in shock, stunned by the loss of the *Hood*. It demanded retaliation. Churchill, reflecting the public mood, issued his famous battle cry: 'Sink the *Bismarck!*'

A fleet consisting of four battleships, two battle cruisers, two aircraft carriers, 21 destroyers and 13 cruisers was dispatched.

The chase was on.

27.
4 June 1937,
The Death of Ekaterina Dzhugashvili, Stalin's Mother

Joseph Stalin's mother, Ekaterina Dzhugashvili, born 5 February 1858, married at the age of fourteen. Her first two children, both boys, died within their first year. Her third child, Joseph Dzhugashvili, was born 18 December 1878, and although struck by a bout of smallpox, he survived. History would remember him better as Joseph Stalin.

A sensitive child

Ekaterina Dzhugashvili, known as Keke, dictated her memories in 1935, two years before her death. The transcript was stored by the Georgian archive of the Ministry of Internal Affairs and was only released in 2007 on the specific request of British author, Simon Sebag Montefiore, who, at the time, was writing his second biography of Stalin, *Young Stalin*.

She called her son 'Soso', Georgian for 'Little Joey': 'My Soso was a very sensitive child,' she wrote.

Seeing her son's survival as a gift from God, Keke was determined to see Soso enter church school to train to become a priest, fighting off, often physically, her husband's insistence that he become a cobbler. 'Mummy,' said the young Soso, 'what if, when we arrive in the city, father finds me and forces me to become a shoemaker? I want to study. I'd rather kill myself than become a cobbler.' 'I kissed him,' wrote his mother, 'and wiped away his tears. Nobody will stop you studying, nobody is going to take you away from me.'

Having freed herself from her violent husband, Ekaterina Dzhugashvili moved from one accommodation to another picking up work where she could.

Ekaterina Dzhugashvili, c1892.

Like a tsar

In later life, Stalin arranged for his mother to move into a large mansion in Tiflis, capital of Georgia (now Tbilisi), but a woman of humble needs, she felt uncomfortable with such luxury and confined herself to one small room.

She turned down his requests to visit him in Moscow and Stalin, never fond of travelling, visited her only rarely. She once asked her son, 'Joseph, what exactly are you now?' He replied, 'Do you remember the Tsar? Well, I'm like a tsar.' 'You'd have done better to have been a priest,' she said in response. When he asked her why she had beaten him so much as a child, she shrugged and said, 'It's why you've turned out so well.'

Ekaterina Dzhugashvili died 4 June 1937, aged 79. Stalin upset Georgian tradition and sensibilities by not attending her funeral, sending Lavrentry Beria, a fellow Georgian, in his stead.

28.
16 June 1953,
The Start of the East German Uprising

Stalin had died in March 1953 and a new post-Stalinist era beckoned for those trapped behind the Iron Curtain. But if the workers of East Germany thought that Stalin's death meant change, they were soon disabused as the East German premier, Walter Ulbricht, strove to increase industrial output.

Walter Ulbricht's plan

East Germany's economy was stagnating and Ulbricht, a Stalinist to the core, proposed a range of measures to pump-up the economy – increase taxes, increase prices and increase production by 10 per cent – but with no corresponding increase in wages. If the new quotas were not met, workers were told, wages would be cut by a third. The Kremlin viewed these proposals with concern, advising Ulbricht to tone down the measures and slow down the intense pace of industrialisation that the East German leader insisted was necessary. For the workers of the German Democratic Republic this was a lose-lose scenario.

Citizens of post-war Eastern Europe did as their governments ordered; any protest was silent, whispered in dark corners. But these measures were too much; Ulbricht had gone too far.

Walter Ulbricht, c1946. Deutsche Fotothek.

Strike

On 16 June 1953, East Berlin construction workers downed tools. The following morning, 17 June, the strike had spread with over 40,000 demonstrators marching through the capital. Their demands at first focussed on the economic – a return to the old work quotas. But then as the strike spread to other cities – Leipzig, Dresden and some 400 cities and towns throughout East Germany, their voices gained strength and their hearts courage. They demanded increasingly more – free elections, a new government, democracy. Meetings were held; workers' councils elected. In the East German town of Merseburg, workers stormed the police station and released prisoners from the jails.

Protestors tore down communists flags and carried banners proclaiming, 'We want free elections; we are not slaves', 'Death to communism' and 'Long Live Eisenhower'. This was no longer a strike but an uprising.

Soviet intervention

Ulbricht turned to the Kremlin. Lavrentry Beria, Stalin's former Chief of Secret Police and the man poised to take over now that that Stalin was dead, sent in the tanks. The crews, 20,000 troops based in East Germany, were told by Beria not to 'spare bullets'. This was a revolution and it needed crushing. (Six months later Beria was dead – executed by his Kremlin colleagues. One of the supposed reasons for his arrest was his heavy-handed dealing of the East German Uprising).

East German Uprising, 17 June 1953. German Federal Archives.

Martial law was declared while, on the afternoon of the 17th, the tanks moved in and, alongside the East German police, opened fire. Down the Unter den Linden, people, demonstrators, civilians fell. How many were killed no one knows for sure. The figures vary considerably between sources based in the West and those of the East. But at least 40 were killed, possibly up to 260, and 400 wounded.

The West

If the East German protestors hoped for assistance from the West, they, like their counterparts during the Hungarian Revolution three years later, were to be disappointed. The US were not prepared to risk war over such an issue. But the US did start a food aid programme, distributing over 5 million food parcels during July and August. Winston Churchill's response, at the time prime minister, was also muted. According to German historian, Hubertus Knabe, Churchill feared the resurgence of a united Germany so soon after the Second World War. While publicly supporting a united Germany, a divided one, he felt, was more secure. Churchill considered the regime's response to the uprising as 'restrained'.

Thus without the West's intervention, pockets of resistance continued for a few weeks but the main thrust of the East German Uprising had been crushed within just 24 hours of starting.

And then started the reprisals – thousands arrested, perhaps up to 6,000, tortured and interned. Six ringleaders were executed. Walter Ulbricht took the opportunity of purging his party of seventy per cent of its members.

During the Cold War, the human face of socialism only went so far and today Germany still remembers the uprising of 1953.

29.
16 June 1958,
The Execution of Imre Nagy

Imre Nagy is remembered with great affection in today's Hungary. Although a communist leader during its years of one-party rule, Nagy was the voice of liberalism and reform, advocating *national* communism, free from the shackles of the Soviet Union. Following the Hungarian Revolution of 1956, Nagy was arrested, tried in secret and executed. His rehabilitation and reburial in 1989 played a significant and symbolic role in ending communist rule in Hungary.

Imre Nagy was born 7 June 1896 in the town of Kaposvár in southern Hungary. He worked as a locksmith before joining the Austrian-Hungary army during the First World War. In 1915, he was captured and spent much of the war as a prisoner-of-war in Russia. He escaped and having converted to communism, joined the Red Army and fought alongside the Bolsheviks during the Russian Revolution of 1917.

Agriculture

In 1918, Nagy returned to Hungary as a committed communist and served the short-lived Soviet Republic established by Bela Kun. Following its collapse in August 1919, after only five months, Nagy, as with other former members of Kun's regime, lived underground, fearful of arrest. Eventually, in 1928, he fled to Austria and from there, in 1930, to the Soviet Union, where he spent the next fourteen years studying agriculture.

Imre Nagy's plaque outside the 'House of Terror' museum, Budapest.
Photograph by the author.

Following the Second World War, Nagy returned again to Hungary serving as Minister of Agriculture in Hungary's post-war communist government. Loyal to Stalin, Nagy led the charge of collectivization, redistributing the land of landowners to the peasants.

A *New York Times* journalist, writing in 1956, described Nagy as a 'burly 6-foot 200-pounder... He never made any secret of his fondness for good food, good drink, good clothes. He liked to sit in Budapest cafes and discuss politics or the merits of different Hungarian football teams'.

Prime Minister

In July 1953, four months after Stalin's death and with the Soviet Union's approval, Nagy was appointed prime minister, replacing the unpopular and ruthless, Mátyás Rákosi. Rákosi, 'Stalin's Best Hungarian Disciple', had been responsible for a reign of terror in which some 2,000 Hungarians had been executed and up to 100,000 imprisoned. Nagy tried to usher in a move away from Moscow's influence and introduce a period of liberalism and political and economic reform. This, as far as the Kremlin was concerned, was setting a bad example to other countries within the Eastern Bloc. Nagy quickly became too popular for the Kremlin's liking and in April 1955 Rákosi was put back in charge and the terror and oppression started anew. Seven months later, Nagy was expelled from the communist party altogether.

Hungarian Revolution

A Soviet tank on the streets of Budapest, October 1956.
Central Intelligence Agency

On 23 October 1956, the people of Hungary rose up against their government and its Soviet masters. The Hungarian Revolution had begun. Nikita Khrushchev in Moscow sent the tanks in to restore order while the rebels demanded the return of Imre Nagy. Khrushchev relented and Nagy was back in control, calling for calm and promising political reform, while, around him, the Soviet tanks tried to quash the uprising. On 28 October, Khrushchev withdrew the tanks, and for a few short days, the people of Hungary wondered whether they had won.

On 1 November, Nagy boldly announced his intentions: he promised to release political prisoners, including Cardinal Mindszenty, notoriously imprisoned by Rákosi's regime; he promised to withdraw Hungary from the Warsaw Pact; that Hungary would become a neutral nation; and he promised open elections and an end to one-party rule. Two days later, he went so far to announce members of a new coalition government, which included a number of non-communists. This was all too much for the Kremlin. If Nagy delivered on these reforms, what sort of message would it send to other members of the Eastern Bloc? Its very foundation would be at risk.

On 4 November, Khrushchev sent the tanks back in; this time in far greater numbers. Nagy appealed to the West. While the US condemned the Soviet attack as a 'monstrous crime', it did nothing, distracted by presidential elections; while Britain and France were in the midst of their own calamity, namely the Suez Crisis. Anyway, the West was never going to risk war for the sake of Hungary.

The Hungarian Uprising was crushed. Nagy was replaced by Janos Kadar, a man loyal to Moscow, and who would remain in charge of Hungary for the next 32 years, until ill health forced his retirement in May 1988.

With the uprising defeated, the communists returned, the Hungarian secret police, the AVO, re-emerged in their uniforms and, with their Soviet friends, plucked out leading insurgents for execution and scores more for deportation to Russia. They exhumed the bodies of their fallen colleagues, killed during the revolution, and reburied them with full military honours. By the end of the year the Iron Curtain was back in place but not before over 200,000 men, women and children had escaped into Austria and the West.

In November 1958, the communists won 99.8 per cent in a single-party election. Everything in Hungary was back to normal.

Secret Trial

Nagy knew he was in danger and sought refuge in the Yugoslavian Embassy in Budapest. Despite receiving a written assurance from Kadar guaranteeing him safe passage out of Hungary, on 22 November 1956, Nagy, along with others, was kidnapped by Soviet agents as he tried to leave the embassy. He was smuggled out of the country and taken to Romania.

Two years later, Nagy was secreted back into Hungary and along with his immediate colleagues, put on a trial that was as secret as it was pointless. The trial, which lasted from 9 to 15 June, was tape-recorded in its entirety –

52 hours. Charged with high treason and of attempting to overthrow the supposedly legally-recognised Hungarian government, Nagy and his 'fascist counter-revolutionary' colleagues were found guilty and sentenced to death. On 16 June 1958, Imre Nagy, amongst others, was hanged; his body unceremoniously dumped, face down, in an unmarked grave. He was 62. (Even as late as 1988, on the thirtieth anniversary of Nagy's death, the police had to use violence to break up a ceremony in honour of his memory.)

1989

Exactly thirty-one years after his execution, on 16 June 1989, Imre Nagy and his colleagues were rehabilitated, reinterred and afforded a public funeral. The whole of the country observed a minute's silence. Six coffins were placed on the steps of the Exhibition Hall in Budapest's Heroes Square. One coffin was empty – representative of all revolutionaries that had fallen in '56.

Imre Nagy bust, Budapest. Photograph by the author.

It was an emotional and symbolic event attended by over 100,000 people. People lined the routes of Budapest and crowded into Heroes' Square, paying their respects to the great man who, more than anyone, had symbolised the hope and the ultimate defeat of the Uprising. Shops and businesses were closed, schools given the day off. In the square, flowers and wreaths lay everywhere, Corinthian pillars were decked in black and white, Hungarian flags, with the central Soviet emblem removed, fluttered at half-mast, and Hungarians with bowed heads felt united by grief and ingrained memories. People listened to the eulogies and watched the solemn laying of flowers. They listened to the speeches – words criticising the government and the continued interference of the Soviet Union, and demands for multi-party elections – echoes of 1956; words inconceivable even a few weeks earlier.

The writing was on the wall for Hungary's communist rulers. Sure enough, on the 33rd anniversary of the start of the revolution, 23 October 1989, the People's Republic of Hungary was replaced by the Republic of Hungary with a provisional parliamentary president in place. The road to democracy was swift – parliamentary elections were held in Hungary on 24 March 1990, the first free elections to be held in the country since 1945. The totalitarian government was finished – Hungary, at last, was free.

Meanwhile, on 6 July 1989, the Hungarian judicial acquitted Imre Nagy of high treason. The very same day, Janos Kadar died.

1950s Hungarian flag with the central Soviet emblem torn out, Budapest. Photograph by the author.

30.
18 June 1974,
The Death of Georgy Zhukov

Georgy Zhukov achieved fame as perhaps the most successful Soviet military commander of the Second World War. In the post-war Victory Parade in Moscow's Red Square, Zhukov stole the show, inspecting the troops mounted on a white stallion.

Adored by the public and respected by international opinion, Zhukov's position was always going to be vulnerable given Stalin's innate jealousy. Sure enough, in 1946, Zhukov, heavily criticised for being 'politically unreliable', was dismissed and dispatched to a position of diminished responsibility in Odessa.

Known for his uncompromising discipline, Georgy Zhukov placed strategic objective far above the safety of the men he put into battle. Yet, despite his toughness, he could be rendered a wreck by a single harsh word from Soviet dictator, Joseph Stalin. During the early days of the war, he was once reduced to tears by an angry Stalin and had to take the handkerchief offered by Vyacheslav Molotov.

Born 1 December 1896, Zhukov first saw action during the First World War, where, renowned for his bravery, he was twice decorated. He then fought with the Red Army against the Whites during the Russian Civil War of 1917-23 and quickly rose through the ranks. Stalin's great 1930s purge of the military was for Zhukov 'the most difficult emotional experience of my life'. Like many others, he kept a small packed suitcase near his front door should the NKVD come for him. But, unlike many of his contemporaries, he survived and indeed benefited by being able to step into the shoes of men purged, 'dead men's shoes'.

Georgy Zhukov, 1941. Novosti Archive

World War Two

He played a major role during the Great Patriotic War, as Russians call the Second World War, commanding forces in the defence of Leningrad, holding the Germans at bay at Moscow, and instrumental in defeating the Germans at the Battle of Stalingrad. He went on to command victory at the Battle of Kursk and led the Red Army's capture of Berlin in May 1945. 'Where you find Zhukov, you find victory,' became a popular saying within the Red Army. He was the only one of Stalin's generals capable of standing up for himself, even to the point of putting his career and possibly his life at risk. Conversely however, his stubbornness impressed Stalin, and he gained his boss's respect.

Zhukov had his compassionate side. On being told of Goebbels's six dead children in the bunker of the Reich Chancellery, poisoned by their parents, Zhukov said: 'I had not the heart to go down and look at the children'. Zhukov was there, representing the Soviet Union, when, on 8 May 1945 in Berlin, Germany signed its unconditional surrender.

Post-war

Zhukov's stubbornness, which served him well during the war, served him less so post-war. Stalin's basis of rule, throughout his time in power, was fear. For four years, 1941 to 1945, war had kept people in a state of constant fear. Now, in 1945, with the war over, it was necessary to re-establish the fear. What better way than to announce it than to have Zhukov, of all people, war hero extraordinaire, purged. Zhukov, at least, was spared arrest and interrogation and all the trappings of a full purge, he was merely demoted. On arriving in Odessa to start his new, much humbler life, he suffered a heart attack, probably brought on by the stress of his ordeal.

Following Stalin's death in 1953, Zhukov returned to the fore and helped Nikita Khrushchev to power, arresting Khrushchev's main rival for power, Lavrentry Beria. Bursting into a meeting to make the arrest, as pre-arranged, Zhukov shouted at Beria, 'Shut up, you are not the commander here. Comrades, arrest this traitor!' Beria was executed in December 1953 and with Khrushchev now in power, Zhukov was called back to the Kremlin as Deputy Defence Minister, elevated two years later to Defence Minister. However, Zhukov was never comfortable as a politician, much preferring the life of a soldier. He argued with Khrushchev's vision of how the military should be developed and tried to diminish the Politburo's influence on how the military was run. Zhukov was again side-lined.

He published his memoirs, *Reminiscences and Reflections*, in 1969. The book was an immediate bestseller and Zhukov received some 10,000 letters from fans and admirers.

Georgy Zhukov died on 18 June 1974 and his ashes were buried within the Kremlin Wall with full military honours.

Georgy Zhukov Monument, Moscow's Red Square.

In 1995, celebrating the fortieth anniversary of the end of the war, Russia unveiled a statue of Zhukov in Moscow's Red Square.

31.
20 June 1756,
The Black Hole of Calcutta

On 20 June 1756, 123 Britons perished in a tiny dungeon cell in the city of Calcutta. The incident, which soon became known as the Black Hole of Calcutta, illustrated only too well that the Indian race, when left without Britain's civilising influence, was barbaric in the extreme.

In April 1756, the nawab (provincial governor) of Bengal died and the throne passed to his 20-year-old grandson, Siraj-ud-Daulah, a name that was soon to become infamous in Britain as the ultimate in perfidy and cruelty. (In his book, A History of Britain: The British Wars 1603-1776, historian Simon Sharma writes that as a schoolboy, he and his friends referred to Siraj-ud-Daulah as 'Sir Roger Dowler').

The British had been hastily strengthening Fort William in Calcutta (Kolkata) against possible future French incursion into the city. When Siraj-ud-Daulah demanded that the British desist, the British refused – it was they, after all, that had, in 1690, established Calcutta in the first place. Siraj-ud-Daulah marched into the city with 50,000 men and 500 elephants and, imposing his authority, took it with relative ease.

Black Hole

The British fled – but not all managed to escape in time. On the 20 June 1756, those left behind, 146 soldiers and civilians, including two women, surrendered. Despite assurances that they would be protected, they were imprisoned on the apparent orders of Siraj-ud-Daulah in a tiny military cell within Fort William measuring only 18 feet by 14 feet, 10 inches, with only two small windows. Screams and appeals for water were ignored. The prisoners were left to suffocate in the oppressive summer heat, sucking the perspiration from their shirts for liquid or drinking their own urine.

Siraj-ud-Daulah, Nawab of Bengal.

When, the following morning, the door was opened only 43 were still alive. The dead, with no room to fall, remained on their feet. One of the survivors was John Zephaniah Holwell, an Irish-born doctor and commander of the city and a future, albeit briefly, governor of Bengal. Returning to England eight months later, Holwell spent the five-month voyage writing up the tragedy of the Black Hole of Calcutta in his narrative, *A Genuine Narrative of the Deplorable Deaths of the English Gentlemen and others who were suffocated in the Black Hole*. Holwell writes of 'a night of horrors [which] I will not attempt to describe, as they bar all description', and then proceeds to describe the night in detail. 'We had been but few minutes confined,' wrote Holwell, 'before every one fell into a perspiration so profuse, you can form no idea of it. This brought in a raging thirst, which increased in proportion as the body was drained of its moisture.'

Exaggeration

The story caused uproar in Britain. It was not for another century and a half that historians began to question Holwell's narrative, pointing to various flaws in his account. If not the event itself, then certainly the numbers involved were questioned – no more than sixty-nine could possibly have been imprisoned. Holwell may well have exaggerated the event as a means of deflecting blame for having surrendered in the first place. The nawab was shown to have had no knowledge or input into the incarceration of the prisoners.

But in 1756, people were too busy braying for Siraj-ud-Daulah's blood to be too concerned about precise numbers or details. British pride had to be restored and it was to Robert Clive, 'Clive of India', they turned.

The Battle of Plassey

Robert Clive, painted by Nathaniel Dance.

141

In January 1757, Clive retook Calcutta without difficulty, forcing Siraj-ud-Daulah to flee.

Six months later, on 23 June 1757, in a village called Plassey (now Palashi), 90 miles north of Calcutta, the opposing armies met. Clive's force of just 3,000 men seemed, on paper at least, outnumbered 17 to 1 by Siraj-ud-Daulah's 50,000 men, which included a sizeable French element. But Clive had struck a bargain with Siraj-ud-Daulah's disaffected army chief, Mir Jafar.

As battle was joined, Mir Jafar held his men back and Siraj-ud-Daulah's men, poorly trained, ill-equipped and many dosed up on opium, were no match for the British who suffered little more than 70 killed or wounded. The Indian commanders strode around on bejewelled elephants intended to instil fear in the enemy but the British simply shot at the beasts causing them to stampede and wreak havoc within the Indian lines. Siraj-ud-Daulah, who had fled the field of battle on a camel, was soon caught and, on 2 July 1757, executed.

Britain had got its revenge and the Battle of Plassey ensured that it was the British, in the guise of the East India Company, that now oversaw the administration of Bengal, an area the size of France and Germany combined. Clive was appointed governor and ensured that his puppet, the new nawab, Mir Jafar, paid his dues.

The Monument

Meanwhile, John Zephaniah Holwell commissioned a fifty-foot high obelisk, erected at the site of the Black Hole of Calcutta, to commemorate those who lost their lives that night. It was removed in 1821.

In 1902, the new Indian viceroy, Lord Curzon, ordered that a replica should be built on the same spot. In 1940, at the insistence of the Indian independence movement, the memorial was moved to the grounds of St John's Church in Calcutta, a church built by the East India Company in the 1780s, where it can still be seen today.

Black Hole of Calcutta Memorial

32.
22 June 1940,
France Surrenders

On 11 November 1918, the French and British allies accepted Germany's surrender and, between them, signed the armistice that ended the First World War. The signing took place in a railway carriage in the middle of the picturesque woods of Compiègne, fifty miles north-east of Paris. The humiliation of that event ran deep into the psyche of Germany, and none more so than in Adolf Hitler, at the time a corporal in the Imperial German Army.

On 22 June 1940, Hitler, now the German *Führer*, got his revenge – it was the turn of the French to surrender, and Hitler made sure that it was done in the most demeaning circumstances possible – in exactly the same train carriage and in the same spot as the signing twenty-two years earlier.

The Fall of France

Following the 1914-1918 war, the French had built a defensive 280-mile long fortification, the Maginot Line, all along the Franco-German border as protection against a future German attack. The Battle of France began on 10 May 1940. The Germans rendered the Maginot Line obsolete within a morning by merely skirting round the north of it, through the Ardennes forest. Because of its rugged terrain, the French considered the forest impassable. Reaching the town of Sedan on the French side of the Ardennes on 14 May and brushing aside French resistance, the Germans pushed forward, not towards Paris as expected, but north, towards the English Channel, forcing the French and their British allies further and further back. In 1916, the Germans had failed to take Verdun despite ten months of trench warfare; in May 1940, it took them but a day.

Elsewhere, Hitler's armies were enjoying victory after victory – the Netherlands capitulated on 15 May, followed two weeks later by the surrender of Belgium. Allied forces, with their backs to the sea in the French coastal town of Dunkirk, were trapped. But the Germans, poised to annihilate the whole British Expeditionary Force, were inexplicably ordered by Hitler to halt outside the town. Between 26 May and 2 June, over 1,000 military and civilian vessels rescued and brought back to Britain 338,226 Allied soldiers. But not without scenes of panic, broken discipline and soldiers shot by their officers for losing self-control. Meanwhile, Hitler's puzzled generals watched, rueing a missed opportunity.

Winston Churchill may have viewed Dunkirk as a 'deliverance' but the French considered the British cowards for what they saw as a betrayal at Dunkirk. Hitler too thought little of the British soldier: 'They can certainly beat their colonial subjects with a whip but on the battlefield they are miserable cowards'.

The swastika flies over Paris

The fall of France was dramatic in its speed. German Chief of General Staff, Franz Halder, who had organised the invasion of Poland eight months earlier, warned Hitler of the folly of attacking France. Privately, he believed it to be 'idiotic and reckless'. In the event, Hitler's forces entered a largely deserted Paris on 14 June, over two million Parisians having fled south. Soon the swastika flag was flying from the Arc de Triomphe.

On 16 June, the French general, Charles de Gaulle, escaped France to begin his life of exile in London. He was later sentenced to death – *in absentia* by the French Vichy government.

German soldiers in Paris, June 1940. German Federal Archive.

In Britain, Winston Churchill, appointed prime minister only on 10 May, urged the French to keep on fighting and discussed the possibility of France and Great Britain becoming one unified nation. When French prime minister, Paul Reynaud, put the idea of the union to the French government, now based in Bordeaux, the idea was ridiculed. Marshal Philippe Pétain, hero of the 1916 Battle of Verdun, preferred to surrender – to continue the fight would destroy the country and a union with Britain would be akin to a 'marriage with a corpse'. French general, Maxime Weygand, believed that following the fall of France, the British would soon have 'its neck wrung like a chicken' by the Germans.

On 17 June, Reynaud resigned, to be replaced by the 84-year-old Pétain, whose first acts were to seek an armistice with the Germans and order Reynaud's arrest. France had been defeated.

Weeping Frenchman. National Archives and Records Administration.

The Forest of Compiègne

On 20 June, the Germans prepared the text for the French-German armistice, with Hitler dictating its preamble. The venue for the signing was to be the forest of Compiègne, where, 22 years before, at the end of the First World War, the Germans had surrendered to the French and signed the armistice of 11 November 1918. Hitler, with a flair for the dramatic, ordered that the signing ceremony should take place in the in the very same railway carriage that had been used in November 1918, now on display in a Parisian museum. The carriage, once a dining car which had been transformed into a conference room, split into two by a glass partition, was transported north.

About 200 yards from the carriage stood the Alsace-Lorraine statue, commemorating the 1918 signing, featuring a fallen German eagle, impaled by the sword of the victorious allies. Now, in June 1940, it was adorned by the Nazi swastika. Nearby stood a statue of Marshal Ferdinand Foch, the French commander-in-chief, who had led the negotiations in 1918.

At 3.15 on the afternoon of 21 June, a warm summer's day, the German delegation arrived and emerged from their Mercedes: Hermann Goring, Rudolph Hess, Joachim von Ribbentrop, Wilhelm Keitel, Erich Raeder, Alfred Jodl amongst others and, last of all, Hitler, his First World

War Iron Cross pinned upon his tunic.

The American journalist and writer, William Shirer, author of the excellent, *Rise and Fall of the Third Reich*, originally published 1959, was witness to the occasion. Shirer describes the expression in Hitler's face: 'grave, solemn, yet brimming with revenge… There was something else, difficult to describe, in his expression, a sort of scornful, inner joy at being present at this great reversal he himself had wrought.'

Hitler and his entourage stopped to read the French inscription of a granite block, which read in capitals, 'HERE ON THE ELEVENTH OF NOVEMBER 1918 SUCCUMBED THE CRIMINAL PRIDE OF THE GERMAN EMPIRE – VANQUISHED BY THE FREE PEOPLES WHICH IT TRIED TO ENSLAVE.'

The German delegation took their place in the carriage, Hitler pointedly sitting where Foch had sat 22 years before. Then arrived the French delegation, headed by General Charles Huntziger. Shirer noticed that the German guard of honour, 'snapped to attention for the French as they passed but did not present arms'.

With everyone sitting, Keitel, with a monocle in his eye, read aloud Hitler's preamble of the armistice, a translator relaying it to the French. At the glass partition, one of Hitler's henchmen, Otto Günsche (who took on the responsibility of burning Hitler's body following his leader's suicide on 30 April 1945), kept guard with orders to shoot anyone who 'should dare to conduct himself in an improper manner towards Hitler'.

Hitler uttered not a word. With the reading of the preamble done, Hitler and most of his entourage made their exit with a Nazi salute, and left to the sound of the German national anthem and the *Horst Wessel* song (a Nazi favourite composed in memory of a Nazi 'martyr') ringing in their ears. The French delegates stood, some with tears in their eyes.

The French sign the Armistice

Keitel and Jodl stayed behind to discuss the details of the armistice with Huntziger. France was to be split into two – the northern half occupied by the Germans and the southern half run by a French government answerable to the Germans. This government, headed by Pétain, was to be based in the spa town of Vichy.

At 18:30, the following day, with the Germans getting impatient, the

French were given one hour to sign or face a resumption of hostilities. Huntziger, speaking to General Weygand in Bordeaux, insisted that he should be *ordered* to sign the armistice and not merely *authorized* to sign it, thereby removing the responsibility from his shoulders. At 18:50, Huntziger and Keitel duly signed the hateful document.

On hearing the news, Hitler was thrilled, slapping his knee with delight. (Exactly one year later, he would launch the German invasion of the Soviet Union.)

Straight afterwards, on Hitler's orders, the railway carriage and the monument commemorating the 1918 signing were destroyed. The following day, Hitler enjoyed a three-hour whistle-stop tour of Paris. Having taken in the main sites and been photographed with the Eiffel Tower behind him, he left. It was, he said, 'the dream of my life to be permitted to see Paris. I cannot say how happy I am to have that dream fulfilled today.' On visiting Napoleon's tomb, he said: 'That was the greatest and finest moment of my life'. Before departing, he ordered the demolition of two Parisian First World War monuments, including the monument to Edith Cavell, the British nurse shot by the Germans in Brussels in October 1915.

The German occupation of France would last four long years until in August 1944, two months from the start of the Normandy landings, the first parts of France were finally liberated.

Hitler and entourage in Paris, 23 June 1940. German Federal Archives.

33.
22 June 1941,
Hitler Launches Operation Barbarossa,
Germany's Invasion of Russia

On 22 June 1941, Adolf Hitler launched Operation Barbarossa, Germany's invasion of the Soviet Union. What followed was a war of annihilation, a horrific clash of totalitarianism, and the most destructive war in history.

Hitler's intention was always to invade the Soviet Union. It was, along with the destruction of the Jews, fundamental to his core objectives – living-space in the east and the subjugation of the Slavic race. He stated his intentions clearly enough in his semi-autobiographical *Mein Kampf*, published in 1925. This was meant to be a war of obliteration – and despite the vastness of Russian territory and manpower, Hitler anticipated a quick victory (his generals had predicted ten weeks). So confident the Nazi hierarchy, that they provided their troops with summer uniforms but made no provision for the fierce Russian winter that lay further ahead.

'You have only to kick in the door,' said Hitler confidently, 'and the whole rotten structure will come crashing down'. Two tons of Iron Crosses were waiting in Germany for those involved with the capture of Moscow. This was always going to be the most brutal war, one which could not be 'conducted with chivalry', as Hitler told his generals, but 'conducted with unprecedented, unmerciful, unrelenting harshness'.

Unprecedented, unmerciful, unrelenting

Two years earlier, on 23 August 1939, the Nazis and Soviets had signed a non-aggression pact. But both sides knew it was never more than a postponement of hostilities. For the Soviets, it gave them time to build up their defences (in the event little was achieved); and for Hitler the pact gave him time to concentrate on the West (the planned defeats of France, Britain and elsewhere) before turning his attention eastwards.

German soldier, a fallen Russian and a burning Russian tank, June 1941.
German Federal Archives.

May God Bless Our Weapons

Now, in June 1941, with his Western objectives achieved (with the exception of Britain), the time had come.

On the eve of attack, Joseph Goebbels, Hitler's Minister for Propaganda, wrote in his diary, 'One can hear the breath of history... May God bless our weapons!'

Stalin's spies had forewarned him time and again of the expected attack but he refused to believe it, dismissing it all as 'Hitler's bluff'. When warned of the imminent German invasion from a high-ranking Luftwaffe spy, Stalin responded, 'Tell your "source" to go fuck his mother.' He ordered another shot for spreading 'misinformation'.

Stalin strenuously forbade anything that might appear provocative to the Germans, even insisting on the continuation of Russian food and metal exports to the Germans, as agreed in the 1939 Pact. He prohibited the evacuation of people living near the German border and forbade the setting up of defences.

So when, at 4 a.m. on 22 June 1941, Operation Barbarossa was launched, progress was rapid. (Barbarossa was the nickname given to Frederick I, 1122-1190, king of Germany and Holy Roman Emperor). At first, more frightened of Stalin's prohibition of 'provocative' acts than the German armies, Soviet soldiers didn't dare fire back. When one desperate Soviet border guard signalled, 'We're being fired on. What do we do?', the response came back, 'You must be mad; and why isn't your signal in code?'

At 6 a.m. that morning, the German Ambassador in Moscow handed over the declaration of war to Vyacheslav Molotov, Stalin's foreign minister. Molotov spat on the piece of paper, tore it up, and ordered his secretary to 'show this gentleman (the ambassador) out through the back door'.

(22 June was not the most auspicious date on which to launch an attack on the Soviet Union. It was on 22 June, exactly 129 years before, that Napoleon started his ill-fated invasion of Russia.)

For the good of humanity

Operation Barbarossa was the largest attack ever staged – three and a half million Axis troops, including Romanian and Hungarian, along a 900-mile front from Finland in the north to the Black Sea in the south. The Germans employed their *Blitzkrieg*, or lightning attacks, that had proved so successful against Poland and France. Their tanks were advancing 50 miles a day and, within the first day, one quarter of the Soviet Union's air strength had been destroyed – the Russians had left rows of uncamouflaged planes sat on their airfields, providing easy targets for the *Luftwaffe*.

German soldiers were excited by the prospect of defeating Stalin's mighty Bolshevik empire. One 18-year-old German tank driver wrote, 'It's a German's duty for the good of humanity to impose our way of life on lower races and nations'. They, like Hitler, expected an easy victory. An SS sergeant wrote, 'My conviction is that Russia's destruction will take no longer than France's; I assume I'll still get my leave in August'.

By the end of October, Moscow was only 65 miles away; over 500,000 square miles of Soviet territory had been captured and, as well as huge numbers of Soviet troops and civilians killed, 3 million Red Army soldiers had been taken prisoner of war, where, unlike in the West, the rules of captivity held no meaning for the Germans. (Of the five million Soviet PoWs taken during the course of the war, 3½ million were to die of malnutrition, disease and brutality. Those who survived returned home to the Soviet Union to be immediately branded as traitors and, in many instances, sent to the gulags.)

Stalin, once his generals had persuaded him that his country was under attack, controlled the Soviet response. His first acts were to order the execution of those who retreated and to send Molotov to formally announce the war to his people. Molotov's radio broadcast, relayed across cities by loudspeaker, announced this 'act of treachery unprecedented in the history of civilised nations'.

The Great Patriotic War

Stalin attempted to control every aspect of operations but only for the first week before suddenly giving up. 'Lenin founded our state,' he declared, exhausted, 'and we've fucked it up.' This 'bag of bones in a grey tunic', as Nikita Khrushchev later described him, disappeared to his dacha where, many believe, he suffered a mental breakdown. Nothing could be done without him, nothing issued in the way of direction.

When, after three days, his Politburo came for him, Stalin feared he was about to be arrested. Instead, they came to ask him what to do. Once stirred, Stalin re-emerged. On 3 July, in his first public address since the invasion, perhaps the most important speech of his life, Stalin spoke of 'The Great Patriotic War'.

By the end of June, Finland, Hungary and Albania had all declared war on the USSR. For Finland it was a 'holy war', an opportunity to avenge their defeat the previous year during the Finnish-Soviet 'Winter War'.

Joseph Stalin, August 1945. US Army Signal Corps.

The sides had been drawn, the invasion launched. What followed was the most ferocious war ever known which was to last three years and claim the lives of over five million Axis troops, nine million Soviet troops, and up to 20 million civilian deaths.

34.
28 June 1914,
The Assassination of Archduke Franz Ferdinand

On Sunday, 28 June 1914, the 50-year-old heir to the Austrian-Hungarian throne, the Archduke Franz Ferdinand and his wife, the Countess Sophie, paid an official visit to Sarajevo, capital of Bosnia, to inspect troops of the Austrian-Hungarian army. And it was the assassination of Franz Ferdinand and his wife on this day in this city that would unleash a chain of events that rapidly escalated into the most devastating war the world had seen – the First World War.

Archduke in love

The Emperor of the Austrian-Hungarian (Habsburg) Empire, Franz Joseph, had ruled since 1848, and was to do so until his death in 1916, aged 86, a rule of 68 years. When, in 1899, his nephew and heir presumptive, Archduke Franz Ferdinand, announced his desire to marry Sophie Chotek, a Czech, it sent shockwaves through the royal family. For Sophie, although a countess, was a commoner. But the archduke was in love and no amount of family pressure would dissuade him from taking her hand. They married on 28 June 1900. Sophie, as a non-royal, would never become queen, and the archduke had to sign away the right of his future children to succeed him. To add to the indignity, Sophie was barred from attending royal occasions, the only exception was in regard to the archduke's position of field marshal when, acting under his military capacity, he was allowed to have his wife at his side. Thus, together, on 28 June 1914, they made their way to Sarajevo.

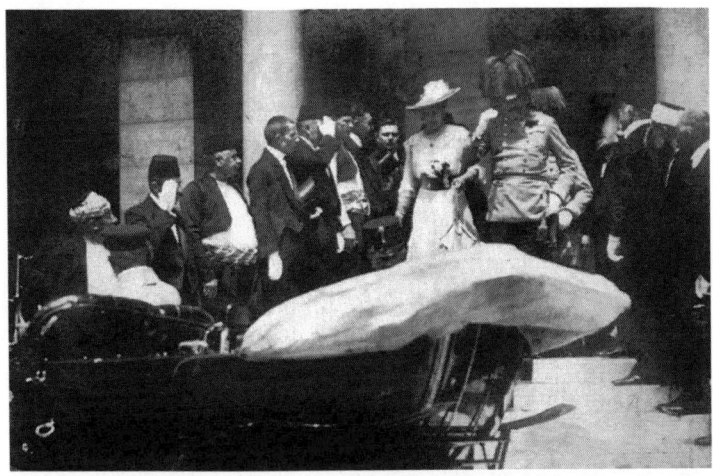

The archduke and Countess Sophie moments before their assassination, 28 June 1914.

The Black Hand

Six years previously, Bosnia had been annexed to the Habsburg Empire. Aggrieved Bosnian Serbs dreamt of freedom and incorporation into the nation of Serbia. The 28 June was also a significant day for Serbia – it was their national holiday and the anniversary of the 1389 Battle of Kosovo, in which Serbia were defeated by the Turks. Thus, the chosen date was provocative, and the Austrians knew it. The Serbs warned the Austrians against the visit, saying that the archduke would be putting himself in danger. One Serb freedom fighter / terrorist, Borivoje Jevtic, wrote 'How dared Franz Ferdinand, not only the representative of the oppressor but in his own person an arrogant tyrant, enter Sarajevo on that day?' Only in 1878, after five hundred years of Turkish rule, had Serbia gained its independence – but not the Bosnian Serbs who remained first under Turkish rule, then, from 1908, Austrian-Hungarian rule.

A Serbian nationalistic group calling itself the Black Hand decided to strike at the hated Austrian-Hungarians by assassinating the heir to the Habsburg throne. (Jevtic, quoted above, was a member). Indeed, they had tried to assassinate Emperor Franz Joseph three years earlier. Dispatched to Sarajevo were a number of young freedom fighters, including a 19-year-old named Gavrilo Princip. And it was in Sarajevo that Princip would change the world.

Each armed with a revolver, a hand grenade and, in the event of failure, a vial of cyanide, the would-be assassins joined, at various intervals, the mass of spectators lined along a six-kilometre route and waited for the six-car motorcade to come into view. The first lost his nerve, whilst the second, Nedeljko Cabrinovic, managed to throw his bomb causing injury to a driver and a few spectators but leaving the archduke and his wife unharmed. Cabrinovic swallowed his cyanide and jumped into the River Miljacka behind. But the poison, so old, failed to work and the river only came up to his ankles. Arrested, he was attacked by several bystanders. Meanwhile, Princip, witnessing the failure of the mission, traipsed to a local inn.

Franz Ferdinand, Library of Congress.

Understandably shaken, Franz Ferdinand arrived, as planned, at the City Hall, where he complained to the city mayor, 'Mr Mayor, I come to Sarajevo on a visit, and I get bombs thrown at me. It is outrageous.' Then, in delivering a speech, he ended with the words, 'I see in the people of Sarajevo an expression of joy at the failure of the attempt at assassination'.

On the countess's suggestion, Franz Ferdinand decided to visit the injured lying in hospital. On the way, his chauffeur took a wrong turning and found himself the wrong way down a one-way street, ironically named after the emperor, Franz Josef. On realizing his error, the chauffeur tried to reverse the car but stalled next to the very inn where Princip was planning his next move.

On seeing the archduke's car in front of him, Princip jumped onto its running board and fired, hitting the countess in the stomach. 'Sophie, don't die,' wailed the archduke, 'stay alive for the children'. The second bullet caught him in the throat.

One of the royal couple's bodyguards, Count Franz von Harrach, riding on the car's running board, gave this account: 'As the car quickly reversed, a thin stream of blood spurted from His Highness's mouth onto my right check. As I was pulling out my handkerchief to wipe the blood away from his mouth, the Duchess cried out to him, "In Heaven's name, what has happened to you?" At that she slid off the seat and lay on the floor of the car, with her face between his knees. I had no idea that she too was hit and thought she had simply fainted with fright.'

As the car hurried to the governor's residence, a member of his staff asked the archduke if he was OK, to which the archduke replied several times, 'It is nothing', before breathing his last.

The arrest of Gavrilo Princip, 28 June 1914.

Princip was bundled to the ground, his revolver seized from his hand. He managed to swallow the cyanide but, again, the poison, being so old, had no effect. (Although happy to have assassinated Franz Ferdinand, Princip was sorry to have killed the archduke's wife).

The Road to War

Austria reeled in shock, the assassination prompting several anti-Serb demonstrations. Serbia's government denied any involvement. Since 1912, Austria-Hungary had been concerned with Serbia's growing military strength so the crime presented the perfect opportunity for the Habsburg Empire to affirm its authority over its neighbour. With the backing of its powerful ally, Germany, Austria-Hungary sent an ultimatum to Serbia which, in the words of Britain's foreign secretary, Sir Edward Grey, was the 'most formidable document ever sent from one nation to another'. Serbia had 48 hours to respond. Shocked by the demands of the 'July Ultimatum', as it became known, Serbia turned to its ally, Russia, who recommended complete acceptance. Unable to do so entirely, Serbia agreed to eight, suggesting, quite reasonably, that the Hague Tribunal decide the other two. Not good enough, said the Austrian-Hungarians, breaking off diplomatic relations. On 28 July they declared war on Serbia.

And now, all the alliances formed in the preceding decades fell into place. Russia, protector of Serbia, began to mobilise. France, Russia's ally in the Triple Entente, felt obliged to offer its support. Germany gave Russia twelve hours to halt its mobilisation. The deadline passed, thus on 1 August, Germany declared war on Russia and, two days later, on France.

Germany's determination to invade France through Belgium brought in Great Britain, who, in 1839, had signed a treaty guaranteeing Belgium neutrality. Would Britain really risk war with a 'kindred nation' over a 'scrap of paper', a treaty signed 75 years before? Britain prevaricated but yes, it would, declaring war on Germany on 4 August. Sir Edward Grey, gazing out from the Foreign Office, remarked, 'the lamps are going out all over Europe. We shall not see them lit again in our lifetime'.

Within a matter of weeks, what started off as 'some damn foolish thing in the Balkans', as the former German chancellor, Otto von Bismarck, had once predicted, had escalated into a major conflict, one that would last 1,568 days, from 28 July 1914 to 11 November 1918, and cost over 9 million lives. The Great War had begun.

At the time of the assassination, both Nedeljko Cabrinovic and Gavrilo

Princip were still only nineteen. Their age saved him from execution as Austrian-Hungarian law decreed that the death penalty could not be applied to those aged under 20. Instead, they were sentenced to the maximum penalty of twenty years to be served at Theresienstadt prison (later used by the Nazis as a death camp). Both men died of tuberculosis while in prison – Cabrinovic in 1916 and Princip two years later. They share the same grave. After the war, their remains were re-interred in St Mark's Cemetery in Sarajevo.

Gavrilo Princip's gun; the car in which the Archduke and the countess was riding; and his blood-stained sky blue uniform and plumed cocked hat are all on permanent display in the Museum of Military History in Vienna, Austria.

35.
30 June 1934,
The Night of the Long Knives

The Night of the Long Knives was Adolf Hitler's great purge, eliminating the Nazi Party of those he distrusted, together with anti-Nazi figures within Germany and members of his paramilitary wing, the SA. Its most notorious victim was Ernst Rohm, once his loyal friend and devotee. So what had brought Hitler to such a critical moment so early in his twelve-year reign?

Hitler had come to power in January 1933 and immediately started, piece-by-piece, tearing up the Weimar constitution, squashing opposition and ridding Germany of democracy.

The End of Democracy

In the last parliamentary elections of the Weimar Republic, in March 1933, the Nazis polled 44 per cent of the vote — not enough for a majority but enough to squash any future political resistance. Within a fortnight Hitler proposed the Enabling Act, a temporary dissolution of the constitution whilst he dealt with the problems facing the nation. The Reichstag passed the proposal by 441 votes to 84. There would be no more elections or a constitution to keep Hitler in check. The Reichstag had, in effect, voted away its own power.

The temporary became permanent. Within a matter of weeks it had become illegal to criticize the government. A new secret police force, the Gestapo, immediately began arresting 'unreliable' persons, and Dachau, the first concentration camp, was opened to cater for their custody. Trade unions were banned, freedom of the press curtailed, and all other political parties declared illegal. Germany had become a one-party state with Hitler its leader, and soon its dictator.

Ernst Rohm

A year later, with Hitler's power almost absolute, only the excesses of the SA and their bull-necked leader, Ernst Rohm, troubled him. Their violence, which as a revolutionary during the 1920s, Hitler would have endorsed, had become an embarrassment to the Chancellor. Having gained power through the proper process Hitler wanted to win over the German people and international opinion through legitimate means not by force.

Ernst Rohm.

But Rohm and the SA felt that Hitler was going soft and had not given them their due reward for helping the Nazis into power. They started talking of a 'second revolution' with Rohm the leader of the People's Party, greatly alarming the industrialists and businessmen that Hitler had managed to woo. Rohm wanted also to merge the army with the SA under his command, which, in turn, alarmed the army and its chief, Werner von Blomberg.

Rohm felt confident. Writing to a friend in January 1934, he said, 'Hitler can't walk over me as he might have done a year ago; I've seen to that. Don't forget that I have three million men, with every key position in the hands of my own people. Hitler knows that I have friends in the Reichswehr, you know! If Hitler is reasonable I shall settle the matter quietly; if he isn't I must be prepared to use force – not for my sake but for the sake of our revolution'.

In April 1934, Hitler and Blomberg signed a secret pact: Hitler promised Blomberg and the army full control of the military (ahead of Rohm's SA); and, in return, Blomberg promised Hitler the army's support when the time came for Hitler to claim the presidency following the anticipated death of 86-year-old Paul von Hindenburg.

Heinrich Himmler and Hermann Goring, who also feared Rohm, concocted false evidence that Rohm was planning a coup against Hitler. The SA's agitation was beginning to undermine the country's stability, and Hindenburg threatened to bring in martial law unless Hitler could bring the situation under control. In other words – deal with Rohm and the SA.

Hitler acts

On the weekend of 30 June – 1 July 1934, in what was to become known as the 'Night of the Long Knives', Hitler acted. Members of the SS stormed a hotel in the village of Bad Wiessee where the SA had gathered for a weekend of debauchery, pulled Rohm and his henchmen from their beds and had them arrested. Many were promptly executed on the spot. Rohm was not. Hitler took it upon himself to arrest Rohm personally, marching into his hotel room and, brandishing a revolver, yelling, 'You're under arrest, you pig'.

Rohm was taken to a Munich prison, along with other SA leaders, and there awaited his fate. But Hitler, in a fit of nostalgia, found it difficult to order his murder. Instead, he offered Rohm the chance to kill himself. On 1 July, a revolver was left on the table in his cell and he was given ten minutes. Rohm refused, saying, 'If I am to be killed, let Adolf do it himself'. When the ten minutes had elapsed and no shot heard, an SS officer marched in and killed the bare-chested Rohm at point blank range.

Hitler took the opportunity to purge anyone whom he disliked or had crossed him in the past, including the second to last Chancellor of the Weimar Republic, Kurt von Schleicher who, along with his wife, was gunned down at his home. Another victim was Edgar Jung, Franz von Papen's speechwriter, shot in the cellar at Gestapo headquarters; his body was found the following day dumped in a ditch near Berlin. The Night of the Long Knives claimed over 200 lives. Hindenburg congratulated his chancellor for having acted so swiftly. The army, relieved to be freed from its main rival, sided with Hitler, and Blomberg applauded 'the Fuhrer's soldierly decision and exemplary courage'.

All Hitler had to do now was to wait for old Hindenburg to die. He did not have long to wait.

36.
1 July 1916,
The First Day of the Battle of the Somme

Within the collective British and Commonwealth psyche, no battle epitomises the futility of war as much as the Battle of the Somme. Almost 20,000 men were killed on the first day, 1 July 1916, alone.

It started with the usual preliminary bombardment. Lasting five days, and involving 1,350 guns and 52,000 tonnes of explosives fired onto the German lines, British soldiers were assured that the 18-mile German frontline would be flattened – it would just be a matter of strolling across and taking possession of the German trenches.

The Battle of the Somme was designed to relieve the pressure on the French suffering at Verdun. The British army at the Somme consisted mainly of Kitchener recruits. Most had received only minimal training and many had still to grasp the skill of shooting accurately.

At 7.20 am on Saturday 1 July 1916 (a 'lovely, intensely hot day', according to one diarist), the first of seventeen mines was detonated; a huge explosion on the German lines at Hawthorn Ridge. The explosion was captured on film by official war photographer Geoffrey Malins and the Hawthorn Crater is still visible today.

The advance started ten minutes later, at 7.30 am. The massive explosions certainly alerted the German defenders of what was about to come.

German soldier at the Battle of the Somme, 1916.
German Federal Archives.

To the right of the British, a smaller French force, transferred from the Battle of Verdun. As ordered, the men advanced in rigid lines. The bombardment combined with heavy rain the previous days had ensured that the ground was akin to a sea of mud and many an advancing soldier, lumbered with almost 70 pounds of equipment, drowned.

Dead men cannot move on

Far from being decimated by the artillery, the German trenches ahead were brimming with guns pointing towards the advance. What followed went down as the worse day in British military history – 57,000 men fell on that first day alone, 19,240 of them dead. In return, the Germans suffered 185 casualties that first day. The Royal Newfoundland Regiment, for example, suffered ninety per cent casualties – of the 780 Newfoundlanders that advanced on 1 July, only 68 were available for duty the following day.

One of Britain's generals at the Battle of the Somme, Sir Beauvoir de Lisle, wrote, 'It was a remarkable display of training and discipline, and the attack failed only because dead men cannot move on'. Despite the appalling losses, Britain's commander-in-chief, Field Marshal Douglas Haig, decided to 'press [the enemy] hard with the least possible delay'. Thus the attack was resumed the following day. And the day after that.

Re-enactment of Canadian troops 'going over the top', Battle of the Somme, 1916.
Imperial War Museum.

Cavalry and tanks

On 14 July, following a partially successful night-time attack, the British sent in the cavalry – a rare sight on the Western Front of the First World War and one that stirred the romantic notions in old timers such as Haig. But the horses became bogged down in the mud, the Germans opened fire and few survived, either horse or man.

On 15 September, Haig introduced the modern equivalent of the cavalry onto the battlefield – the 'landship'. Originated in Britain, and championed by Winston Churchill, the designers tried to disguise them as water storage tanks giving them the codename 'tanks'. The name stuck. Despite advice to wait for more testing, Haig had insisted on their use at the Somme. He got his way and the introduction of 36 'Mark I', thirty ton tanks with a top speed of five mph, met with mixed results – many broke down but a few managed to penetrate German lines, 'frightening the Jerries out of their wits and making them scuttle like frightened rabbits', as one witness described it.

But, as always, the Germans soon plugged the hole forged by the tanks.

Nonetheless, Haig was impressed and immediately ordered a thousand more. One witness described three of these 'huge mechanical monsters' firing on its own trench. 'Giving no thought to his own personal safety as he saw the tanks firing on his own men, the colonel ran forward and furiously rained blows with his cane on the side of one of the tanks.'

Badly shelled terrain, Battle of the Somme 1916.
Imperial War Museum.

The Battle of the Somme ground on for a further two months. Nine Victoria Crosses were awarded on the first day alone; another 41 by the end of the battle. Soldiers from every part of the Empire were thrown into the melee – Australian, Canadian, New Zealanders, Indian and South African all took their part. The battle finally terminated on 18 November, after 140 days of fighting. 400,000 British and Commonwealth lives were lost, 200,000 French and 400,000 German. For this the Allies gained five miles. The Germans, having been pushed back, merely bolstered the already heavily-fortified second line, the Hindenburg Line.

As AJP Taylor put it in his *First World War*, first published in 1963, 'Idealism perished at the Battle of the Somme. The enthusiastic volunteers were enthusiastic no longer'.

37.
4 August 1944,
The Betrayal of Anne Frank

'I hope I shall be able to confide in you completely, as I have never been able to do in anyone before, and I hope that you will be a great support and comfort to me.'

Her voice has come to symbolise the Holocaust, one victim among the six million who spoke for them all, a testament to all who perished with her.

Anne Frank died aged 15 in the Bergen-Belsen concentration camp in early March 1945.

Born 12 June 1929, Anne and her older sister, Margot, lived their early years in Frankfurt. But in 1933, following Hitler's appointment as Chancellor, the Franks, as a Jewish family, became concerned for their safety as the Nazis introduced increasingly fanatical anti-Semitic legislation.

The Franks Move to Amsterdam

In late 1933 Anne's father, Otto, was offered and accepted a business opportunity in Amsterdam. In February 1934 his wife and daughters joined him in the Netherlands. Of the half million Jews living in Germany in 1933, about 320,000 had emigrated by 1939.

In May 1940 Hitler launched his attack against France and the Low Countries. Rotterdam was heavily bombed and, on 15 May, the Dutch, fearing further losses, surrendered.

Statue of Anne Frank in Utrecht by Pieter d'Hont, unveiled 12 April 1960.

Occupied Netherlands

Life for the Jewish population in Nazi-occupied Netherlands became increasingly intolerable and dangerous. In July 1942, Otto Frank received an order to report his eldest daughter for a work camp. The Franks, fearing for their lives, decided they had no option but to go into hiding.

On 6 July 1942, the Franks moved into their secret annex, behind Otto's business premises at 263 Prinsengracht, and in doing so left their flat in a state of chaos to give the impression of a family on the run. The annex consisted of three floors, its entrance concealed by a large, wooden bookcase. They were to live in this self-imposed incarceration for over two years. From the outside the Franks were provided with food, provisions, news and humanity by a small group of trusted business associates of Otto's. A week after moving in, they were joined by Hermann and Auguste van Pels and their 16-year-old son, Peter. On 16 November, they were joined by a German dentist and veteran of the First World War, Fritz Pfeffer.

The Anne Frank House, 263 Prinsengracht, Amsterdam.

Anne and Peter had a brief flirtation, which, although pleasurable, was, for such a young girl, perplexing. For Anne, becoming aware of her sexuality but in such a confined and claustrophobic atmosphere and tainted with the lack of normality and the constant nag of fear, it must have been unbearably confusing and difficult. But there was always the solace and consolation of her diary.

The Diary

Anne had always shown a propensity to write and on her thirteenth birthday, a month before their flight, she received from her father an autograph book. With its thick blank pages, tartan cover and lock and key, Anne was delighted by her present and immediately began using it as a diary.

As with many a teenager, a diary is a constant companion and source of comfort, allowing the writer to express their feelings, their frustrations, their fears and hopes for the future, and their beliefs and changing attitudes. And so it was for Anne, an ordinary girl with an extraordinary talent, in extra-ordinary circumstances. The last entry in Anne's diary is dated 1 August 1944:

Believe me, I'd like to listen, but it doesn't work, because if I'm quiet and serious, everyone thinks I'm putting on a new act and I have to save myself with a joke, and then I'm not even talking about my own family, who assume I must be sick, stuff me with aspirins and sedatives, feel my neck and forehead to see if I have a temperature, ask about my bowel movements and berate me for being in a bad mood, until I just can't keep it up anymore, because when everybody starts hovering over me, I get cross, then sad, and finally end up turning my heart inside out, the bad part on the outside and the good part on the inside, and keep trying to find a way to become what I'd like to be and what I could be if... if only there were no other people in the world.
    Yours, Anne M. Frank

Three days later, 4 August, Nazi security police, led by an Austrian called Karl Josef Silberbauer, burst into the annex and arrested the Franks and their companions. They had been betrayed but by whom we will never know. The call was taken by Silberbauer's commanding officer, a SS lieutenant called Julius Dettmann, who merely said the call had come from a 'reliable source'. (Following the end of the war, Dettmann was arrested and interned as a prisoner of war. He committed suicide in July 1945). Otto Frank was giving Peter van Pels an English lesson when the Nazis entered the annex. On seeing Anne, Silberbauer said to Otto, 'You have a lovely daughter'. He couldn't believe that the Franks and their friends had been in the annex for over two years. As proof, Otto showed Silberbauer the pencil lines where he had charted Anne and Margot's growth since 1942.

Auschwitz and Bergen-Belsen

The Franks, the van Pels and Fritz Pfeffer, the German dentist, were taken to a prison in Amsterdam, then to the Westerbork transit camp, in the northeast of the country. On 3 September 1944, all eight were deported to Auschwitz-Birkenau in Poland on the last train to leave the Netherlands for the extermination camp. Immediately, on arriving at Auschwitz, Otto was separated from his wife and daughters – he never saw them again. He did, however, remain with Peter van Pels and was reunited with Pfeffer. Pfeffer died in Auschwitz on 20 December 1944 while Peter was put on a death march out of Auschwitz in January 1945 and died in Mauthausen, Austria, aged 18, on 5 May 1945, the very day the camp was liberated. Peter's parents both died as well, his father gassed.

In October 1944, the girls were relocated to Bergen-Belsen whilst their mother remained in Auschwitz where she was to die on 6 January 1945 from starvation.

Margot and Anne, already weak, deteriorated further and when a typhus epidemic swept through Belsen killing almost 20,000 inmates, the sisters were amongst the victims. The exact date of their deaths is not known but it was early March 1945, just weeks before the camp's liberation.

Otto Frank and his daughter's diary

Otto Frank, 1968. Dutch National Archives.

Otto, the only resident of the annex to survive, returned to Amsterdam following the war knowing that his wife was dead but unsure of his daughters' fates. He learnt, on returning home, of their deaths and received from friends Anne's diary. This man, his life devastated by cruelty and inhumanity, sat down and read the secret diary of his deceased daughter.

He read of Anne's desire to be published, to be known as a writer, and decided to devote the rest of his life to Anne's work. He was to die in 1980, aged 91.

The diary was first published in the Netherlands in 1947 and five years later in the US and the UK. The name Anne Frank rapidly became known throughout the world.

Seventy years later and her name lives on, and Anne's diary, recognised as a timeless classic, remains essential reading for all humanity.

38.
9 August 1942,
The Greatest Performance:
The Leningrad Symphony

Poised with his baton, the conductor pauses a moment. His orchestra, instruments at the ready, watch him. Somewhere in the audience, someone coughs. The conductor waits for absolute silence knowing that this is the biggest occasion of his life. Finally, he brings the baton down with a whoosh and starts the performance.

But this is no ordinary conductor, no ordinary orchestra and no ordinary audience. They were all on the verge of death, suffering from the advanced stages of starvation. To hold, let alone play, an instrument for over an hour took every ounce of their strength. But the music they played that night was proof of their spirit and that ultimately their city would survive.

The city was Leningrad; the music was Dmitry Shostakovich's Seventh Symphony, and on 9 August 1942, it saw its Leningrad premier at the height of the most devastating siege of modern times.

A year earlier, Dmitry Shostakovich made a radio announcement in which he said, 'An hour ago, I completed the score of two movements of my new, large symphonic work.' This new work was his Seventh Symphony, later to be called the *Leningrad*.

Dmitry Shostakovich, 1950. Deutsche Fotothek.

The siege of Leningrad had just started; it was to last 872 days, or twenty-nine months. Hitler had declared his intention to 'wipe the city of Petersburg from the face of the earth'. Over a million civilians and soldiers would die – the number of deaths in Leningrad exceeds those who died from the atomic bombs at Hiroshima and Nagasaki combined, and constitutes the largest death toll ever recorded in a single city.

Now I am ready to take up arms

The city authorities had tried to make Shostakovich leave but, loyal to the city, he stayed, working on his composition and volunteering for the People's Army, stating, 'Until now I have known only peaceful work. But now I am ready to take up arms.' But his good intentions were dashed by the military – rejected because of his poor eyesight. He was allowed instead to take his turn on fire warden duty. The American magazine, *Time*, featured the composer on its cover, wearing a golden helmet and holding a fireman's nozzle, with the caption, 'Fireman Shostakovich'. Eventually, he was ordered to leave. On 1 October, with his wife and children and the manuscript of his score stuffed in his suitcase, he bid farewell to the city of his birth. While he was gone, his dog was eaten.

Evacuated to the town of Kuibyshev (modern-day Samara), 900 miles south-east of Leningrad, Shostakovich worked feverishly on the symphony while producing short works to entertain the troops on the frontline, tunes with catchy titles, such as *The Fearless Guards Regiment is on the Move*. By the end of the year, the symphony was done. Dedicated to '…our struggle against fascism, to our coming victory and to my native city of Leningrad', it received its world première, broadcast to the nation, in Kuibyshev on 5 March 1942, followed by a performance in Moscow three weeks later.

A microfilm of the score was smuggled out of the Soviet Union and flown to Teheran and from there to Europe, where conductors fought for the privilege of conducting the work. It was performed first in London, conducted by Sir Henry Wood, then in New York on 19 July, conducted by Arturo Toscanini. The symphony was an immediate hit and Shostakovich's face appeared in newspapers and magazines all over the world.

The Symphony Comes to Leningrad

Then came the decision to play the Leningrad Symphony in Leningrad itself. It would be, according to Andrey Zhdanov, Stalin's man in Leningrad, good for the city's morale. A Soviet plane, dodging the German guns, delivered the score to Zhdanov. The city's principle orchestra, the Philharmonic, had already been evacuated out of the city but the reserve orchestra, the Leningrad Radio Orchestra, was still available. Its conductor, 42-year-old Karl Eliasberg, was charged with reassembling his musicians. But of its 100 members, only 14 remained. The others had all died or been killed. Replacements had to be found. The call went out urging soldiers who could play an instrument to report for duty.

The score, complex and mammoth, was 75 minutes long and involved a 90-piece orchestra. Given the weakness of the musicians who had gathered for the first rehearsal in March 1942, Eliasberg knew the difficulty of the task that lay ahead. 'Dear friends,' he began, 'we are weak but we must force ourselves to start work.'

And it was hard work – despite extra rations, many, especially the brass players, passed out with the effort of playing their instruments. Eliasberg was tough on his players – those who played badly or, worse, failed to turn up for the three-hour long rehearsals, were docked a bread ration. Through discipline and coaxing, Eliasberg got his skeletal orchestra to perform

Shostakovich's huge work. But only once during rehearsals did the orchestra have enough strength to play the whole work throughout – three days before the big day.

The date for the performance was fixed – 9 August 1942, which was also the date set by the Nazis for a huge party in Leningrad's Astoria hotel to celebrate their anticipated capture of the city. The invitations had already been printed. They were never sent out.

The Leningrad Première

Karl Eliasberg.

The Philharmonic Hall was packed – people came in their finest clothes; city leaders and generals took their places. The musicians, despite the warm August temperature, wore coats and mittens – when the body is starving, it is continually cold. Outside, throughout the city, people gathered to listen at loudspeakers. Hours earlier, Leonid Govorov, Leningrad's military commander since April 1942, ordered a barrage of artillery onto the German lines to ensure their silence for the work to be performed without interruption. Loudspeakers, on full volume, pointed in the direction of the

Germans – the city wanted the enemy to hear.

'This performance,' announced Eliasberg in a pre-recorded introduction, 'is witness to our spirit, our courage and readiness to fight. Listen, Comrades!' And the city listened, as did the Germans nearby. They listened as the city of Leningrad reasserted its moral self.

At the end – silence. Then came the applause, a thunderous applause that lasted over an hour. People cheered and cried. They knew they had witnessed a momentous occasion. It was, as Eliasberg described later, the moment 'we triumphed over the soulless Nazi war machine.' Later, Eliasberg and his orchestra were invited to a reception hosted by Zhdanov where, laid out before them, was a huge banquet. They gorged themselves, only to be sick soon afterwards.

Years after the war, Eliasberg met some Germans who had been sitting encamped in their trenches outside the city. On hearing the music, they told the conductor, they had burst into tears, 'Who are we bombing?' they asked themselves, 'We will never be able to take Leningrad because the people here are selfless.'

39.

19 August 1969,
The East German Athlete Who Made a Dash
for Freedom

The 19-year-old man had spent a week watching the guards, learning their routine, as they patrolled the beach on the Baltic seaside resort of Boltenhagen.

The area was known by the East German secret police, the Stasi, as a favoured spot from which to escape to the West. He knew that each hour the guards had to switch off their spotlights for a few minutes to allow the bulbs to cool down.

The young man, Axel Mitbauer, a champion swimmer and member of the East German national swimming team, had already suffered at the hands of the Stasi. Known for his fraternisation with West Germans, he had been locked-up in solitary confinement for seven weeks, deprived of light and beaten up. But Mitbauer was made of strong stuff. On the night of 17 August 1969, he made his move.

When the right moment came, Mitbauer, smeared with 30 tubes of Vaseline against the cold water, slipped into the icy Baltic. Once the spotlights returned, he swam underwater. Using the stars as his guide, he swam 15 miles until, after four hours, he reached a lifebuoy and climbed aboard to rest. Six hours later, at 7 am the following morning, he was picked up by a West German ship. He'd made it.

In 1984, 24-year-old East German, Ines Geipel, along with her teammates, had broken the world record for the women's 4×100 metre relay, clocking-up a time of 42.2 seconds.

It was the crowning moment of her career. Ahead of them lay the Los Angeles Olympics and the chance for further glory. But Geipel fell in love with a Mexican athlete, a walker, and dreamt of living in the West. She soon came to the attention of the Stasi and back in East Germany was made to undergo an operation to remove her appendix. There, they took the opportunity to mutilate her stomach, thus destroying her career and her dreams and leaving her with debilitating stomach cramps.

East Germany's women's 4×100 metre relay team, 1984, with Ines Geipel far left. German Federal Archive.

Twenty years later, Geipel, whose own father had worked for the Stasi, renounced her world record, citing that it had been gained under the influence of drugs.

Success

Germany had been split into East and West in 1949, yet until 1964, the two nations were represented at the Olympics as one team, the 'Unified Team of Germany'. It was only from the Mexico City Summer Olympics of 1968, did the two Germanys appear as separate entities.

The German Democratic Republic (East Germany) saw the

propaganda opportunity that sport, particularly the Olympics, could provide them. At the 1968 Mexico Olympics, the East Germans won nine gold medals; just 20 years later, at the Seoul Olympics of 1988, they won an astonishing 37. Within those two decades, the East German Summer and Winter Olympic teams won 587 medals, 203 of them gold, which for a country of less than 16 million was, on paper at least, a spectacular achievement. In the Summer Olympics of 1976, 1980 and 1988, East Germany notched up second position on the medals' table.

For the East German state, sport was not simply a matter of a bit of patriotic pride but firm proof of the superiority of the socialist state; sport was nothing less than a political weapon. Other nations of the Eastern Bloc followed suite, the USSR, Romania, Yugoslavia, etc, but no one took it as seriously as the East Germans.

The reason was the inbuilt rivalry with their neighbours and co-nationalists, the West Germans (and we all know that feeling of wanting to beat the Germans). West Germany seemed to be winning the Cold War and was doing better economically and materially, but here was the one sphere in which the East Germans felt it could win. And where better to prove the superiority of socialism than on the biggest sporting stage of them all – the Olympics?

Training

The success of East German sportsmen and women was no accident – the state went to great lengths to achieve such astonishing feats, funding and prioritising sport clubs and training facilities, and taking under their wing, from the earliest age, the sporting stars of tomorrow.

The state focussed on individual sports, particularly swimming and weightlifting, rather than team sports, purely on an economical basis – a whole team uses up a lot of resources yet can only win the one medal between them.

Potential youngsters were targeted and put through years of intense training to the exclusion of almost everything else. To be talented in East Germany meant giving up your childhood. Those that won something were rewarded by even greater pressure to maintain their winning ways, becoming boarders at their training grounds, rarely allowed to see friends or family, and deprived of time off, even to celebrate birthdays or family occasions.

But it wasn't just intense physical training these youngsters had to endure but also ideological training, groomed to go abroad, spout the party line and talk animatedly of the socialist utopia they lived in while deploring the ways of the capitalist, imperialist West. For these youngsters were more than just sports stars – they were the country's 'tracksuit diplomats', ambassadors for their nation, models for socialism.

But there was an inherent risk for the state – performing abroad meant that the athletes came into direct contact with Westerners and could fall prey to capitalist indoctrination. They also had the means to escape, and many did. From tracksuit diplomats they became tracksuit traitors. These players became forgotten people within East Germany; their names erased from the sporting history books and their faces blanked out of photographs.

Doping

But success didn't just come through intensive investment and training – it came in the form of a little blue pill – vitamin tablets, or so the athletes were told, even the youngest ones, to help stave off colds and keep them fit. The youngsters, trusting of their coaches, took them. The pills were of course steroids, Oral-Turinabol. There was no parental consent involved; indeed the youngsters were under strict instruction not to tell anyone they were taking them, let alone their parents. Then came the injections. Refusal was not an option.

When young girls started to grow facial hair and stop menstruating, and boys grew breasts and found their testes shrinking, parents who did question the coaches were threatened and told in no uncertain terms to desist. Many of these young girls, whose voices had become so deep, were prohibited from talking to foreign journalists. An estimated 10,000 East German athletes were doped.

Their foreign rivals watched with astonishment as an hitherto unheard of East German with an unnaturally-shaped body came along and wiped the board with them, not just winning but winning by huge margins. No amount of training could compete with these superhuman athletes. The work and dreams of dedicated and decent athletes were shattered by a nation intent on cheating.

British swimmer, Sharron Davies, was cheated of a gold medal in the 1980 Moscow Olympics, losing the 400 metre individual medley by a whole ten seconds to East German, Petra Schneider. Years later, Schneider admitted she'd been doped. In a newspaper interview in 2006, Davies said, 'I don't feel any anger towards Petra at all. In fact, I feel truly sorry for her. But I do feel angry with the IOC [International Olympic Committee] who let down two groups of people. People like myself, whom they should have been protecting and who didn't receive the medals they won cleanly, and the East Germans themselves, who were victims of a system over which they had no control whatsoever'.

Among the extreme cases was that of Heidi Krieger who won the shot put gold at the 1986 European Athletics Championships. Krieger had been fed so many pills, she suffered a serious gender imbalance to the point that, in 1997, she underwent sex reassignment surgery and changed her name to Andreas. In 1986, with the help of steroids, she could throw a shot put over 21 metres. Now, as a man in his mid-40s, he can tolerate only the mildest exertion. But for Krieger, he's content with his new identity, has found love and is comfortable with his past.

Heidi Krieger, 1986. German Federal Archives.

Not so fortunate was 16-year-old, Joerg Sievers. A potential Olympic swimmer, on 17 January 1973, Sievers was found drowned at the bottom of a swimming pool in his hometown of Magdeburg. His grieving parents were told he had been swimming while ill with influenza. But they had seen their son just hours before and he wasn't ill and, furthermore, the boy had, only a few weeks before, been given a flu vaccination. Their request to see the autopsy report was denied. If they had, they would have seen that their poor son had suffered from an enlarged heart, damage to his liver and an infection of the spleen – all brought on as a direct consequence of state-authorized doping.

The Swimmer

Renate Vogel, a swimmer, was another much feted by the regime. During the 1972 Munich Olympics she was part of the 4×100 metre relay team that won silver and, a year later, she won two golds at the inaugural World Swimming Championships in Belgrade, where the East German women swept the board, winning ten gold medals in fourteen events.

But, in 1974, in the European Swimming Championships, despite being the favourite to win, she won silver, losing out to a West German rival. It wasn't good enough for the authorities back home and she was severely criticised and ostracised. She realised that she had been used as a political weapon and with the realisation came the determination to defect. In September 1979, under an assumed name, Vogel boarded a plane from Budapest to Munich and fled to freedom.

The Footballer

Falko Götz, a footballer, took the opportunity of an away match in Belgrade in 1983 to seek asylum in the West German embassy. As a consequence, his mother, back home, was interrogated by the Stasi for 16 consecutive hours; everywhere she went she was followed – not at a discreet distance but right behind. His family lost their jobs and were publicly shunned.

But Götz had no regrets and went on to win the UEFA Cup in 1988 with his new West German team, Bayer Leverkusen. But life in the West did not mean he, or others, had escaped the clutches of the Stasi (indeed, he later found out that the Stasi had, within their files, photographs of his new home in West Germany). Cases of defectors drugged and smuggled back East, although rare, were not unheard of. A friend of Götz in West Germany, a fellow East German, was killed in a car accident. Götz, suspecting it was no accident, feared for his own life.

Returning East after unification Götz read through his Stasi files, a process that took three whole days, to discover that while playing in the East, the secret police were kept informed of his movements and conversations by a number of informants which, to his horror, included several former teammates and even family acquaintances.

East v West at the World Cup

While in athletics, the East Germans were dominant, in football the West Germans were easily favourites. Their first round match during the 1974 FIFA World Cup finals was one of the most politically-charged sporting clashes of the Cold War. East Germany were surprise winners, beating their Western cousins 1-0, providing further proof that when it came to sport, socialism always triumphed. (Ultimately, however, East Germany was knocked out of the competition and West Germany, playing on home soil, went on to lift the trophy).

The goalscorer, Jürgen Sparwasser, later wrote, 'Rumour had it I was richly rewarded for the goal, with a car, a house and a cash premium. But that is not true'. In 1988, one year before the fall of the Berlin Wall, Sparwasser defected to the West – another tracksuit traitor.

For many of East Germany's athletes, experimented upon like human guinea pigs, years of doping have left them with a catalogue of health issues: infertility, cancer, diabetes, organ failure, heart disease and depression are some of the extreme but sadly not uncommon legacies still suffered by these pawns in East Germany's political game.

Those deemed responsible got their justice – of sorts. In an infamous case in Germany in 2000, several were found guilty of knowingly causing harm to persons, including minors. They suffered only minor fines and suspended sentences, leaving many of their victims further embittered.

40.
20 August 1968,
The USSR Invades Czechoslovakia

On the night of 20-21 August 1968, Soviet troops appeared in Czechoslovakia and on the streets of Prague to quell the growing movement of liberalization, a movement known as the 'Prague Spring'.

Socialism with a Human Face

On 5 January 1968, amongst growing discontent of economic failure, the Czechoslovakian communist party appointed Alexander Dubcek as its new chairman. Dubcek promised reform, democratisation and, using Nikita Khrushchev's phrase, 'socialism with a human face'. He eased press censorship, allowed greater artistic and cultural freedom, pardoned victims of political purges, eased travel restrictions, promised to guarantee civil rights and liberties and permitted a degree of democratic reform.

But while urging democratic communism, Dubcek remained loyal to Moscow and at no point was he advocating the dismissal of his or the country's socialist principles. The Soviet leadership, under Leonid Brezhnev, saw it otherwise, becoming increasingly concerned with what they considered Dubcek's treachery and Czechoslovakia's counterrevolution.

Evidence of the transformation was immediately apparent – young men grew their hair, women wore miniskirts, anti-state newspapers appeared, films and plays long since banned by the regime reappeared, including the work of dissident playwright, Vaclav Havel.

In July 1968, Brezhnev, fearing Czechoslovakian independence, met with Dubcek and demanded that he re-imposed strict communist control over his people and ordered Dubcek to reign in his 'counter-revolutionary' methods. Dubcek promised to compromise but over the coming weeks, it came clear to Moscow that nothing was being done. Brezhnev applied greater pressure, often ringing Dubcek and bellowing at him down the telephone.

Leonid Brezhnev, 1967. German Federal Archive.

Soviet Invasion

Meeting on 15 August, the politburo decided that enough was enough. Dubcek's failure to bring Czechoslovakia back in line angered the Soviet Union, and on 20 August 1968, Brezhnev, with support from other Warsaw Pact leaders, ordered in the tanks. The politburo arranged it so that loyal members of the Czechoslovakian government requested Soviet help in dealing with the counterrevolutionary threat. The politburo did not want to appear as occupiers but merely responding to pleas for help.

Half a million Soviet troops (including token numbers from Bulgaria, Hungary, East Germany and Poland) and 2,000 tanks moved in quickly, taking control of Prague's airport and vital points of communication before making a forceful presence on the streets of the capital. Dubcek told his people not to resist. But if the Soviet soldier expected a warm welcome by the good people of Czechoslovakia, as Moscow had told them, they were soon disabused of the idea as Czechoslovakian youths threw stones at their tanks. But faced with such a show of strength, unarmed resistance, limited as it was, soon crumbled. Eleven Soviet soldiers and 72 civilians were killed.

Russian tank on the streets of Prague, 20 August 1968.

You have let us all down

Dubcek, rendered powerless, was, along with his immediate colleagues, arrested at gun point, hit with a rifle butt and bundled unceremoniously into an aeroplane and taken to Moscow. In Moscow, Brezhnev, with tears in his eyes, shouted at Dubcek, 'I trusted you,' he said, 'you have let us all down.'

Dubcek and colleagues were forced into signing declarations of renewed loyalty to Moscow. He was returned to office in Prague, his work carefully censured. Within the year, however, he was removed from power and exiled to a minor post, first as ambassador to Turkey, then further still as a forestry inspector in Bratislava. He was replaced by Gustav Husak, a man more loyal to Moscow and devoted to the socialist cause. Czechoslovakia's brief flirtation with reform and democracy, its Prague Spring, was over.

Alexander Dubcek, 1968. National Archives.

Husak immediately reversed Dubcek's reforms, rid the party of its more liberal members, and imposed greater authoritarian control over the country, a process referred to as 'normalization'. (Husak was to remain in power until the collapse of Czechoslovakia in December 1989.)

Brezhnev Doctrine

Brezhnev, in a speech in November 1968, reiterated the right of the Warsaw Pact to intervene if any Soviet satellite compromised the hegemony of the Eastern bloc by looking West. Known as the 'Brezhnev Doctrine', it ushered in another period of suppression, and the straitjacketing of the arts and ideological strictness.

The writers and artists that led the cultural revolution of the Prague Spring had their works banned. Members of a dissident group, Charter 77, including Vaclav Havel, were imprisoned. A fan of The Beatles, Havel said he was not so much a Leninist as a Lennonist.

The Soviet invasion prompted, within the Soviet Union, the first open demonstration in its history – on 25 August 1968, several Russians demonstrated on Moscow's Red Square, shouting 'Shame on the invaders!' and 'Long live the free and independent Czechoslovakia!' The demo lasted but a few minutes but it was a start.

In Czechoslovakia also, there were minor protests against the re-imposition of authoritarian rule, most notably on 16 January 1969 when a student, Jan Palach, set himself on fire in Prague's Wenceslas Square. Palach was to die of his injuries three days later.

41.
21 August 1940,
The Assassination of Leon Trotsky

Stalin wanted Trotsky dead. He'd got rid of Bukharin, Kamenev and Zinoviev and several other old Bolsheviks, but his greatest enemy, Leon Trotsky, was still alive. He'd thoroughly defeated his rival and had chased him out of the country. But still it wasn't enough. He didn't care how long it took as long as Trotsky was liquidated. In August 1940, in faraway Mexico City, a NKVD agent buried an ice pick into the back of Trotsky's head. Stalin had got his wish.

Born Lev Bronshtein on 7 November 1879 in the village of Yanovka in the Ukraine, Leon Trotsky, the son of a prosperous Jewish farmer, became involved in politics from a young age. Arrested in 1898, the 19-year-old Trotsky was exiled to Siberia where he married and had two daughters, both of whom predeceased him. In 1902, he escaped exile using a forged passport bearing the name Trotsky, the name, he later claimed, of a prison guard he had met in Odessa. He made his way to London where, for the first time, he met Vladimir Lenin and joined the Russian Social Democratic Labour Party. Following the split of the RSDLP, Trotsky's loyalty floated between the two factions, the Bolsheviks and Mensheviks, often repudiating any party ties and holding a stance of non-allegiance. He opposed Lenin on many issues, a stance that was later held against him.

Following the outbreak of disturbances throughout Russia in 1905, Leon Trotsky arrived in St Petersburg and there joined its council of workers, or 'Soviet', becoming its chair until its forced break-up by tsarist troops in December. Trotsky, along with other leaders, was arrested and again sentenced to exile in Siberia. But en route, he escaped and made his way to London before settling in Vienna where he founded and wrote a newspaper for Russia's workers, *Pravda*, 'Truth', earning the nickname, 'the Pen', for his writing. With the outbreak of war in 1914, Trotsky, as a Russian, was forced to leave Austria. He lived in Paris until, expelled for his anti-war writings, he emigrated to Spain and then New York, arriving in January 1917.

Leon Trotsky, 1915.

Revolution

Trotsky returned to Russia and Petrograd (as St Petersburg was now known) in March 1917 and became, in effect, Lenin's second-in-command as the Bolsheviks overthrew the Provisional Government and set up a new socialist order. (Trotsky turned 38 the day of the October Revolution.)

In forming the Council of People's Commissars, Russia's new government, Lenin initially offered the post of chair, in effect head of state, to Leon Trotsky but Trotsky declined the offer, fearing that having a Jew in charge of a country that was still strongly anti-Semitic could be problematic. Instead, Trotsky was appointed the People's Commissariat for Foreign Affairs.

Following Russia's withdrawal from the First World War, Trotsky was appointed War Commissariat, responsible for strengthening and injecting much-needed discipline into the Red Army. His use of former officers of the tsar's imperial army caused much disquiet within the party, Joseph Stalin being particularly critical, and was another tool later used against him.

The most capable man

Trotsky seemed the natural successor to Lenin. In Lenin's 'Testament', he was described as having 'outstanding ability' and 'perhaps the most capable man in the present Central Committee' but was prone, according to Lenin, of displaying 'excessive self-assurance'. But Trotsky's succession was blocked by a troika consisting of Stalin, Lev Kamenev and Grigory Zinoviev. Trotsky greatly underestimated Stalin, once referring to him as 'an excellent bit of mediocrity'.

Following Lenin's death in January 1924, Stalin ensured he was centre place during the funeral arrangements and the funeral itself. Trotsky had been ill and was recovering in a resort in the Caucasus and Stalin's telegram to him purposefully gave the wrong date for the funeral.

Trotsky was increasingly marginalised by the party to the point in January 1925, he was relieved of his ministry. Kamenev and Zinoviev, two-thirds of the troika, themselves fell out with Stalin and belatedly joined forces with Trotsky. In October 1927, Trotsky was expelled from the Central Committee and the following month from the Communist Party altogether.

Exiled

In January 1928, Trotsky, accompanied by his wife, Natalia Sedova, was exiled to Kazakhstan and finally banished from the Soviet Union altogether in February 1929. After four years in Turkey, two years in France and two in Norway, always heavily under guard, Trotsky settled in Mexico. For a while, he lived in the house of the artist Diego Rivera and, while there, had an affair with Rivera's wife and fellow artist, Frida Kahlo. Moving into a house in a leafy suburb of Mexico City, Trotsky began writing prolifically – penning, amongst several books and articles, an autobiography, a history of the Russian Revolution and embarking on a biography of Stalin, in which he described Stalin as having 'played a dismal role during the 1917 revolution'. (The book remained unfinished).

Meanwhile, Moscow hosted the first of the infamous Show Trials in which old Bolsheviks, such as Kamenev and Zinoviev, confessed to various anti-state conspiracies and having acted under the instructions of Trotsky. All were sentenced to death, including Trotsky who was found guilty *in absentia.*

Trotsky's two sons from his second marriage both predeceased him. Sergei Sedov was eliminated in 1937 during Stalin's 'Great Purge' while, in February 1938, his brother, Lev, died on the operating table from a supposed acute appendicitis (very likely on the orders of the NKVD).

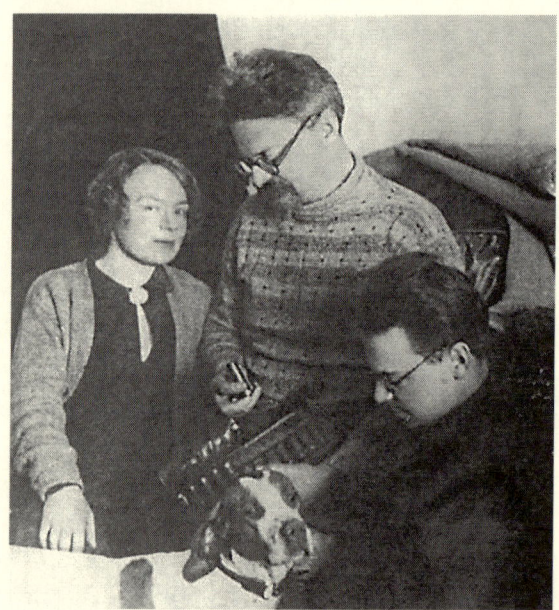

Leon Trotsky, Natalia Sedova and their son, Lev Sedov, 1928.
State Museum of Russian Political History.

Assassination

Despite having up to ten guards at a time, in May 1940, Trotsky survived a raid on his house in Mexico, in which his 25-year-old assistant was abducted, tortured and later murdered, and his grandson, Esteban Volkov, was shot in the foot. Trotsky was unharmed but he was less fortunate three months later.

During this time, Trotsky and his wife were befriended by a Canadian called Frank Jacson, who was introduced to them by Trotsky's secretary who happened to be Jacson's lover. Jacson was, in fact, Jaime Ramón Mercader del Río, a Spanish communist and agent for Stalin's NKVD, who had seduced Trotsky's secretary in order to get close to his intended victim.

On 20 August, about 5.30 pm, Ramon Mercader turned up at Trotsky's home, asking if Trotsky would read something he'd written. A hot day, Sedova, Trotsky's wife, asked him, 'Why are you wearing your hat and topcoat?' Refusing Sedova's offer of tea, Mercader followed Trotsky into the study. Sitting down, Trotsky began to read Mercader's work. Mercader then retrieved the ice pick he'd been hiding within his coat (he had shortened its handle to better conceal it) and struck such a heavy blow to the back of Trotsky's head that it impacted the brain. Having heard a 'terrible, soul-shaking cry', Sedova found her husband 'leaning against the door.... His face covered with blood, his eyes, without glasses, were sharp blue, his hands were hanging'.

Rushed to hospital, Leon Trotsky died in hospital the following day. Stalin had got his man.

Sedova hoped that 'retribution will come to the vile murderers'. Claiming he had acted alone, Ramón Mercader served twenty years in a Mexican prison but never suffered much by way of retribution. Released in 1960, he received a warm welcome from Fidel Castro in Cuba before making his way to the Soviet Union where he was presented with a 'Hero of the Soviet Union' award.

The house in which Trotsky was attacked was later made into a museum, run by Esteban Volkov, the grandson who had been shot in the foot.

42.
30 August 1918,
Fanny Kaplan Tries to Kill Lenin

Late in the evening of the 30 August 1918, Vladimir Lenin, the Bolshevik leader, emerged from a meeting at the Hammer and Sickle factory in Moscow when he was approached by an unknown woman who called out his name. Detained momentarily by a colleague, who was remonstrating about bread shortages, Lenin was about to get into his car, his foot on the running board, when the woman produced a revolver and fired three shots. One shot missed him, ripping through his coat and hitting his colleague in her elbow, but the other two struck him down – one bullet went through his neck, the other into his left shoulder. Lenin survived – just. It had been the second attempt on Lenin's life in just seven months.

Vladimir Lenin's would-be assassin was 28-year-old Fanny Kaplan. Born Feiga Chaimovna Roytblat in the Ukraine on 10 February 1890, Kaplan, one of seven children, was drawn to revolutionary politics from a young age.

Dora / Fanny Kaplan

At the age of sixteen, Kaplan joined an anarchist group based in Kiev, was given the name Fanny Kaplan, sometimes Dora Kaplan, and charged with assassinating the city's governor. But the bomb she was preparing detonated in her room, almost blinding her. She was arrested and, had she not been so young (she was still under twenty-one), she would have faced

198

the death penalty. Instead, she was sentenced to 'eternal penal servitude' in Siberia. During her time of forced labour, her eyesight deteriorated to the point of near blindness.

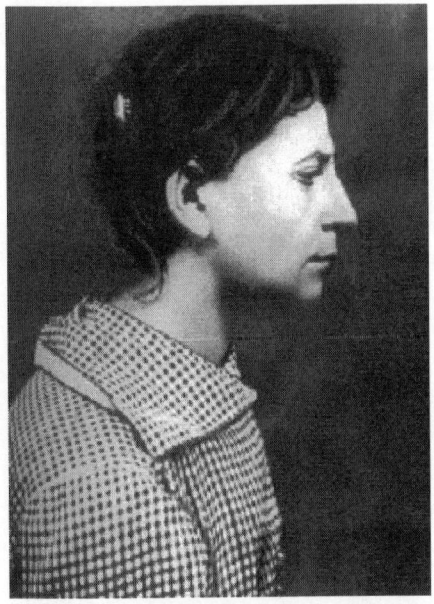

Fanny Kaplan.

Following the February Revolution of 1917 and the overthrow of the last Russian tsar, Nicholas II, Kaplan was released as part of a post-revolutionary political amnesty. She suffered from severe headaches and bouts of blindness but, following an intensive course of treatment, she regained partial sight.

Socialist Revolutionary

She made her way to Moscow and there fell in with the Socialist Revolutionary Party (SR), who, following the October Revolution, had fully expected to share power with their socialist colleagues, the Bolsheviks. Indeed, a Constituent Assembly consisting of SRs, Bolsheviks and others met in Petrograd on 18 January 1918, but when the assembled gathering rejected most of Lenin's suggestions, he had it dissolved within the day.

And so, the embittered SRs plotted to undermine the Bolsheviks by targeting their leader. Thus, on 30 August 1918, Fanny Kaplan shot Lenin.

Having done the deed, she followed SR protocol and allowed herself to be arrested, prepared to sacrifice her life for the cause.

Today I shot at Lenin

Interrogated by the Cheka, the Bolsheviks' newly-formed security wing, Kaplan said, *'Today I shot at Lenin. I did it on my own. I will not say from whom I obtained my revolver. I will give no details. I had resolved to kill Lenin long ago. I consider him a traitor to the Revolution.'*

Vladimir Lenin, July 1920. German Federal Archives.

The Cheka, desperate to know who Kaplan was working for, got nothing out of her. So, at 4 am on 3 September, Fanny Kaplan was escorted into a garage and executed with a single bullet to the back of her head. Her corpse was bundled into a barrel, and set alight. There were to be no remains of Kaplan, no identifiable martyr to the SR cause. The order came from Yakov Sverdlov who, just six weeks before, had ordered the execution of Tsar Nicholas and his family.

Did Fanny Kaplan really shoot Lenin?

But did Fanny Kaplan really shoot Lenin? We will never know for sure but doubts are so rooted that the answer is almost taken as a no – she did not. Why would the SR entrust such an important mission to a poorly-sighted woman, who had never handled a firearm before, to shoot Lenin in the dark? Despite the large crowd milling around Lenin's car, not one of the eighteen witnesses questioned actually saw Kaplan firing her revolver. The bullet removed from Lenin's neck, almost four years after the event, was found not to have been fired from the Browning revolver alleged to have been used by Kaplan.

But Lenin's near death at the hands of a deranged woman suited the Bolsheviks at a time when their survival looked far from certain. Lenin profited from a surge of sympathy that served both him and his party well.

Red Terror

Kaplan's act took place the same fortnight as the successful assassination of leading Bolshevik, Moisei Uritsky. The two events jumpstarted the Bolshevik campaign of 'Red Terror': 'It is necessary, secretly and urgently, to prepare the terror,' urged Lenin. Felix 'Iron' Dzerzhinsky, the first head of the Cheka, openly declared, 'We stand for organized terror – this should be frankly admitted. Terror is an absolute necessity during times of revolution.' Grigory Zinoviev, another leading Bolshevik and friend of Lenin's, added, 'We must carry along with us 90 million out of the 100 million of Soviet Russia's population. As for the rest, we have nothing to say to them. They must be annihilated'. As the Soviets were keen on saying – you can't make an omelette without breaking eggs. (Zinoviev would fall victim to the Soviet system, executed on Stalin's orders in 1936).

Meanwhile, Lenin survived Kaplan's attempt on his life, physically and politically, but his injuries, together with his intense workload, contributed to a series of strokes, the first in May 1922, and ultimately led to his early demise, aged 53, on 21 January 1924.

43.
31 August 1939,
World War Two's First Death

World War Two began with a single death; a death that Hitler would use as the justification for going to war and invading Poland. The victim's name, largely forgotten to history, was Franciszek (or Franz) Honiok.

Eastward ambition

The signing of the Nazi-Soviet Non-Aggression Pact on 23 August 1939, had been the penultimate piece in Hitler's grand jigsaw. With the Soviet Union safely out of the way, Hitler was now free to pursue his ambitions in the West.

Three days later, on 26 August, Hitler ordered the invasion of Poland. Troops had begun to mobilize only for Hitler, nervous of Britain's response, to rescind the order. He knew he couldn't simply march in – he needed a pretext. In the event he made one up.

On 28 August, Hitler revoked the German-Polish Non-Aggression Treaty of 1934. The Poles knew what was coming.

On the nights leading up to 31 August / 1 September there were no less than 21 incidences along the German – Polish border faked by the Germans which, to a gullible world, would seem like acts of Polish aggression for which retaliation was perfectly justifiable.

Operation Himmler

These acts of farce, codenamed Operation Himmler, were organised by Heinrich Himmler and Reinhard Heydrich. The most notorious was the Gleiwitz Incident, the faked attack on the radio transmitting station, a few miles inside Germany, near the border town of Gleiwitz in the Silesia region. Early evening on 31 August 1939, SS soldiers, dressed up as Polish partisans and led by a notorious Nazi thug, Major Alfred Naujocks, 'attacked' the German transmitter and its German guards (more SS men dressed up), and broadcast in Polish a brief anti-German message.

To make the attack look more authentic, the Germans had brought along an inmate from the Dachau concentration camp, the 43-year-old Franciszek Honiok, a farmer and a known Polish sympathizer, arrested by the Gestapo just the day before. The unfortunate Honiok was, what the Germans called, 'canned goods', kept alive until the Gestapo had need for a dead but still warm body.

Franz Honiok.

Having dressed Honiok as a Polish bandit, they drugged him unconscious, shot him at the scene and then left his body there as evidence of the supposed attack. Local police and press found the body and the news spread across Europe. 'There have been reports of an attack on a radio station in Gleiwitz,' reported the BBC. 'Several of the Poles were reported killed, but the numbers are not yet known.' The attack made the *New York Times* the following day.

Hitler knew that the falsehood of Operation Himmler was highly transparent but, as he lectured his staff the week before, 'I need a propagandistic cause for declaring war, whether convincing or not. The victor will not be asked whether he told the truth'.

4.45 a.m. World War Two starts

The following morning, 1 September, at 4.45 German troops attacked Poland. Hours later Hitler spoke to the nation, referring to the 'Polish atrocities'. He continued, 'This night for the first time Polish regular soldiers fired on our own territory. This group of Polish Army hooligans has finally exhausted our patience. Since 5.45 a. m. we have been returning the fire… I will continue this struggle, no matter against whom, until the safety of the Reich and its rights are secured.' Whether by accident or design, Hitler was an hour out.

Rudolph Hess, getting carried away in hyperbole, declared, 'There is bloodshed, Herr Chamberlain! There are dead! Innocent people have died. The responsibility for this, however, lives with England, which talks of peace while fanning the flames of war. England that has point blank refused all the Fuhrer's proposals for peace throughout the years.'

Technically, Franciszek Honiok had been killed during peacetime but his death can be considered the first in a conflict that would, over the ensuing six years and a day, claim over 50 million victims.

The Second World War had begun.

44.

18 September 1931,
The Suicide of Geli Raubal, Hitler's Niece

On 18 September 1931, a 23-year-old woman was found dead in a sumptuous nine-room Munich apartment, a single shot wound into her heart. Her name was Geli Raubal, the apartment was rented to Adolf Hitler, and the young woman happened to be Hitler's niece. Cause of death – suicide. Naturally.

Geli Raubal was the daughter of Hitler's half sister, Angela. Angela and Adolf grew up together; both products of the same father, Alois Hitler, and his second and third wives respectively.

Uncle Alf

In 1928, Hitler offered his sister the position of housekeeper in his Bavarian mountain retreat. Angela arrived with her two daughters, Elfriede and 19-year-old Angela, known as Geli. Hitler immediately took a shine to the carefree Geli and, in order to remove her from her mother's watchful eye, installed her into his Munich apartment. Nineteen years Hitler's junior, she was, according to one of Hitler's aides, 'of medium size, well developed, had dark, rather wavy hair, and lively brown eyes… it was simply astonishing to see a young girl at Hitler's side.'

Geli, who called Hitler 'Uncle Alf', had been born in Linz; the town Hitler always considered his hometown, on 4 June 1908.

Geli Raubal.

One colleague wrote, 'When she was there, Hitler rarely started on his dreadful and often endless monologues... Geli's presence relaxed and released him.' Another wrote, 'No one else was ever allowed to tease him as much as she did, because no one else made him feel so secure. He hated nothing more than being laughed at, but when Geli laughed, she was laughing with him, not at him.' Hitler's English nephew, Patrick, described Geli as looking 'more like a child than a girl. You couldn't call her pretty exactly, but she had great natural charm. She usually went without a hat and wore very plain clothes, pleated skirts and white blouses. No jewellery except a gold swastika given to her by Uncle Adolf.'

Hitler once told his photographer, Heinrich Hoffman, 'I love Geli and could marry her.' He liked to be seen with his attractive niece, taking her to meetings, and to restaurants and theatres, but their relationship was a stormy one. Both were consumed by jealousy – Geli of Hitler's relationship with a 17-year-old Eva Braun, one of Hoffman's models; and Hitler by Geli's flirtatious conduct and numerous admirers.

Hitler controlled her life and dictated whom she was allowed to see and when. Geli found her uncle's overbearing influence suffocating. He refused Geli permission to move to Vienna to study music (Vienna was where, as a young man, Hitler twice unsuccessfully applied to the art academy).

When Hitler suspected Geli of dating his chauffeur, an ex-convict called Emil Maurice, he flew into a rage and had the man sacked (although he was at some point later re-instated). What we don't know for sure was whether Hitler had a sexual relationship with his niece. His sexuality has always been a subject for debate – was he homosexual or even asexual? Hitler often maintained he was wedded to the German nation and had no time for women. (He only married Eva Braun in the bunker beneath the Reichstag in Berlin just forty hours before their joint suicide in 1945.)

Sickened

With regards to Geli, Wilhelm Stocker, an SS guard, decades later, wrote, 'She admitted to me that at times Hitler made her do things in the privacy of her room that sickened her but when I asked her why she didn't refuse to do them she just shrugged and said that she didn't want to lose him to some woman that would do what he wanted.' The 'things' that 'sickened' her, so speculation has it, included sexual games involving urination. Certainly, one of Hitler's opponents within the party, Otto Strasser, said how Geli had had a similar conversation with him, in which urination was mentioned. But then, as an opponent, can Strasser's word be trusted?

In 1929, Hitler wrote Geli an explicit letter. The letter, had it been exposed to the press, would have spelt the end of Hitler's career. It fell to a Catholic priest, Father Bernhard Stempfle, a fervent anti-Semite who had helped Hitler edit his biographical *Mein Kampf*, to rescue the letter. (Fr Stempfle would later fall victim to Hitler's purge, the Night of the Long Knives, probably for simply knowing too much about Hitler's deepest secrets. His body was found in a forest near Munich with a broken neck and three bullets in the heart).

For the last time – no

On the afternoon of 18 September 1931, witnesses heard Hitler and Geli have a row. As he got into his car to go to a meeting ahead of attending a conference in Hamburg, Hitler was heard shouting, 'For the last time – no.'

After Uncle Alf's angry departure, staff at the apartment heard Geli stomping around and may have heard a noise that sounded like a shot from a revolver.

Adolf Hitler. Artist unknown.

The following morning, when Geli failed to emerge for breakfast, they knocked on her door, but found it locked from the inside. When there was no answer, they either broke the door down or called in a locksmith (accounts vary). The exact sequence of events is unclear. Inside they found Geli lying face down in a pool of blood with a single bullet wound to her heart. The gun, lying nearby, had been Hitler's revolver. It looked like suicide. Yet, on the writing desk, was an upbeat letter Geli was in the process of writing to a friend. It was left unfinished in midsentence.

The seeds of inhumanity

There was no inquest into her death nor an autopsy. The passage of the bullet was not consistent with suicide, yet suicide was the verdict. There were several rumours – that her nose was broken, that she was pregnant.

The first police officer on the scene, Heinrich Muller, was seen pocketing the letter and the pistol into his coat. He was later appointed head of the Gestapo. An anti-Nazi journalist, Fritz Gerlich, claimed that Hitler never did leave for his meeting, and that he and Geli had lunch together at a local restaurant. On returning to their apartment, they had a row that resulted in Geli's death. (Gerlich and, apparently, the owner of the restaurant, was another killed during the Night of the Long Knives.)

When Hitler was told of his niece's death, by Rudolf Hess, he fell into a deep depression, almost comatose, and talked of taking his own life. Colleagues kept watch over him. He became a vegetarian because, apparently, the sight of meat reminded him of her corpse. Her bedroom was sealed off and maintained as a shrine. Each year, on the anniversaries of her birth and her death, the room was decked with flowers.

How Geli's mother, Angela, reacted to the news is not recorded but one can imagine. She stayed on working for Hitler until, in 1936, she left his employ to marry an architect. Hitler, upset by her departure, did not send a wedding present.

Heinrich Hoffman, Hitler's official photographer, later stated that Raubal's death 'was when the seeds of inhumanity began to grow inside Hitler'.

Sixteen months after the death of Geli Raubal, on 30 January 1933, Hitler was appointed chancellor.

45.
12 October 1915,
The Execution of British Nurse, Edith Cavell

When the First World War broke out, Edith Cavell was working as a matron in a Brussels nursing school, a school she had co-founded in 1907 and where she'd helped pioneer the importance of follow-up care. But at the time, July 1914, she was on leave, holidaying with her family in Norfolk, England. On hearing the news of war, her parents begged her not to return to Belgium – but of course she did.

Following the German occupation of Brussels, Cavell refused the German offer of a safe conduct into neutral Netherlands. She continued her work and in the process hid refugee British, Belgian and French soldiers and provided over 200 of them the means to escape into the Netherlands from where most managed the journey back to England. Her network knew it was dangerous work and discussed whether they should continue. Cavell insisted they should: 'If we are arrested we shall be punished in any case, whether we have done much or little'. And so they carried on. With the Germans watching the work at the hospital and its comings and goings, her arrest was inevitable. It duly came on 3 August 1915. Edith Cavell, arrested by the Germans, readily admitted her guilt.

Edith Cavell.

Patriotism is not enough

Cavell was remanded in isolation for ten weeks, not even being allowed to meet the lawyer appointed to defend her until the morning of her trial, a trial which lasted only two days. Cavell, along with 34 others also arrested, was found guilty. Her case became a *cause célèbre* but the British government, realising the Germans were acting within their own legality, was unable to intervene. However, the Americans, as neutrals, pointed to Cavell's nursing credentials and her saving of the lives of German soldiers, as well as British, but to no avail. Along with her Belgian accomplice, Philippe Baucq, the nurse was found guilty and sentenced to be shot.

On the evening before her execution, Cavell was visited by an army chaplain. She told him, 'Patriotism is not enough. I must have no hatred or bitterness towards anyone.' The words are inscribed on Cavell's statue, near Trafalgar Square in London.

On 12 October 1915, about to face the firing squad, Cavell said, 'My soul, as I believe, is safe, and I am glad to die for my country'. She was 49.

The Edith Cavell Memorial, London. Photographed by the author.

Judged justly

The German foreign secretary, Alfred Zimmermann, expressed pity for Cavell but added that she had been 'judged justly'. 'I can assure you,' wrote Zimmermann in a newspaper article, 'that the case was conducted with the utmost thoroughness. No war court in the world could have given any other verdict.' The fact that Cavell was a woman was of no relevance. But the decision to execute Cavell, however legal, was a localized one, unknown to the German army's High Command or Wilhelm II, the German Kaiser. On hearing of the execution the Kaiser was appalled, considering the sentence a political error.

Indeed, the British made propaganda capital out of the nurse's execution, stoking up anti-German feeling by exploiting the image of the gentle nurse slaughtered by the German barbarian. Following the backlash, all of the others had their death sentences commuted to imprisonment. In the weeks following Cavell's execution, recruitment into the British Army doubled. The name Edith became popular – Edith Piaf, born two months after Cavell's execution, was reputably named after her.

British propaganda poster depicting the German 'murder' of Edith Cavell.

After the war, Cavell's body was brought back to England where, in May 1919, she was afforded a state funeral at Westminster Abbey in London, attended by packed streets of mourners. A statue was erected in near Trafalgar Square, another in the grounds of Norwich cathedral, and a third in Paris. In June 1940, following Nazi Germany's invasion and occupation of France, Adolf Hitler personally ordered the destruction of Edith Cavell's monument. The London memorial, designed by Sir George Frampton, was not well received on its unveiling in 1920. One reviewer wrote, 'the figure of Edith Cavell is a beautiful conception, finely executed, but it is overshadowed and dwarfed by the great mass of granite which forms the background; and the squat figure representing Humanity, surmounting it, is as unpleasing as it is curious'.

Edith Cavell is buried at Norwich cathedral and each October, on the anniversary of her death, a service of remembrance is held at her grave.

46.
15 October 1946,
The Suicide of Hermann Goring

Born in Bavaria, 12 January 1893, to a well-to-do Prussian family, Hermann Goring fancied himself as a cut above the rest, a cultured man, fond of fine living, the arts and women. Indeed, as a young fighter pilot during the First World War, Goring cut a dashing figure and in June 1918, won the *Pour le Mérite*, otherwise known as the Blue Max, Prussia's highest award.

At the time of his birth, Goring's parents were stationed in Haiti, his father working for the German consul there. His mother returned to Germany to give birth, then promptly headed back to Haiti, leaving baby Hermann with a friend, not to see her child again for three years.

After the First World War, Goring worked as a commercial pilot in Denmark and Sweden, where he met his future wife, the Swedish baroness Carin von Kantzow. They married in Munich on 3 February 1923. Serving as a Prussian deputy in the German Reichstag, he met the young Adolf Hitler and soon afterwards, in 1922, joined the fledging Nazi Party.

Austria

A year later, on 8 November 1923, Goring was shot in the leg and badly injured during the Munich *Putsch*, Hitler's failed attempt to seize power by force. From there, together with his wife, Goring escaped to Austria. In Innsbruck, his wound was operated on but such was the pain he was given morphine, thereby starting an addiction which would last until his final days. At one point, during his forced sojourn in Austria, and later Italy, where he met Italy's fascist leader, Benito Mussolini, Goring's addiction had become so severe he had to be incarcerated in a mental hospital, occasionally having to be restrained by means of a straitjacket.

In 1927, after four years away, Goring returned to Germany.

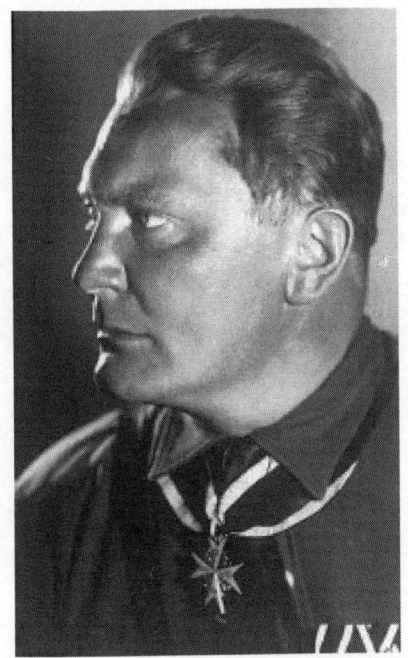

Hermann Goring, 1932. German Federal Archives.

Elections

Following the national elections of May 1928, Goring entered the Reichstag, occupying one of only twelve seats won by the Nazis (out of a total of 491).

Following the more successful elections of July 1932, in which the Nazis gained 230 seats, Goring was made president of the Reichstag. Then, following Hitler's appointment as chancellor on 30 January 1933, Goring established the first concentration camps for the imprisonment of the Nazi's political opponents and founded the Nazi secret police, the feared Gestapo. (He ceded control of the Gestapo to Heinrich Himmler in 1934).

Goring's wife, Carin, died on 17 October 1931, and four years later, on

10 April 1935, Goring married for the second time. His second wife, Emmy, bore him his only child, a girl called Edda (rumoured to have been named after Mussolini's daughter), born 2 June 1938, who is still alive today (2015) and believed to be living in Munich.

Emmy Goring, née Sonnemann. German Federal Archives.

You can call me Meyer

Goring helped Hitler in destroying the SA and liquidating its leader, Ernst Rohm, during the Night of the Long Knives in June 1934. Hitler repaid Goring's loyalty by appointing him in 1935 Commander-in-Chief of the *Luftwaffe*, the German Air Force. The following year he was also appointed Economics Minister. Goring's grasp of economics was questionable but, with Hitler's prompting, he introduced the Four-Year-Plan, a more aggressive policy to prepare Germany for war.

In August 1939, a month before the outbreak of Second World War, Goring boasted about the strength of the *Luftwaffe*, declaring, 'Not a single bomb will fall on the Ruhr. If an enemy plane reaches the Ruhr, my name is not Hermann Goring, you can call me Meyer.'

Initially, Goring's *Luftwaffe* enjoyed a string of successes, playing crucial roles during the Nazi invasions of Poland and France during the first year of the war. However, reverses during the Battle of Britain and on the Eastern Front, particularly the *Luftwaffe's* failure to relieve stranded German troops trapped in Stalingrad, saw the decline of Goring's influence. His Meyer boast came back to haunt him as, later in the war, the *Luftwaffe* failed to prevent the bombing of German cities. German civilians suffered terribly under the barrage of bombing inflicted by the US Air Force and the Royal Air Force's Bomber Command, most notably in Cologne, Hamburg and, in February 1945, Dresden.

Goring and his medals

Goring enjoyed a lavish and wealthy lifestyle. He collected art, much of it stolen from Jewish collectors, adored his uniforms and loved receiving and bestowing medals. In October 1938, he proudly presented the Grand Service Cross of the Golden Eagle award to the US aviation hero, Charles Lindbergh. (In 1941, Lindbergh was to suggest to President Roosevelt that the US struck a 'neutrality pact' with Hitler). Goring was the only ever recipient of Germany's highest military award for heroism, the Grand Cross to the Iron Cross, awarded on 19 July 1940 in recognition of his services with the *Luftwaffe*. (Days before his suicide on 30 April 1945, Hitler revoked Goring's medal).

Anti-Semitic

Although not so furiously anti-Semitic as most of his colleagues (his godfather and mother's lover, Hermann Epenstein, was of Jewish ancestry) Goring's role certainly accelerated Hitler's desired destruction of Germany's Jewish population. Following the nationwide pogrom against the Jews, *Kristallnacht*, on the night of 8 – 9 November 1938, Goring didn't see why German insurance companies should have to pay out and so ordered the Jewish community to collectively pay compensation to the tune of one billion marks.

It was Goring who, in July 1941, ordered Reinhard Heydrich to prepare a set of proposals on how to deal with the 'Jewish Question'; an order that led, six months later, to Heydrich chairing the one-day Wannsee Conference, in which the plans for the Final Solution were officially

217

adopted.

Downfall

In 1941, having made Goring *Reichsmarschall*, 'Reich Marshal of the Greater German Reich', Hitler named him as his deputy and successor. In the event, in his last days, Hitler declared Goring a traitor for having suggested that he take full command, and stripped him of all his decorations, titles and offices, and placing him under house arrest. In his last will and testament, dictated the day before his suicide, Hitler stripped Goring of his party membership.

*Hermann Goring, front row, far left, at the Nuremberg Trials, 1946.
Seated next to him is Rudolph Hess. US National Archives.*

Following Germany's final defeat and surrender, Goring gave himself up to the Americans. Tried at the post-war Nuremberg trials, Goring was charged with various accounts, including war crimes and crimes against humanity.

After a trial lasting 218 days, during which he was finally cured of his morphine addiction, Goring was found guilty. The judgement described his guilt as 'unique in its enormity'. He was sentenced to hang. Goring's plea for death by firing squad, a 'soldier's death', was refused. Two hours before his execution was due to take place, he took his own life using poison that had either been smuggled into him or hidden all the while in a container of pomade. He was 53.

Ten of his fellow accused, all high-ranking Nazis, were hanged on 16 October in a 'small brightly-lit gymnasium in the gaol yard', where, only a couple days before, American soldiers had played a game of basketball.

47.
20 October 1952,
The Start of the Mau Mau Uprising

In 2013, half a century on, Kenyans tortured by the British colonial authorities during the Mau Mau Uprising of the 1952 – 1960 received pay-outs totalling £20m from the British government. The High Court had rejected the British government's claim that too much time had passed for there to be a fair trial. But what exactly was the Mau Mau Uprising?

After the Second World War, Britain began the difficult and lengthy process of decolonisation. In African countries that were entirely black in population, such as Ghana, the process was relatively straightforward. Where it was more difficult were the nations that had sizeable population of white settlers. Rhodesia being an example of this latter category, as was Kenya.

The Crown Colony

Kenya's official association with Britain had started in 1895, when the country became British East Africa. The British government encouraged the settlement of Kenya's fertile highlands by Europeans, utilising the labour of the very peoples they had dispossessed, such as the traditional tribes of the Kikuyu. In 1920, British East Africa became an official crown colony of the British Empire. The white settlers were given preference in all spheres of politics, administration and society, and Africans were barred from political involvement until 1944 when a small number were appointed (not elected) onto the legislature.

Resentment of white expansion and settlement deepened. During the late 1940s, the Kikuyu established a secret society bound by oaths whose aim was the eventual expulsion of the white settlers by means of force. The society was known as the Mau Mau. The taking of an oath bound people to the cause, with severe penalties, including death, for those who broke their oaths. These oaths, elaborate affairs, involved eating the hearts and drinking the blood of goats.

The Mau Mau's acts of violence, although isolated, needed dealing with. Thus, on 20 October 1952, Kenya's governor, Evelyn Baring, declared a state of emergency. The declaration only made a potentially volatile situation worse and, in effect, elevated the situation into a full-scale uprising. The Mau Mau fled to the forests to re-group before launching a series of violent attacks on whites and loyalist blacks, including murder and arson. An attack on the town of Lari in March 1953, resulted in almost 100 deaths of Kenyans who had refused to take the oath, including the local chief known to be loyal to the British.

The British authorities responded by rounding up thousands of alleged Mau Mau members and subjecting many to torture, rape and castration and at least one reported case of a Kenyan being roasted alive. One official document describes an African employee of Special Branch who 'pushed pins into their sides, buttocks, fingers and, on at least one occasion, the head, and ... pinched the sides of their bodies, penis and scrotum with pliers. He crushed the fingers of one detainee'.

The man the British suspected of being the Mau Mau leader, although he himself denied it, was Jomo Kenyatta, leader of the Kenya African National Union (KANU). Kenyatta, a graduate from University College London and once an extra in a film directed by Alexander Korda, became the focal point of the uprising. Baring, determined to have Kenyatta imprisoned, bribed the judge to the tune of £20,000 (about £500,000 / US$770,000 in 2015), bribed witnesses and threatened Kenyatta's defence lawyers. The sentence of seven years hard labour, which Kenyatta served almost in its entirety, only elevated his standing among the rebels.

Jomo Kenyatta, 1966. German Federal Archive.

The primarily targets and victims of the Mau Mau's insurgence over the next four years were not so much the whites but fellow Kikuyu and Africans whom they suspected of collaborating with the British. Thus the Mau Mau alienated the support of many of their countrymen. Many Africans, victims themselves and appalled by the level of violence, sided with the British. British settlers responded by turning into vigilantes and hunting down Mau Mau insurgents. As one white farmer said, 'We take out our sten guns and we let the bloody vermin have it'. But it began backfiring – the greater and more violent the reprisals, the greater the sympathy for the Mau Mau. Violence bred violence.

In mid-May 1953, the British sent in George Erskine to deal with the situation for once and for all. Armed with twelve battalions, artillery and the RAF, the sustained show of force made the difference. RAF Lincoln bombers, for example, dropped some 6 million bombs onto the Kenyan forests over a two-year period.

The Hola Camp Massacre

By 1956, the British had all but squashed the uprising but its detainees were detained further until the state of emergency was finally lifted in January 1960. The British treatment of its prisoners was harsh and brought widespread condemnation. The British massacre at the Hola Camp in 1959 being an example of colonial abuse. The camp in the town of Hola in the south east of the country contained 506 of what the British considered the 'hardcore' insurgents and their aim was to brainwash these detainees into accepting the right of the British to rule. When on 3 March 1959, eighty-eight prisoners refused to carry out labour as ordered by the camp commandant, John Cowan, guards set upon them with clubs, killing eleven and severely injuring the rest. (No one was reprimanded for the incident, let alone prosecuted. Indeed, Cowan was later awarded the MBE).

The Hola incident, although it gained particular coverage, was only one of many and the camp at Hola only one of about 150 across the country holding some 150,000 Mau Mau suspects. The Kenya Human Rights Commission said up to 90,000 Kenyans were executed, tortured or maimed during the uprising.

Independence

Following the defeat of the Mau Mau, the British authorities in Kenya reformed land tenure, allowing greater number of Kenyans access to and ownership of land. In 1957, the authorities staged the first direct elections for Africans to the Legislative Council but based on a limited suffrage, too fearful to permit universal suffrage. Finally, on 12 December 1963, Kenya was handed its independence with Jomo Kenyatta its first president. Kenya, which two years later was declared a republic, became a member of the British Commonwealth.

But the scars inflicted on the Mau Mau ran deep and were still felt half a century later. 'I would like to make clear now, and for the first time on behalf of Her Majesty's government,' said William Hague, the then foreign secretary, to the House of Commons in 2013, 'that we understand the pain and grievance felt by those who were involved in the events of the emergency in Kenya'.

48.
23 October 1956,
The Start of the Hungarian Revolution

In October 1956, the people of Hungary stood up against the oppression of Soviet rule. The subsequent uprising almost succeeded but the Soviet Union, in a full show of force, re-established its control and the revolution was quashed as quickly as it had erupted.

Slices of Salami

From March 1944, during the Second World War, Hungary was occupied by the forces of Nazi Germany, being liberated by the Soviet Union's Red Army on 4 April 1945. Backed by Joseph Stalin, Hungary's fledging communists, led by Mátyás Rákosi, the self-styled 'Stalin's best pupil', bullied their way into power. Having destroyed all political opponents by 'cutting them off like slices of salami,' as Rákosi later boasted, the communists consolidated their grip on power and in 1949, Hungary had officially become the People's Republic of Hungary with Rákosi at its helm.

In just a matter of years, over 300,000 Hungarians were purged under Rákosi's rule: exiled, imprisoned or killed. Stalin would have thoroughly approved of Rákosi's hard-line tactics but within four months of the Soviet leader's death, on 5 March 1953, the Soviet politburo replaced Rákosi with Imre Nagy, whose softer approach gained him popular consent. Life improved, goods appeared in shops, and political prisoners were released. But Nagy became too popular for the Kremlin's liking and in April 1955

Rákosi was put back in charge and the oppression started anew. But Nagy remained a hero.

Mátyás Rákosi. German Federal Archive.

A year after his re-appointment, Rákosi was replaced by fellow hard-line Stalinist, Erno Gero. (The Kremlin, finally realising how unpopular Rákosi was, told him to resign on grounds of ill health and fly to Moscow for treatment. He did, never to return to his home country. He was not missed). But under Erno Gero, nothing changed – arrests continued, the AVO, the Hungarian secret police, was busier than ever, while discontent simmered and people longed for the return of Imre Nagy.

Speaking in 1957, Peter Fryer, member of Great Britain's communist party, described the situation in pre-revolutionary Hungary: 'Hypocrisy without limit; medieval cruelty; dogmas and slogans devoid of life or meaning; national pride outraged; poverty for all but a tiny handful of leaders who lived in luxury, with mansions on *Rózsadomb*, Budapest's pleasant Hill of Roses, special schools for their children, special well-stocked shops for their wives – even special bathing beaches at Lake Balaton, shut off from the common people by barbed wire.' (Fryer resigned from the communist party over what happened in Hungary.)

In June 1953, the Poles demonstrated against Stalinist rule. Soviet tanks went in, there were shootings, many were killed, but then Nikita Khrushchev, Stalin's successor, withdrew the tanks and granted the Poles a degree of concession and reform. If the Poles could do it, why couldn't the Hungarians?

Russians go home!

On 23 October 1956, students in Budapest staged a peaceful demonstration, having, the night before, drawn up a list of sixteen demands. Among them, the demand for a new government led by Imre Nagy; that all criminal leaders of the Stalin-Rákosi era be immediately relieved of their duties; general elections by universal and secret ballot to elect a new National Assembly with all political parties participating; for the Russian language to cease being a compulsory subject in Hungarian schools; and for the removal of Soviet troops from Hungarian soil.

The students met at the statue of General Jozsef Bem, a national hero of the 1848 Hungarian Revolution. By the evening of the 23rd, the demonstration had reached 200,000 in number. 'Russians go home!' they shouted. Red stars were torn down from buildings. A 30-foot bronze statue of Stalin in the city's Hero Square, erected five years previously as a gift to the dictator from the Hungarian People, was pulled down, leaving only his boots on the plinth. A delegation of protestors tried to broadcast their demands on national radio, demanding that the radio should belong to the people. The police opened fire and killed several demonstrators. Erno Gero condemned the protest, saying, 'We shall defend the achievements of the people's democracy under all circumstances from whichever quarter they may be threatened. Today the chief aim of the enemies of our people is to shake the power of the working class, to loosen the peasant-worker alliance, to undermine the leadership of the working class in our country and to upset their faith in its party, in the Hungarian Workers' Party.' Gero sent in the troops, but, to his dismay, found that many of his soldiers sided with the demonstrators.

At 2 am, at Gero's request, the Soviet tanks began arriving. Martial law was imposed. What had began as a peaceful demonstration had turned very quickly into a full-scale revolution. The Kremlin responded by putting Imre Nagy back in charge believing that 'limited concessions' were necessary to satisfy the Hungarian people. Nagy promised his people reform in return for an end to the violence.

We lied by night

On 28 October, Khrushchev withdrew his troops from Hungary – but only as far as over the border. Hungarians sensed victory. Political parties, long since banned, reformed; new newspapers sprung up, most only a side long, plastered up on shop fronts, trees and street lamps. Hundreds of Hungary's secret police were lynched – punishment for their years of torture and oppression of the Hungarian people. A reporter from the *New York Times* recorded the following scene: 'Among those watching this demonstration was a furtive figure clad in a leather coat. Suddenly someone identified him rightly or wrongly as a member of the hated AVO, the Hungarian political police. Like tigers, the crowd turned on him, began to beat him and hustled him into a courtyard. A few minutes later they emerged rubbing their hands with satisfaction. The leather-coated figure was seen no more.'

Nagy, riding the wave of optimism, promised open elections and a coalition government. A few days later he went even further – promising Hungary's withdrawal from the Warsaw Pact.

The citizens of Budapest took control of the radio; the state broadcasters were happy to cede control and confessed to having been instruments of the state: *'We lied by night, we lied by day, we lied on all wavelengths. We, who are before the microphones, are now new men.'*

A Russian howitzer on the streets of Budapest, October 1956. Fortepan.

This went much further than Poland; Nagy had gone too far. The rebels hoped and expected support and aid from the West but Britain and France were distracted by the emerging crisis over the Suez Canal and the US by presidential elections. The aid never materialised. Meanwhile, in China, Chairman Mao heckled Khrushchev for being weak and encouraged him to take a firmer line. So Khrushchev, taking advantage of the West's preoccupations, ordered the tanks back in. They duly reappeared in Hungary on 3 November and entered Budapest the following day. This time, with brutal efficiency, the uprising was crushed.

Our troops are still fighting

Nagy appeared on Radio Budapest early on the morning of 4 November as the tanks started their devastating work in the capital:

'This is Imre Nagy speaking. Today at daybreak Soviet forces started an attack against our capital, obviously with the intention to overthrow the legal Hungarian democratic government. Our troops are still fighting; the Government is still in its place. I notify the people of our country and the entire world of this fact.'

Imre Nagy, 1945. Fortepan.

And that was it. Nagy's voice disappeared – no one ever heard it again. Seconds later, the National Anthem played, not the communist version but the anthem that brought tears to patriotic hearts. A couple hours later, at 8.10, Radio Budapest broadcast its last appeal, 'Help Hungary… help, help, help,' before being taken off air.

The 'entire world' that Nagy had appealed to, ignored him. Western powers spoke loud words; the US condemned the attack as a 'monstrous crime', but did nothing – the risks of venturing into an Eastern European conflict, and the potential for escalation, were too great.

Just after 1 pm on 4 November, Moscow radio announced, 'The Hungarian counter-revolution has been crushed.' Nagy sought sanctuary in the Yugoslavian embassy and was replaced by the harder Janos Kadar, who, loyal to Moscow, welcomed the return of Soviet forces to crush the 'counter-revolutionary threat'. Over 200,000 Hungarians fled across the border into Austria and the West until that escape route was sealed off. Thousands were executed or imprisoned by Kadar's regime in reprisal.

Imre Nagy, lured out of the embassy by a promise of safe passage to Belgrade, a promise written by Kadar himself, was arrested and taken to Romania. Later, he was smuggled back into Hungary, charged with treason, tried and, on the orders of Kadar, was hung on 16 June 1958. He was buried within the prison yard.

49.
27 October 1962,
The Height of the Cuban Missile Crisis

The Cuban Missile Crisis of October 1962 epitomized the Cold War as the two superpowers, the US and the Soviet Union, brought the world to the brink of nuclear war.

In January 1959, after a two-year guerrilla campaign, Fidel Castro, a Marxist, aided by the charismatic Che Guevara, had disposed of Cuba's 30-year-old dictatorship. The Soviet Union's premier, Nikita Khrushchev, was delighted by this turn of events and that a communist coup had taken place without Soviet encouragement (or bullying).

When Castro nationalized American assets in Cuba, the US responded by placing a trade embargo against Cuba. The Soviet Union came to Cuba's rescue and the two nations bonded, Castro aligning Cuba to the Soviet cause. When they met at the United Nations in September 1960, Khrushchev and Castro embraced. 'I do not know if Fidel is a communist,' said the Soviet leader, 'but I know I am a Fidelista.'

Bay of Pigs

The US, alarmed by this communist presence in their backyard, resolved to have Castro removed from power. On 17 April 1961, a US-backed band of Cuban exiles landed at the Bay of Pigs hoping to raise a counter-uprising against Castro, despite the assurances of the new US president, John F Kennedy, five days before, that the US would not intervene militarily to overthrow Castro. The invasion failed and over a thousand Cuban rebels were captured by Castro's forces. Kennedy was heavily criticized, and internal support for Castro deepened as Cuba became firmly anti-American.

Fidel Castro, April 1959. Library of Congress.

Khrushchev decided to use his new ally. In retaliation for America aiming missiles at the Soviet Union from bases in Turkey, Khrushchev sought Castro's permission to place nuclear missiles in Cuba to face America. In Khrushchev's words, he wanted to 'put one of our hedgehogs down the Americans' trousers', and to give the US a 'little of their own medicine'. Castro gave his support and by the end of July 1962, the first Soviet ships had set sail for Cuba. The ships' captains were unsure of their final destination, or what cargo they were carrying, until half way across when, in front of high-ranking security officers, they were allowed to open sealed envelopes disclosing their destination.

Indisputable evidence

By the time, on 22 October, Khrushchev realised that the Americans had uncovered his secret, 42 nuclear missiles had been put into place on the island of Cuba. Soviet officials based in Washington tried to deny their presence but the American public refused to believe them. Kennedy's speech of 22 October, broadcast on radio and television, in which he talked of 'indisputable evidence', shocked the nation. The public clambered to stock up on foodstuffs and essentials, especially in cities, unhelpfully listed by the American media, as the most vulnerable to nuclear attack.

John F Kennedy, July 1963.
National Archives and Records Administration

Washington was fearful of Khrushchev – not because they conceived the Soviet leader as a worthy opponent but because they deemed him, correctly, as erratic and untrustworthy. Although they were not to know this at the time, the responsibility of the Cuban-based missiles had been delegated to local commanders. On his part, Khrushchev underestimated Kennedy and was dismissive of the young president: 'How can I deal seriously with a man who is younger than my own son?' he asked.

We'll all meet together in Hell

Direct intervention, although favoured by the US military and discussed in detail, was eventually discarded for fear of escalating the crisis into war.

Instead, on 24 October, Kennedy's administration implemented a naval blockade, or quarantine, 800 miles from Cuba, later reduced to 500 miles, to prevent the arrival of further Soviet ships carrying missiles. But the US army and its nuclear weapons remained on red alert.

Nikita Khrushchev, June 1961. John Fitzgerald Kennedy Library.

There then came an exchange of letters between Kennedy and Khrushchev. In one eight-page letter, dated 26 October, Khrushchev wrote, 'I assure you that the ships on their way to Cuba are carrying the most innocent and peaceful cargoes.' How he hoped to get away with such bluster and lies is beyond imagination. Khrushchev warned Kennedy against maintaining the blockade, threatening the use of Soviet submarines against US ships. If it came to nuclear war, Khrushchev warned, 'we'll all meet together in Hell.'

The Eve of Armageddon

On 27 October, an American U-2 reconnaissance plane was shot down over Cuba killing the pilot, Major Rudolf Anderson, the only person killed by enemy fire during the Cuban Missile Crisis. The Crisis had become even more precarious. The American public felt it was on the eve of Armageddon.

Kennedy's generals urged him to retaliate and launch an invasion of Cuba. Kennedy, resisting, sent his brother, Robert, to negotiate with the Soviet Union's ambassador to the US, Anatoly Dobrynin. The deal they thrashed out was conveyed to and accepted by their respective masters. Khrushchev would order the withdrawal of Soviet missiles in Cuba in return for the withdrawal of the US missiles in Turkey, and, in addition, an American pledge not to attempt an overthrow of Castro. Despite this latter condition, Fidel Castro was furious at having not been consulted by the Soviets and scornful of what he saw as Khrushchev's defeat. But the world at least had been saved from devastation.

Cut Mr K's balls off

Nikita Khrushchev and John F Kennedy meeting in Vienna, 3 June 1961.
US Department of State.

On 28 October, Moscow announced Khrushchev's intention to remove the missiles from Cuba. The US, however, did not issue a public statement regarding the removal of their missiles from Turkey, so, on the face of it, the Soviet Union, and Khrushchev personally, had suffered a dishonourable defeat. To make matters worse, Soviet ships, returning home with their missiles, were shadowed out of Cuban waters by US planes and subjected to humiliating searches by US patrols. The Cuban Missile Crisis was over and Kennedy crowed that he had 'cut Mr K's balls off'.

Two years later, in October 1964, Nikita Khrushchev, was forced out of office. He was accused, among other things, of having brought 'the world to the brink of nuclear war... Having no other way out, we were forced to accept all the demands and conditions dictated by the US, right down to the humiliating inspection of our ships by the Americans'.

50.
30 October 1979,
The Death of Rachele Mussolini

In 1914, in Milan, the future fascist dictator, Benito Mussolini, married Ida Dalser, a 34-year-old beautician who soon bore him a child, Benito Albino Mussolini. The marriage lasted just a few months and on 17 December 1915, before the birth of Benito Jr., Mussolini, at the time at home on army sick leave, married Rachele Guidi in a civil ceremony. Guidi had been his long-term mistress and mother to his first child, Edda, who had been born in 1910.

Mussolini and Rachele Guidi shared the same place of birth – the town of Predappio in the area of Forlì in northern Italy. Guidi had been born 11 April 1890. She and Mussolini had first met when Mussolini appeared at her school as a stand-in teacher. Guidi's father had warned her against marrying the penniless Mussolini: 'That young man will starve you to death,' he warned. After the death of her father, Guidi's mother began a relationship with Mussolini's widowed father.

In December 1925, a decade later after their marriage, Rachele and Mussolini renewed their vows in a Catholic church. It was less a romantic gesture than an attempt by Mussolini to ingratiate himself with the pope, Pius XI. The Mussolinis were to have five children.

Rachele Mussolini, née Guidi.

As dictator, Mussolini preached about the importance of the family and liked to portray his own family as a model fascist household. But in truth, he had little time for his children and could number his lovers by the hundred. Rachele knew about her husband's many indiscretions. In an interview with *Life* magazine in February 1966, she said, 'My husband had a fascination for women. They all wanted him. Sometimes he showed me their letters – from women who wanted to sleep with him or have a baby with him. It always made me laugh.'

A beautiful companion

In 1923, Rachele took on a lover of her own – according to Edda in an interview in 1995, shortly before her death, and only broadcast in 2001. Rachele, according to Edda, told Mussolini, 'You have many women. There is a person who loves me a lot, a beautiful companion.' Mussolini may have been shocked but he did nothing to stop the affair, which, apparently, lasted several years.

Benito and Rachele Mussolini in 1923 with their first three children.
Edda, their eldest, is on the right.

In fact, it was less Mussolini's dalliances that worried Rachele, than his career in politics: 'You can't be happy in politics… one day things go well,' she said, 'another day things go badly.' She admitted that she had been at her happiest when they were poor. 'She never was,' declared *Life*, 'nor ever wanted to be, anything but a housewife'. She certainly disliked the trappings of being married to Italy's most powerful man. She hated life in Rome and, refusing to live there, avoided the city at all costs. 'If I lived in Rome,' she told *Life*, 'I'd be a communist.'

Mussolini was, by all accounts, fearful of his wife. Once, following an argument, she kicked him out of the house and made him have his dinner on the front steps. One friend remembered, 'The *Duce* was more afraid of her than he was of the Germans.'

In 1930, Edda married Mussolini's foreign secretary, Galeazzo Ciano. (During the Second World War, on 11 January 1944, Mussolini had his son-in-law executed. Edda never forgave her father: 'The Italian people must avenge the death of my husband. If they do not, I'll do it with my own hands'). Another womanizer, Rachele disliked her daughter's husband and made no attempt to disguise it.

The Mistress

In his latter years, while running the Salo Republic, Mussolini had his mistress, Clara Petacci, a woman two years younger than Edda, set up home nearby – much to Rachele Mussolini's disgust. Wife and mistress frequently argued while Mussolini, the diminished dictator, cowered.

Clara Petacci.

Indeed, on one occasion, Rachele, accompanied by a minder, confronted Petacci. On arriving at the villa gates of her rival, Rachele kept her finger on the doorbell until Petacci's own minder came out to tell her to go away. But Rachele forced her way in. On coming face to face with her husband's mistress, she demanded that Petacci move out of the area. Petacci broke down in tears while Rachele called her names. Both minders waited anxiously in the wings. Petacci tried to read to Rachele letters sent to her by Mussolini. Unable to bear this, Rachele lunged at Petacci and had to be restrained by the minders.

Death at Lake Como

In April 1945, Mussolini, knowing the end was in sight, tried to flee to neutral Switzerland. His companion was not Rachele, his wife of thirty years, but Petacci. They were caught close to Lake Como very near to the Swiss border by Italian partisans and executed on 28 April.

Benito Mussolini.

Days after the end of the war, Rachele also tried to flee to Switzerland and was also apprehended at Como by partisans. Handed over to the Allies, she was interned by the Americans, where she volunteered to cook for her fellow inmates before being released within a matter of months. Penniless, she and Edda lived in Rome, surviving on hand-outs before eventually returning to Predappio, her place of birth.

Rachele canvassed the Italian government to allow her to bury her husband's body in Predappio. Finally, her wish was granted and in 1957, Mussolini was returned and buried within the family crypt. Immediately, Mussolini's grave became a shrine for neo-fascists with frequent 'pilgrimages' especially on significant dates – his date of birth, 29 July, and death, 28 April.

Meanwhile, dressed traditionally as a 'black-cad mamma', Rachele Mussolini kept chickens, tendered a garden, and opened a small restaurant within sight of a mock-medieval castle that Mussolini had built at the height of his power. The restaurant did well, as did a roaring side trade in selling postcards featuring her husband.

Mussolini's brain

In March 1966, Rachele was handed an envelope by an American diplomat. Inside, bizarrely, was a piece of Mussolini's brain which the Americans had removed from Mussolini's corpse presumably, thought Rachele, because they 'wanted to know what makes a dictator'. The *Washington Post* that year had reported that a 'section' of Mussolini's brain had been 'examined by pathologists who described it as average'. She placed the section of the brain in a box above Mussolini's grave.

In 1974, Rachele Mussolini published *Mussolini: An Intimate Biography*. She died, aged 89, on 30 October 1979.

Alessandra Mussolini, 2007.

In 2009, 64 years after Mussolini's death, in another bizarre postscript, Mussolini's granddaughter, Alessandra Mussolini, model turned politician, discovered that the Italian version of the online auction site, eBay, was listing three glass vials containing blood samples and more fragments of her grandfather's brain with a starting price of 15,000 euros. On realising their mistake (eBay forbids the sale of body parts), the listing was immediately removed. Alessandra, niece to Sophia Loren, was, understandably, 'outraged'.

What might have been

In 1910, while working as a journalist, the 27-year-old Mussolini was offered a job as a reporter in America. Rachele was pregnant with Edda at the time and therefore they decided against going. 'I often wish we had,' she said. 'I think my husband might have been very successful in America.'

If only.

51.
8 November 1939,
Georg Elser Almost Assassinates Hitler

The date is 8 November 1939, the location – the *Bürgerbräukeller* beer hall in Munich. With their uniforms freshly-pressed, their buttons gleaming, their shoes polished, Hitler's longest-standing comrades file into the hall, their chests puffed-up with pride, their wives at their sides. This event, on this day, had become an annual occasion in the Nazi calendar, a ritual of celebration and remembrance. The climax of the evening, awaited with great anticipation, would be Hitler's appearance and his speech in which he would praise and pour tribute on these self-satisfied men, his old-timers.

But among the 3,000 devotees, was one man who awaited Hitler's appearance with equal anticipation – but for entirely different reasons. This man was 36-year-old carpenter, Johann Georg Elser, born 4 January 1903. For Elser, a long-time anti-Nazi, had planted a bomb with the full intention of killing Adolf Hitler. And his bomb was due to explode half way through the Fuhrer's speech.

Kill Hitler

Georg Elser had always been quietly defiant in his hatred of the Nazi regime – he'd supported the communists and, once Hitler was in power, refused to give the Nazi salute. He feared Hitler's aggressive warmongering and foresaw the coming of war and resolved himself, in his own way, to do something to prevent it – and that was to kill Hitler.

Each year on 8 November, since 1933, Hitler had come to the same beer hall in Munich and delivered a two-hour speech, starting at 8.30, the precise time that, in 1923, he had bulldozed into the hall brandishing a pistol, interrupting a meeting of Bavarian city officials and, firing two shots into the ceiling, declared revolution. The Beer Hall *Putsch* failed but had come an occasion to honour and remember the Nazis that had fallen that night in Munich.

On 8 November 1938, Elser attended the annual commemoration. And it was this event, he decided, that would provide the perfect opportunity to implement his audacious plan. The following night, he witnessed first-hand the vicious *Kristallnacht*, when Nazis throughout the country terrorized Germany's Jews in a concentrated orgy of killing, vandalism and violence. Seeing for himself this state-sponsored anarchy merely confirmed for Elser that what he was doing was right.

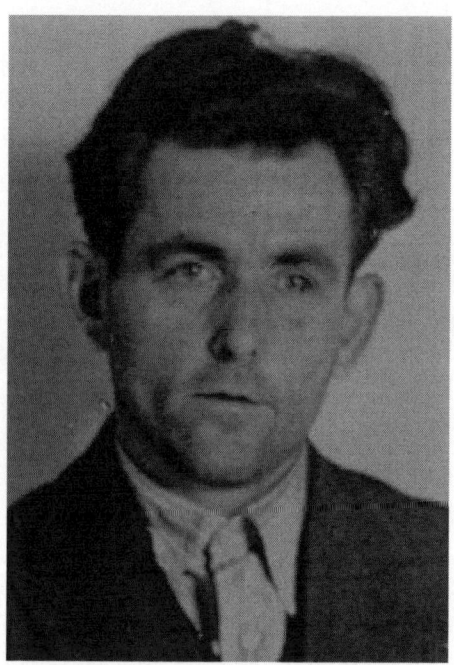

Georg Elser, 8 November 1939.
Polish National Digital Archives.

Thus, Elser spent the next year preparing. Elser, who played the zither and double bass, got a labouring job at a quarry specifically so he could acquire some explosives. Knowing nothing about bombs, he made numerous prototypes and tested them in a secluded orchard belonging to his parents.

Elser would eat his evening meal at the beer hall, then hide within until the building was closed up at night. Working quietly and ensuring each night that he left nothing behind – not even a speck of sawdust, he painstakingly hollowed out a pillar near the speakers' podium. Having finished his night's work, he would doze until the building was re-opened at seven the following morning, when he would exit, often carrying a small suitcase of debris to be disposed of. A week before the big night, he placed within the pillar a timed device set to go off at the point Hitler was midway through his speech.

Thirteen minutes

But sadly for Elser, and indeed for all mankind, Hitler changed his routine. War had broken out two months before and Hitler had more pressing matters to attend to and had to get back to Berlin. Thus, Hitler began his speech half an hour earlier than normal and instead of the usual two hours, spoke only for an hour. He left the building at 9.07. Thirteen minutes later, at 9.20, Elser's bomb went off. It killed eight Nazis and injured over sixty. But Hitler was not one of them.

Elser was arrested just 25 metres away from the Swiss border. The contents of his pockets proved to be his undoing – wire cutters, scribbled notes and sketches of explosives, and a postcard of the interior of the *Bürgerbräukeller*. Sent to Berlin's Gestapo, he was interrogated and brutally tortured by the Gestapo, often in the presence of Heinrich Himmler, who refused to believe that Elser had worked alone and was not part of a wider conspiracy. Elser even rebuilt the bomb as proof that he was capable of it. His interrogators had to admit they were impressed. The owner of the quarry where Elser had worked paid for his negligence, being arrested and badly beaten. His wife lost her mind and died.

Hitler was convinced that Elser was working for the British. Members of Elser's family and an ex-girlfriend were also interrogated. His girlfriend would later recall seeing Elser: 'I was horrified by his appearance. His face was swollen and beaten black and blue, and his eyes were bulging out of their sockets'. They hypnotized him, starved him, drugged him, beat him.

Yet, throughout a year of questioning, Elser kept to his story that he had acted alone.

Finally, after twelve months with Berlin's Gestapo, Elser was sent to Sachsenhausen concentration camp. Although kept in isolation, he was allowed to play his zither, allowed to visit the camp barber for a daily shave and, according to one witness, permitted to visit the camp brothel. The Nazis hoped that their theory of British involvement would come to light and hence kept Elser alive. But in early 1945, with defeat staring the Germans in the face, Elser was transferred to Dachau concentration camp where he was shot on 9 April 1945, weeks before its liberation.

56-foot steel memorial to Georg Elser by German artist, Rolf Hochhuth, unveiled in Berlin in 2011.

Hellmut G Haasis's book, *Bombing Hitler: The Story of the Man Who Almost Assassinated the Führer*, originally published in German in 1999, was only released in English in 2013. Piecing together contemporary transcripts, personal testimonies and family recollections, Haasis puts together a compelling story of the doomed hero, a testament to a man who almost singlehandedly changed the course of twentieth century history – almost. It is a story of quiet courage, determination and tragedy. One closes the book wondering what might have been had this simple carpenter with a mission had set his bomb to go off just thirteen minutes earlier.

By such thin threads, hangs the destiny of mankind.

52.
9 November 1970,
The Death of Charles de Gaulle

When, in 1940, Charles de Gaulle first arrived in London, Winston Churchill asked a colleague, 'Why have you brought this lanky, gloomy brigadier?' The man replied: 'Because no one else would come.'

De Gaulle had fought with great distinction during the First World War, and was thrice wounded. At the Battle of Verdun he served under Philippe Pétain, whom he greatly admired and who was to become his mentor. During the Battle of Verdun, on 2 March 1916, de Gaulle was taken prisoner by the Germans. He tried unsuccessfully to escape five times and was only released following the armistice in November 1918.

Following the Great War, de Gaulle served in Poland, Germany and the Middle East. He became convinced that future wars should rely on tanks and aircraft, thus avoiding the static stalemate of the previous war. The same conclusion had been reached in Germany but while, from 1939 the Germans acted on it, the French did not, putting far too much faith in the Maginot Line, France's fortified line of defence along the Franco-German border built during the 1930s. Indeed, de Gaulle's belief in mobile warfare, which he espoused in a number of books, won him many enemies within the French high command, not least from his old friend, Pétain, and may have been the cause for the lack of further promotion within the army.

Charles de Gaulle, c1942. Library of Congress.

Leader of all free Frenchmen

With the German invasion of France in 1940, de Gaulle, in command of a tank division, put up a gallant defence but, outnumbered, finally succumbed. France's French prime minister, Paul Reynaud, appointed de Gaulle to the ministry of war, thus de Gaulle's military career abruptly gave way to politics.

Having served for just ten days in Reynaud's government, de Gaulle fled to England shortly before his country's surrender to Germany. On his arrival in London, Churchill recognised him as the 'leader of all free Frenchmen, wherever they may be'.

On 17 June, Reynaud was replaced by the 84-year-old Phillippe Pétain. Pétain immediately sought an armistice with the Germans, labelled de Gaulle a traitor, had him stripped of his rank and ordered him executed *in absentia*.

On 18 June, in a broadcast from London, de Gaulle extolled his countrymen to continue the fight, asserting that France was not alone. In what became known as the Appeal of 18 June, he declared, 'The flame of the French resistance must not be extinguished and will not be extinguished.' De Gaulle returned the following day and this unknown Frenchman with his patriotic-sounding name boldly announced, 'I, General de Gaulle, a French soldier and military leader, realise that I now speak for France'. His words soon spread and became the battle cry of the Free French movement.

He became the self-appointed leader of the 'Free French'. In May 1943, de Gaulle moved to Algiers, a French colony, and there established the French Committee for National Liberation, with himself as its president. A year later, the ever-confident de Gaulle renamed the FCNL the Provisional Government of the French Republic.

Man of destiny

Winston Churchill considered de Gaulle as a 'man of destiny' but their relationship was never an easy one. De Gaulle's relationship with US president, Franklin D Roosevelt, was even worse. Roosevelt was furious that de Gaulle should take it upon himself to assume the role of president of a provisional government, and refused to acknowledge de Gaulle's self-appointed political title.

Roosevelt had instructed Churchill to exclude de Gaulle from having any input into the planned Allied invasion of France. On the eve of the invasion in June 1944, however, Churchill decided that de Gaulle had to be informed. On 4 June, de Gaulle was in Algiers and Churchill sent a plane to bring him back to London. At first, de Gaulle refused to return until, with a bit of arm-twisting, he was persuaded. De Gaulle had been angered by Roosevelt's insistence that come liberation, he planned to install, not a provisional government headed by de Gaulle, but a provisional Allied military government. When Churchill urged de Gaulle to seek a rapprochement with Roosevelt, de Gaulle responded angrily, 'Why should I lodge my candidacy for power in France with Roosevelt? The French government already exists.'

De Gaulle's fear was that if he didn't act fast enough, the French communists, who had also been active within the resistance, would seize power come liberation.

Winston Churchill and Charles de Gaulle, Morocco, 13 January 1944.
Imperial War Museum.

In London, de Gaulle was asked to broadcast a message to the Free French. But on reading Eisenhower's planned speech, due to be delivered before his, de Gaulle was furious that the American had made no mention of him or the Free French. Finally, however, de Gaulle made his speech.

De Gaulle wanted to return to France at the first possible opportunity. Churchill refused permission until a week after D-Day. On 14 June, almost four years to the day since leaving, de Gaulle stepped foot on French soil, and, visiting the recently-liberated town of Bayeux, was greeted with much enthusiasm.

Paris liberated!

Two months later, on 25 August, Paris was liberated. The following day, de Gaulle made his triumphant return. In his speech, he proclaimed, 'Paris outraged, Paris broken, Paris martyred, but Paris liberated! By herself, liberated by her people, with the help of the whole of France!' His administration was officially recognised by the Allies but de Gaulle was deeply offended that France was still not considered one of the Great Powers or invited to the 'Big Three' conferences with Churchill, Roosevelt and Stalin at Yalta and Potsdam.

On 15 August 1945, Pétain was tried for his collaboration with the Nazis and found guilty. The 89-year-old Marshal was sentenced to death by firing squad. De Gaulle however stepped in and taking into account Pétain's age and his First World War record, commuted Pétain's death sentence to life imprisonment. (Pétain was imprisoned, in relative luxury, on the island of Île d'Yeu, on the Atlantic coast of France. Increasingly frail, he needed constant care. He died on 23 July 1951, aged 95.)

On 10 September 1944, the Provisional Government of the French Republic was formed. At its head as prime minister – Charles de Gaulle. A year later, on 13 November 1945, following elections, de Gaulle was confirmed in his post as provisional head. However, he didn't last long. Disillusioned with coalition politics, de Gaulle resigned in January 1946.

France is a widow

Charles de Gaulle, July 1963. German Federal Archives.

In 1947, he formed his own party, the right-wing Rally of the French People (RFP) but, failing to gain support, de Gaulle resigned in 1951. The party disbanded in 1953.

Returning to politics in 1958, after seven years of retirement, de Gaulle was again elected president. This time, he remained in power for ten years during which time he granted independence to all thirteen of France's colonies, most notably Algeria following the seven-year Algerian War; survived several assassination attempts; advanced France's atomic capabilities; and negotiated France's inclusion into the European Economic Community, and its removal from NATO. He survived the political turmoil caused by the student riots during 1968, and resigned in April 1969.

He didn't have long to enjoy his second retirement. Charles de Gaulle died of a heart attack on 9 November 1970, two weeks short of his 80th birthday. Upon his death, Georges Pompidou, the president, announced his predecessor's death with the words, 'General de Gaulle is dead. France is a widow.'

53.
10 November 1918,
The Abdication of Kaiser Wilhelm II

The Kaiser would 'like every day to be his birthday' was Otto von Bismarck's damning assessment of Wilhelm II.

Hot head

Wilhelm II, Tsar Nicholas II of Russia and King George V of Britain were all cousins. George and Wilhelm were both grandsons of Queen Victoria, and Nicholas's wife, the Empress Alexandra, was Victoria's granddaughter. They met, as a threesome, only twice. Winston Churchill described Wilhelm as a 'very ordinary, vain but on the whole a well-meaning man'. Queen Victoria's judgment was somewhat harsher, calling her grandson 'such a hot-headed, conceited and wrong-headed young man'.

Like a victim of unrequited love, Wilhelm loved the English and hated and resented them at the same time. In 1889, Grandmother Victoria made Wilhelm an honorary admiral of the Royal Navy. Gushing with thanks, Wilhelm promised he would always take an interest in Britain's fleet as if it was his own. He had a chest made of oak from Nelson's *Victory*.

Born on 27 January 1859 with a paralyzed left arm, considerably shorter than the right, Wilhelm needed help with eating and dressing throughout his life, and went to great lengths to hide his disability. He had, for example, a specially-made fork to help him with his food. He owned over 30 castles throughout Germany and would visit them all occasionally, indulging in socialising and hunting – he was capable of killing a thousand or more animals in the course of a weekend's hunt.

Kaiser Wilhelm II, 1902. Imperial War Museum.

Wilhelm loved all things military. He reputably owned some 600 uniforms, many he designed himself. But his military knowledge was superficial at best and as the war progressed, he was increasingly side-lined by his generals. His knowledge of political matters was equally shallow, having neither the enthusiasm nor attention span to read lengthy or detailed reports.

Wilhelm's power, he firmly believed, was God-given. Any criticism of him or his policies was, in effect, an act of blasphemy. Germany, he said, 'must follow me wherever I go.'

Britain's foreign secretary, Sir Edward Grey, once said of the Kaiser, 'The German Emperor is like a battleship with steam up and screws going, but with no rudder, and he will run into something some day and cause a catastrophe. He has the strongest army in the world and the Germans don't like being laughed at and are looking for somebody on whom to vent their temper and use their strength. It is 38 years since Germany had her last war, and she is very strong and very restless, like a person whose boots are too small for him.'

The Kaiser's War

The assassination of Archduke Franz Ferdinand on 28 June 1914 by Gavrilo Princip, a member of a Serbian terrorist group, had given Austria-Hungary the opportunity to assert its authority over Serbia. But first it sought reassurance from its powerful ally, Germany. Wilhelm II gave Austria-Hungary the assurance it needed then promptly went off on a cruise around Norway. By the time he returned from holiday, the whole of Europe was teetering on the edge of war.

In late 1918, with the tide of war turning against Germany, the Kaiser's generals, especially Erich Ludendorff, were tempted by US president Woodrow Wilson's Fourteen Points – a blueprint for a post-war peace that would have avoided overly-punitive terms on a vanquished Germany. But Wilson was demanding democracy in Germany. On 3 October, on Ludendorff's urging, Wilhelm appointed the liberal Prince Maximilian of Baden chancellor of Germany. But Wilhelm's nod towards parliamentary democracy was not enough for the US president – he demanded the Kaiser's abdication.

In November 1918, Paul von Hindenburg and Wilhelm Groener (Ludendorff's replacement) went to see Wilhelm, who had bolted to army headquarters in the Belgium town of Spa. Hindenburg, a monarchist, bowed his head in shame and left Groener to do the talking.

Wilhelm remained defiant until the news came through – in Berlin, Prince Max had proclaimed a socialist republic – the new Germany had no room for a monarch. Thus, on 10 November, Kaiser Wilhelm II abdicated. The 500-year rule of the Hohenzollern dynasty had come to an end. Wilhelm fled to the Netherlands and into exile, never again to step on German soil.

The following day at 5 am, Paris time, the Western Front armistice was signed and came into effect six hours later at 11 am. War was over.

Exile

Following the war and his forced abdication, the ex-kaiser lived in exile in the Dutch town of Doorn. King George V described his cousin as 'the greatest criminal in history'. The Dutch queen, Queen Wilhelmina, declined ever to meet the fallen kaiser but when the Paris Peace Conference requested Wilhelm's extradition to face trial for war crimes, she refused to hand him over.

Wilhelm II in exile, Doorn, 1933. German Federal Archives.

In 1940, with Hitler's armies bearing down on the Netherlands, the Dutch royal family fled to Britain. Wilhelm however did not, even refusing Winston Churchill's offer of asylum. In fact, Wilhelm rather admired what Hitler was doing and supported the 'elimination of the British and the Jews' from Europe, adding, 'The Jews [are] being thrust out of their nefarious positions in all countries'. Following the fall of France in June 1940, Wilhelm sent Hitler a telegram in which he wrote, 'Congratulations, you have won using *my* troops'. Hitler was unimpressed.

Wilhelm was content to continue living in occupied Holland, believing that the Nazis would restore the monarchy and the kaiser to his throne. Of course they did not, and the 82-year-old embittered private citizen, once a kaiser, died the following year on 4 June 1941. Hitler, despite his animosity towards Wilhelm, wanted to give the old kaiser a state funeral in Berlin but was unable to override Wilhelm's wishes that his body should not be returned to Germany until the monarchy was restored. However, another of Wilhelm's stipulations, that there should be no Nazi regalia at his funeral, was ignored and his funeral was adorned with swastikas.

54.
19 November 1863,
Abraham Lincoln Delivers His
Gettysburg Address

The Battle of Gettysburg, Pennsylvania, 1 – 3 July 1863, was the biggest battle of the American Civil War, in American history, and indeed in the western hemisphere. At the end of it, Union forces, led by General George Meade, emerged victorious but in doing so paid a heavy price – 23,000 men killed or wounded, while the forces of the Confederacy, led by General Robert E Lee, had lost much the same number, killed or wounded, and were forced into retreat. Most of the dead lay in shallow graves; many not buried at all.

Of these 46,000 casualties, 7,963 Americans lost their lives during the three days of battle at Gettysburg.

A few appropriate remarks

Shortly after the battle, seventeen acres of land were purchased to establish the Soldiers' National Cemetery of Gettysburg where the Union dead were moved from their shallow graves to more honourable places of rest. The mammoth task of reinternment was only half done when, four and a half months after the battle, the new cemetery was dedicated on Thursday, 19 November 1863. The principle speech, lasting over two hours, was delivered by the former US secretary of state, Edward Everett. Following Everett, came the president, Abraham Lincoln, invited as an afterthought to deliver 'a few appropriate remarks', or, as listed in the programme for the event, 'Dedicatory Remarks'.

Abraham Lincoln, 1863. Library of Congress.

Lincoln's speech, in contrast to Everett's marathon, consisted of only ten sentences, 272 words, and lasted barely two minutes. In his Gettysburg Address, Lincoln summarized the principles of human equality as declared in the Declaration of Independence ('all men are created equal'), and expressed the Civil War in terms of a struggle for 'a new birth of freedom'.

A flat failure

Lincoln, feeling weak with the onset of smallpox, was conscious of the inadequacy of his efforts, and returned to his seat, reputedly muttering to a colleague, 'It is a flat failure'. His speech was met by a silence which some interpreted as admiration for what they had just heard, while others saw it was an awkward, anti-climatic response.

Edward Everett was evidently impressed; writing the following day to the president, 'I should be glad if I could flatter myself that I came as near to the central idea of the occasion in two hours as you did in two minutes.'

Written transcript of Abraham Lincoln's Gettysburg Address,
November 1863.

Lincoln's speech, subsequently known as the Gettysburg Address, has gone down in history as one of the most famous oratories of modern times:

Four score and seven years ago our fathers brought forth on this continent a new nation, conceived in liberty, and dedicated to the proposition that all men are created equal.

Now we are engaged in a great civil war, testing whether that nation, or any nation, so conceived and so dedicated, can long endure.

We are met on a great battlefield of that war.

We have come to dedicate a portion of that field, as a final resting place for those who here gave their lives that that nation might live.

It is altogether fitting and proper that we should do this.

But, in a larger sense, we can not dedicate, we can not consecrate, we can not hallow this ground.

The brave men, living and dead, who struggled here, have consecrated it, far above our poor power to add or detract.

The world will little note, nor long remember what we say here, but it can never forget what they did here.

It is for us the living, rather, to be dedicated here to the unfinished work which they who fought here have thus far so nobly advanced.

It is rather for us to be here dedicated to the great task remaining before us—that from these honoured dead we take increased devotion to that cause for which they gave the last full measure of devotion—that we here highly resolve that these dead shall not have died in vain—that this nation, under God, shall have a new birth of freedom—and that government of the people, by the people, for the people, shall not perish from the earth.

55.
22 November 2011,
The Death of Svetlana Alliluyeva,
Stalin's Daughter

22 November 2011 saw the death of Lana Peters in Wisconsin. To those who came into contact with her, she was simply a lonesome frail 85-year-old with a rather strange accent. But she was, in fact, once known by the name of Svetlana Stalina and she was the daughter of Joseph Stalin.

Peters' arrival in the US in 1967 gave the West a huge propaganda coup – the defection of Stalin's own daughter was the ultimate proof of how terrible life was behind the Iron Curtain. She had even been prepared to leave behind her two adult children, aged 22 and 17, in the Soviet Union.

I have come here to seek self-expression

In her first US press conference, in 1967, Peters acknowledged her father's monstrous rule but insisted that the blame for the murder of millions of Soviet citizens could not be laid purely on one man – it was the regime and its ideology. 'I have come here to seek the self-expression that has been denied me for so long in Russia,' she said. Shortly afterwards, she wrote *Twenty Letters To A Friend*, which went on to become a bestseller. A follow-up autobiography, *Only One Year*, sold equally well. With time she became more critical of her past – she publicly burnt her Soviet passport and accused her father of being 'a moral and spiritual monster'.

Svetlana Alliluyeva with her father, 1935.

In 1970, she married Wes Peters, and was to keep his name for the rest of her life. Peters' first wife had died in a car crash. She was also called Svetlana and her mother, the widow of the architect, Frank Lloyd Wright, saw in Alliluyeva a divine substitution for her deceased daughter. Under her urging, her new Svetlana and Peters married. They had one child, Olga, and although fond of each other, Svetlana Peters felt too suffocated by her husband's former mother-in-law's domineering presence and the marriage ended within three years.

Back in the USSR

In 1982, Peters and her daughter moved to Cambridge, England. Two years later, to the delight of the Soviets, she moved back to the USSR, wanting to be reunited with the children she had left behind 15 years before. Her life in the West, she told reporters, had not afforded her 'one single day' of freedom. Having had her Soviet citizenship restored, she lived in Tbilisi in Georgia. Stalin had been a Georgian but had felt little affinity for his homeland, spending his whole life as dictator cooped-up in the Kremlin. Peters had never been to Georgia and perhaps she felt the need to connect to her ancestral home. But life didn't work out, she feuded with her family and after just two years, she requested to be allowed to leave again.

By 1984 she was back in the US and was never again to step on

Russian soil.

Nadezhda Alliluyeva

Svetlana was born 28 February 1926, the second child to Stalin and his second wife, Nadezhda Alliluyeva. Her brother, Vasily, was almost five years older. She also had a half-brother, Yakov, born 1907, a product of Stalin's first marriage.

Svetlana Alliluyeva with her father and brother, Vasily, 1935.

Being brought up in the stifling atmosphere of the Kremlin must have been difficult for a young girl. Her parents' marriage was often strained and her mother, Nadezhda Alliluyeva, a manic depressive and prone to violent mood swings, never showed her any affection. In November 1932, when Svetlana was only six, her mother committed suicide. Nadezhda had had a public row with Stalin during a dinner party. In a foul mood, she retired to bed early and was found the following morning dead with a revolver at her side. History has always implied that Stalin was responsible for his wife's death but eyewitnesses report his genuine grief and guilt – what had he done, he asked aloud, to have been so punished?

But Peters was never told that her mother had taken her own life, being fed the official line that Nadezhda had died from appendicitis. Ten years later she found out quite by accident from a magazine article.

Stalin died in 1953. Peters gave a graphic description of his final moments: 'He suddenly opened his eyes and looked at everyone in the room. It was a terrible gaze, mad or maybe furious and full of fear of death... Then something incomprehensible and frightening happened. ... He suddenly lifted his left hand as though he were pointing to something above and bringing down a curse on us all. ... The next moment, after a final effort, the spirit wrenched itself free of the flesh.'

Following her father's death, she took her mother's name and became Svetlana Alliluyeva.

In 1963, Peters met Brijesh Singh, an Indian Communist visiting the Soviet Union. The two fell in love and although in a later interview she referred to him as her husband, they were never allowed to marry. Singh died in 1966 and Alliluyeva was at least permitted to take his ashes back to India. It was in India she embraced Indian mysticism and made the decision that she did not want to return to Moscow and a life of forced atheism. 'It was impossible to exist without God in one's heart,' she said afterwards. She walked into the US embassy in New Delhi and requested asylum.

A very simple man

Of her father, Alliluyeva described Stalin in a 2010 interview as a 'very simple man. Very rude. Very cruel. There was nothing in him that was complicated. He was very simple with us. He loved me and he wanted me to be with him and become an educated Marxist.'

But like many a possessive father, that love was mixed with jealousy and paranoia as would be expected from the twentieth century's most paranoid despot. She may have been his 'little sparrow' but as a young woman, Peters often fell in love with older and unsuitable men. One infamous case, in 1942, was that of Alexei Kapler. A dashing and confident 39-year-old, Kapler had made his name as a filmmaker and screenwriter and the previous year had won the much-coveted Stalin Prize.

Kapler was, in Peters' words, 'the cleverest, kindest, most wonderful person on earth'. He lent her risqué literature, novels and poetry full of love and yearning, and took her out to the cinema and art galleries. Kapler was certainly brave – it takes a sort of perverse courage for a womanising, married man to seduce a 16-year-old girl, and to boast about it, when her domineering father is never too far away, especially when that father is Joseph Stalin. Sure enough, the inevitable happened. Stalin had had their telephone conversations taped and armed with the evidence he flew into a rage. It was bad enough that Kapler was married and old enough to know better, but what really irked was that Kapler was a Jew.

'But I love him,' protested Alliluyeva meekly. 'Love?' Stalin bellowed, slapping her twice across the face. Their father / daughter relationship died that day. Kapler was arrested as a British spy and sentenced to five years, released, then promptly sentenced to another five.

My father's name

In the late forties Peters married twice. Stalin disproved of her first husband, refusing to meet him, but he did allow the marriage to go ahead. It wasn't to last. Nor would a second marriage to the son of Andrey Zhdanov, one of Stalin's closest aides. Both marriages produced one child.

'You can't regret your fate,' Ms. Peters once said, 'although I do regret my mother didn't marry a carpenter.'

She never truly found peace and never managed to escape her father's shadow, 'Wherever I go,' she said, 'I will always be a political prisoner of my father's name'. 'You are Stalin's daughter,' she said on another occasion. 'Actually you are already dead. Your life is already finished. You can't live your own life. You can't live any life. You exist only in reference to a name.'

56.
Winston Churchill,
Born 30 November 1874,
and the First World War

Winston Churchill rather enjoyed war. In July 1914, as Britain prepared for the oncoming catastrophe, Churchill, at the time the First Lord of the Admiralty, wrote to his wife, 'I am interested, geared up and happy. Is it not horrible to be built like that?' And in 1916, in a letter to David Lloyd George's daughter, Churchill admitted: 'I think a curse should rest on me — because I love this war. I know it's smashing and shattering the lives of thousands every moment, and yet, I can't help it, I enjoy every second of it'.

Churchill had been appointed to the Admiralty in October 1911, and had continued the policy established by his predecessor of keeping Britain ahead of the Germans and strengthening the navy by expanding the number of Dreadnoughts, the most powerful battleship of the time.

But despite these preparations, Britain suffered a number of setbacks during the first months of the First World War – on 22 September 1914, the German navy sunk a number of British ships at Dogger Bank (sixty miles off the east coast of England in the North Sea), killing 1,459 sailors; and on 16 December, German ships penetrated close enough to British shores to attack Scarborough, Hartlepool and Whitby causing 137 fatalities. Churchill, in his role at the Admiralty, took the brunt of the blame and the public's anger.

Winston Churchill, 1904. Imperial War Museum.

Antwerp

In October 1914, with German forces bearing down on Antwerp, the British government dispatched Churchill to Belgium. Although, through his efforts, he helped delay the fall of the city by about a week, allowing the Belgian Army to escape and the vital Channel ports to be saved, he was still heavily criticised at home for failing to save the city.

Stung by the criticism, Churchill offered to resign from the government in return for a post as an army officer in the field. His offer, met with derision and loud guffaws, was refused.

The Landship

Throughout the war, Churchill furthered the cause of the newly-developed 'landships', or, to use its original code word, the 'tank'. On 15 September 1916, during the Battle of the Somme, the British commander-in-chief, Sir Douglas Haig, introduced the tank onto the battlefield.

Gallipoli

In 1915, the British planned to use the Royal Navy to take control of the Dardanelles Straits from where they could attack Constantinople, the capital of the Ottoman Empire. The Dardanelles, a strait of water separating mainland Turkey and the Gallipoli peninsula, is sixty miles long and, at its widest, only 3.5 miles.

As First Lord of the Admiralty, Churchill insisted that the Royal Navy, acting alone, could succeed. On 19 February, a flotilla of British and French ships pounded the outer forts of the Dardanelles and a month later attempted to penetrate the strait. It failed, losing six ships, half its fleet. Soldiers, it was decided, would be needed after all, and Horatio Kitchener was called in.

Finally, in January 1916, after the loss of some 220,000 Allied casualties, the curtain fell on the whole sorry 'side show' that was Gallipoli. Although Churchill's responsibility in Gallipoli had, by and large, ceased once the army had been deployed, he was still much criticised for his involvement, and the disaster at Gallipoli was a severe setback to Churchill's reputation. Indeed, his wife, Clementine, said that 'the Dardanelles haunted [Churchill] for the rest of his life. I thought he'd never get over the Dardanelles. I thought he would die of grief.'

The humiliation of Gallipoli, together with a scandal about the supply of shells, forced the Liberal prime minister, Herbert Asquith, to form a coalition government. One of the conditions, as laid down by the Conservatives, was that Churchill, a Liberal, be relieved of his cabinet duties. He was. Appointed to the rather meaningless post of Chancellor of the Duchy of Lancaster, Churchill bemoaned, 'I am finished'.

Lieutenant Colonel

Demoted and demoralised, Churchill handed in his resignation from the coalition government and, although he remained an MP, joined the frontline troops as a lieutenant colonel of the Royal Scot Fusiliers on the Western Front. By all accounts, although unorthodox as an officer, he was popular and courageous, and improved morale by organising entertainment for the troops and reducing punishments.

In January 1916, his battalion moved onto the front line. Although he spent only about 100 days at the front, Churchill led by example, venturing thirty times or so into no man's land, often flirting with death. His comrades noticed he never ducked while at the front. But, as Churchill said, 'It's no damn use ducking. The bullet has gone a long way past you by now!'

Winston Churchill, centre, in army uniform with colleagues, 1916.

In March 1916, Churchill, eager to get back to politics, resigned his army commission and returned to London. But things did not go according to plan. In December 1916, Asquith was replaced as the coalition's prime minister by David Lloyd George but there was still no position for the eager Churchill. Lloyd George's welcome was not one to lift his hopes, writing to Churchill: 'You do not win trust even where you command admiration'.

Finally, in July 1917, despite protests and strong vocal disproval from the Conservatives, Churchill was appointed Minister of Munitions but it was still a post outside the cabinet and his duties there were mainly administrative.

Winston Churchill as Minister of Munitions meeting workers near Glasgow,
9 October 1918. Imperial War Museum.

Red Peril

In January 1919, following the end of the war, Churchill was appointed
Secretary of State for War and Secretary of State for Air.

Deeply alarmed by the Bolshevik threat, the 'red peril', following the
Russian Revolution and the downfall of the tsar, Churchill poured troops
into Russia to assist the counter-revolutionary cause during the Russian
Civil War. 'The foul baboonery of Bolshevism', as he called it, must be
'strangled in its cradle'. Churchill was concerned lest Bolshevism should
spread to Germany and so urged his colleagues at the Paris Peace
Conference to treat Germany as friends in the post-war world: 'Kill the
Bolshie, Kiss the Hun,' as he wrote to Violet Asquith.

But the Bolsheviks survived and, following the defeat of the 'Whites',
the last remaining British troops were withdrawn in 1920.

Inter-war

Losing his seat as a Liberal MP, Churchill swapped sides and served a
Conservative government as Chancellor of the Exchequer until their defeat
in the election of 1929. Although the Conservatives were re-elected in 1931,
Churchill, considered too much a loose canon, was side-lined – again. He

remained in the shadows throughout the thirties, writing and painting, until recalled to the Admiralty in 1939, by which time the Second World War had begun.

57.
7 December 1941,
Pearl Harbor, the Day of Infamy

How Japan's hollow victory spelt the end for Hitler

On 7 December 1941, Japan launched a surprise attack on the US. In just two hours it destroyed a large part of the US fleet docked in Pearl Harbor and, in one stroke, forever destroyed US isolationism and made the conflict global.

The US may have been expecting war but the attack on Pearl Harbor still took it totally by surprise. Yet 11 months before, a lone voice had predicted such a possibility. On the 27 January 1941, the US ambassador in Japan, Joseph Grew, cabled the White House warning that the Japanese *might* 'attempt a surprise attack on Pearl Harbor using all their military facilities'.

As 1941 wore on, the likelihood of war became more apparent but the US ignored Grew's prediction, believing that conflict, if it came, would either start in the US-controlled Philippines or the Dutch or British possessions in Southeast Asia.

Certainly, US president, Franklin D. Roosevelt, believed war was a distinct possibility – 'They [the Japanese] hate us,' he said privately. 'Sooner or later, they're going to come after us'. He also feared what would happen to the US if Japan overran Britain's possessions in the Southeast Asia – 'If Great Britain goes down,' Roosevelt said, 'all of us in all the Americas would be living at the point of a gun.'

The USS Arizona *under attack, Pearl Harbor, 7 December 1941.
National Archives and Records Administration.*

Asia for the Asians

On 17 October 1941 the prospect of war became more real – Japan's prime minister, Fumimaro Konoye, known for his restraint and sense of compromise, was replaced by the more aggressive Hideki Tojo. Within a month, Tojo had finalized plans to cripple the US fleet, and invade much of Southeast Asia to secure for Japan its supply of natural resources. Japan had long wanted to rid the area of Western imperialists and rule Asia on behalf of its neighbours – 'Asia for the Asians' became its war cry.

On 26 November, Tojo's plan went into action – a Japanese fleet commanded by Admiral Isoruku Yamamoto, consisting of six aircraft carriers, two battleships and assorted other craft, set off from north-eastern Japan. The Americans had broken Japanese codes but in the event this gave them no advantage as the US fleet was maintaining strict radio silence. Meanwhile, in Washington, the US and Japan were negotiating Japan's withdrawal from China. (Japan and China had been at war since 1931). Japan had no intention of withdrawing but was happy to lure the US into thinking that their intentions were honourable. It was all part of the ruse.

Hideki Tojo, 1940.

With Yamamoto's fleet 275 miles north of the Hawaiian island of Oahu, the first wave of fighters took off, commanded by Lt Commander Mitsuo Fuchida (25 years later, having converted to Christianity, Fuchida became a US citizen). It took them 1½ hours to reach Oahu. At one point dense cloud obscured their route but at the most opportune moment, the clouds parted, and there below them was Pearl Harbor.

Tora, tora, tora!

It was approaching 7 a.m. on Sunday 7 December when the radar station on Oahu first reported to its HQ a number of aircraft on its screen. The reply came back: 'Don't worry about it'. HQ was expecting a squadron of US planes from California to be arriving that same morning. But these were Japanese planes (bombers, dive-bombers and fighters), 181 of them, intent on ripping out the heart of the US fleet quietly moored on this Pacific island, 3,400 miles away from Japan.

Neatly and conveniently lined up along 'Battleship Row', were seven of the US's eight battleships plus a hundred other ships. Fuchida, knowing he couldn't fail, dispatched the pre-arranged victory signal, *Tora, tora, tora* (Tiger, tiger, tiger). Torpedoes and bombs rained down. The general alarm sounded, 'Man your battle stations – THIS IS NO DRILL!' Within minutes, several of the ships had been hit. Men jumped overboard and tried to swim to safety. The previously calm waters of the harbour, now glazed with a layer of oil, erupted into a wall of flame, killing many of those in the water.

The biggest casualty, claiming 1,177 lives, almost half of the victims at Pearl Harbor, was the battleship, the USS *Arizona*. Twenty-three sets of brothers died aboard the ship, plus all 21 members of the *Arizona's* music band. Hit four times by Japanese bombers, the ship's magazine exploded with such intensity that it lifted the entire battleship ten feet out of the water and knocked down people two miles away.

The nearby airfields were also targeted. Row upon row of perfectly-lined aircraft were destroyed. American sailors, queuing up for breakfast and unable to comprehend what was happening, were mowed down as they waited their turn.

At 8.40, the second wave attacked. The Americans, now employing their anti-aircraft guns, managed to hit a few of the incoming planes, but the Japanese fighters inflicted yet more damage.

By 10 a.m. it was all over – three of the eight American battleships had been sunk and four seriously damaged; many other vessels were destroyed together with almost 300 planes. 2,403 Americans died (civilian and military) and over 1,000 wounded. The Japanese lost 29 planes and 100 pilots.

One American admiral admitted to the Americans' preconceived racial stereotyping: 'At first I thought the U.S. Army Air Corps was accidentally bombing us. We were so proud, so vain, and so ignorant of Japanese capability. It never entered our consciousness that they'd have the temerity to attack us. We knew the Japanese didn't see well, especially at night – we knew this as a matter of fact. We knew they couldn't build good weapons, they made junky equipment, they just imitated us. All we had to do was get out there and sink them. It turns out they could see better than we could and their torpedoes, unlike ours, worked'.

At the same time, Japanese forces had attacked the Philippines and the British colony of Hong Kong and violated neutral Thailand. The Pacific islands of Wake and Midway also fell victim to attack as well as British-controlled Malaya. Singapore, on the southern tip of Malaya, had been bombed. Without an official declaration of war, Japan, in just a matter of hours, had secured control of the skies and seas of a quarter of the world's surface. As Winston Churchill described in his war memoirs, 'Over all this vast expanse of waters Japan was supreme, and we everywhere were weak and naked.'

Pearl Harbor, 7 December 1941.
National Archives and Records Administration.

The Sleeping Enemy

But as successful as the operation may have appeared, its triumph was short-lived – a third wave, due to attack the huge stores of fuel and its navy arsenal, was cancelled due to fear of an American counterattack, and the battleships, having been sunk only in the shallow waters of the harbour, were mostly repaired and fully operational before the end of the war (although the USS *Arizona*, for one, remained on the bottom of the harbour where it is still today). None of the aircraft carriers had been hit nor the submarines. While Japan celebrated its supposed victory, Yamamoto knew that in the long term he had failed – 'a military man can scarcely pride himself on having smitten a sleeping enemy'.

The following day, in his address to Congress, Roosevelt declared, 'Yesterday, December 7, 1941, a date which will live in infamy, the United States of America was suddenly and deliberately attacked by naval and air forces of the Empire of Japan'. Congress accordingly voted 470 to 1 to go to war (the one being a pacifist vote from Montana).

Churchill was delighted. 'To have the United States at our side' (he later wrote), 'was to me the greatest joy. Now at this very moment I knew the United States was in the war, up to the neck and in to the death. So we had won after all!... Hitler's fate was sealed. Mussolini's fate was sealed. As for the Japanese, they would be ground to powder.'

Hitler Declares War

Adolf Hitler too was pleased, the teetotaller breaking with habit and toasting the Honorary Aryans, as he called the Japanese, with a small glass of champagne. 'Now it is impossible for us to lose the war,' he announced with glee. On 11 December, less than six months since invading the Soviet Union, Germany declared war on the US. Hitler had not been obliged to – the Tripartite Pact, signed by Germany, Italy and Japan in September 1940, had only stipulated that Germany would declare war if Japan was the *victim* of aggression.

But Hitler wanted to pre-empt the possibility of the US declaring war on Germany. After all, as his Foreign Minister, Joachim von Ribbentrop, explained, 'A great power does not allow itself to be declared war upon; it declares war on others'. Hitler, always hostile to America with its racially diverse and therefore inferior population, believed Germany had nothing to fear, predicting that the US would not be ready for war until at least 1970.

Both acts, the invasion of the Soviet Union and the declaration of war against the US, stand up as Hitler's two greatest blunders. Germany's fate was sealed and the conflict, that had started 27 months before, was now truly global.

58.
23 December 1953,
The Execution of Lavrenty Beria

On 23 December 1953, Lavrenty Beria was executed. Born in Georgia on 29 March 1899, Beria had risen to prominence in Georgia during the Russian Revolution of 1917 and, during the 1920s, became a firm favourite of fellow-Georgian, Joseph Stalin. In 1938 Beria was appointed head of the dreaded secret police, the NKVD.

Perfidy and cunning

A brutish, inhumane man, Lavrenty Beria declared in 1937 that enemies 'of the party of Lenin and Stalin [would] be mercilessly crushed and destroyed'. He was true to his word and played a major role in Stalin's Great Purges of the 1930s, sending countless numbers to the gulags or to be executed. Stalin called Beria 'our Himmler'. It was meant as a compliment.

Yugoslavian writer, Milovan Djilas, described Beria as 'plump, greenish, and pale, with soft damp hands… with [a] square-cut mouth and bulging eyes behind his pince-nez.' Svetlana Alliluyeva, Stalin's daughter, described him as 'more treacherous, more practiced in perfidy and cunning, more insolent and single-minded' than even her own father. One recent historian described Beria as 'an unprincipled careerist, capable of any crime'.

Lavrenty Beria, c1940.

Uncle-figure

A lover of Rachmaninov's music and a cuddly uncle-figure to Svetlana Alliluyeva, Beria had his bodyguards abduct young girls off the streets for his devious sexual pleasure. Those that refused his predatory advances risked being packed off to a gulag.

Beria had risen through the ranks as first secretary of the Georgian communist party, forcing through collectivisation and quashing nationalistic tendencies. His first task as head of the NKVD, was to purge his predecessor, Nikolai Yezhov, and wind down the Great Terror that had reached a climax in 1937. The worst may have been over but the arrests continued and Beria, according to contemporary accounts, was not shy in getting his hands dirty while interrogating suspects; relishing in torture and beatings meted out to the unfortunates brought before him.

Appointed deputy prime minister in 1941, Beria mobilised mass slave labour to produce the urgently needed raw materials for the Soviet Union's war effort.

Lavrenty Beria with Stalin's daughter, Svetlana Alliluyeva, on his knee while Stalin works in the background, c1934.

Beria became Stalin's most trusted and loyal aide, heaping praise on the ageing dictator, and acting with increasing ruthlessness to win the praise of his boss. But only as a means of advancing and protecting his own position. As Stalin lay dying in his dacha, in March 1953, Beria appeared distraught, although he fooled no one. As soon as Stalin was declared dead, Beria spat on the old man's body and left the dacha 'beaming'.

None of us can feel safe

With Lavrenty Beria now favourite to take power, other members of the Politburo feared for their safety: 'As long as that bastard's alive, none of us can feel safe,' said one. Beria implemented an amnesty, releasing many from the gulags, but many saw this as a mere attempt on imposing his claim on succeeding Stalin.

But it wasn't enough – on 26 June 1953, Beria was arrested on trumped-up charges, such as spying for the British. Nikita Khrushchev (who was to replace Stalin) described Beria's reaction when arrested: 'He dropped a load in his pants!'

From his cell, Beria wrote several grovelling letters to his politburo colleagues pleading his innocence and his devotion to the party and the communist cause. Exasperated by the flow of letters, Khrushchev ordered the removal of Beria's pen and paper.

In December 1953, Beria was put on trial. The whole case was a mockery but no more than Beria had subjected so many of his victims. He was, unsurprisingly, found guilty and sentenced to be executed. Beria fell on all fours and begged for mercy. He was taken down and promptly shot. Lavrenty Beria died as so many of his victims had. He has no known grave.

Following his death, subscribers to the *Great Soviet Encyclopaedia* received a letter from its editors, instructing them to cut out and remove the three page article on Beria and to paste in, instead, three enclosed pages that contained extended articles on Friedrich Wilhelm von Bergholz, an 18th-century aristocrat, the Bering Sea, and Bishop Berkeley, the 18th century Irish philosopher.

Beria had been erased.

59.
23 December 1948,
The Execution of Hideki Tojo

On 23 December 1948, former prime minister of Japan, Hideki Tojo, was executed for war crimes.

Born in Tokyo on 30 December 1884, Hideki Tojo, the son of a general, was brought up in a military environment that held little regard for politicians or civilians. An admirer of Adolf Hitler, Tojo advocated closer ties between Japan and Germany and Italy, and in September 1940, the three Axis powers signed the Tripartite Pact.

Appointed Japan's Minister for War in July 1940, Tojo was keen to accelerate the coming war against the US. He viewed the US as a weak nation, populated by degenerate and lazy civilians. Tojo was appointed Japan's prime minister in October 1941 and within two months had ordered the attack on Pearl Harbor, thus turning the war into a global conflict.

As well as prime minister and minister for war, Hideki Tojo was also appointed home and foreign minister. From February 1944 he was also made Commander-in-Chief of the General Staff. Thus, he ruled almost as dictator, answerable only to Emperor Hirohito.

But as the war turned against Japan, Tojo faced mounting pressure from his government and military hierarchy. Eventually, on 18 July 1944, after a string of losses, the Emperor obliged Tojo to resign.

Following the atomic bombs over Hiroshima and Nagasaki in early August 1945, Tojo was amongst those who maintained Japan should still not surrender.

Sorry it is taking me so long to die

In September 1945, following Japan's surrender, Tojo tried to resist capture by the Americans by committing suicide – shooting himself in the heart. With US military police pounding at the door of his Tokyo home, his doctor used a piece of charcoal to draw a circle on Tojo's chest, pinpointing the exact location where Tojo should aim. However, Tojo somehow missed, shooting himself in the stomach. 'I am very sorry it is taking me so long to die', he mumbled as he was arrested. 'I await for the righteous judgment of history. I wished to commit suicide but sometimes that fails.' Nationalists were appalled that Tojo, having advocated suicide to his countrymen, had failed to take his own life. His use of a gun was considered cowardly – it should have been a samurai sword.

Hideki Tojo, c1945.

Having survived his suicide attempt, Tojo was placed in prison. While incarcerated, an American dentist set him up with a new set of dentures.

Unbeknownst to Tojo, the dentist had secretly drilled his teeth with the words 'Remember Pearl Harbor', written in Morse Code.

Having been nursed back to health, Tojo was tried as a war criminal and found guilty. He went out of his way to take responsibility, deflecting all blame from the emperor. At his trial, he declared, 'It is natural that I should bear entire responsibility for the war in general, and, needless to say, I am prepared to do so.'

Along with six other 'Class A' war criminals, Hideki Tojo, a week shy of his 64th birthday, was executed by hanging at Sugamo Prison on 23 December 1948.

In August 2015, on the seventieth anniversary of Japan's defeat, a Chinese ice cream manufacturer celebrated the occasion by selling ice creams depicting Tojo's face.

60.
30 December 1916,
The Assassination of Grigory Rasputin

When Prince Felix Yusupov offered his guest, Grigory Rasputin, refreshments at his palace in St Petersburg on the evening of 29 December 1916, the glass of red wine and Rasputin's favourite cakes were laced with enough poison to kill five men. Rasputin, however, seemed totally unaffected as he gulped back the wine and wolfed down the cakes.

Despairing, Yusupov shot Rasputin in the back and then, satisfied with a job well done, he left to join his fellow conspirators. Here, in his words, is what happened next:

'I was suddenly filled with a vague misgiving; an irresistible impulse forced me to go down to the basement. Rasputin lay exactly where we had left him. I felt his pulse: not a beat, he was dead. All of a sudden, I saw the left eye open. A few seconds later his right eyelid began to quiver, then opened. I then saw both eyes, the green eyes of a viper, staring at me with an expression of diabolical hatred. The blood ran cold in my veins. My muscles turned to stone.

'Then a terrible thing happened: with a sudden violent effort Rasputin leapt to his feet, foaming at the mouth. A wild roar echoed through the vaulted rooms, and his hands convulsively thrashed the air. He rushed at me, trying to get at my throat, and sank his fingers into my shoulder like steel claws. His eyes were bursting from their sockets. By a superhuman effort I succeeded in freeing myself from his grasp.

'"Quick, quick, come down!" I cried. "He's still alive." He was crawling on hands and knees, grasping and roaring like a wounded animal. He gave a desperate leap and

287

managed to reach the secret door which led into the courtyard. Knowing that the door was locked, I waited on the landing above grasping my rubber club. To my horror I saw the door open and Rasputin disappear. Purishkevich sprang after him. Two shots echoed through the night. I heard a third shot, then a fourth. I saw Rasputin totter and fall beside a heap of snow.'

Grigory Rasputin, photographed by Karl Bulla, 1910.

But still refusing to die, Rasputin's attackers resorted to clubbing him senseless then wrapping his body in a blue rug and throwing him in the icy waters of the River Neva.

The subsequent autopsy found that Rasputin had died by drowning, implying he had survived the huge dose of poison, four bullets, and the severe clubbing. Prince Yusupov and his pro-monarchist friends believed they were acting in the best interests of the monarchy.

At least, this is the story that has filtered down through the decades.

In 1932, Prince and Princess Yusupov successfully sued Metro-Goldwyn-Mayer in an English court over the MGM film *Rasputin and the Empress* for portraying the princess as having been seduced by Rasputin.

They won and were awarded the sum of £25,000 (about £1.5 million / US$2.5 million in 2015). (The case set a precedent thereby introducing the 'all persons fictitious disclaimer'.) Appearing in the witness stand, Yusupov was asked whether he'd killed Rasputin. Knowing he was free from prosecution, he freely admitted it: 'Yes, I killed Rasputin. It was my duty to kill him. So I killed him'.

The Russian people will be cursed

Rasputin had a sense of his coming demise, warning the tsar, Nicholas II, weeks before his death:

> *I shall depart this life before January first. If one of your relatives causes my death, then none of your children will remain alive for more than two years. And if they do, they will beg for death as they will see the defeat of Russia, see the Antichrist coming, plague, poverty, destroyed churches, and desecrated sanctuaries where everyone is dead. The Russian tsar, you will be killed by the Russian people and the people will be cursed and will serve as the devil's weapon killing each other everywhere.'*

One of Prince Yusupov's conspirators, the Grand Duke Dmitri Pavlovich, was indeed a cousin of the tsar, and the tsar and his family would be murdered by the Bolsheviks within 19 months of Rasputin's murder.

I have killed the Antichrist

Two years previously, on 28 June 1914 (the very day that Archduke Franz Ferdinand was assassinated in Sarajevo), Rasputin survived an earlier assassination attempt. Visiting his family in Siberia, Rasputin was almost killed by a woman named Khionia Guseva. Guseva, who lacked a nose, may have been urged on by a former friend of Rasputin's, an anti-Semitic monk called Iliodor. Waiting for him outside a church, Guseva stabbed Rasputin in the stomach and cried out, 'I have killed the Antichrist!' Rasputin recovered but became dependent on frequent doses of opium to relieve his pain. Declared insane, Guseva was later committed to an asylum.

Born Grigory Yefimovich Novik in a remote Siberian village on 22 January 1869, Rasputin's adopted name is Russian for 'debauched one', a nickname he earned by his reputed womanizing and drunkenness, which he defended by claiming he was driving out sin with sin. As a boy, he was known for his psychic powers leading some to believe he was possessed by the Devil.

As a young man Rasputin began his pilgrimages, going as far as Greece and Jerusalem, sometimes walking days on end without food or water and wearing shackles to amplify the pain. He reputably practised self-flagellation as a further means of purification.

Grigory Rasputin, c1915. State Museum of Russian Political History.

Rasputin and the Tsarevich

In 1903, Rasputin arrived in St Petersburg, his reputation as a holy man preceding him. Summoned by the Royal Family, Rasputin was able to stem the bleeding of the tsar's youngest child and only son, the heir to the throne, the haemophiliac Alexei. Only Rasputin, it seemed, could treat the poor boy. Thus, he formed a bond with the royal couple and enjoyed their patronage. The tsar dismissed reports of Rasputin's drunkenness and promiscuity as gossip and found the mystic's presence calming, stating that he felt at peace whenever Rasputin spoke with him of God.

Rasputin was certainly victim of malicious rumourmongers – newspaper cartoons portrayed him as devilish and the nobility sought every opportunity to discredit him. The scandals relating to his debauched behaviour would have been passed off as nothing unusual had Rasputin been an aristocrat. His sympathy for Russia's Jews riled the anti-Semitic nobility.

Russian nobility certainly felt that Rasputin had too much influence on royal affairs, especially during the Great War with Nicholas away at the front. The tsarina Alexandra hired and fired ministers on a disconcertingly regular basis, based entirely on Rasputin's recommendations. But Rasputin's influence only went so far – he had tried to persuade the tsar not to go to war and to halt the regular pogroms initiated against the Jews – all to no avail.

Did the British kill Rasputin?

The above story on how Rasputin was killed, accepted as fact for almost a century, has come under increasing scrutiny. The account relies entirely on Felix Yusupov himself, who was keen to take the glory for having killed Rasputin. (Yusupov was a transvestite, who once appeared as a cabaret singer dressed as a woman.)

However, more recent evidence points increasingly to the involvement of a British spy, Oswald Rayner. Rayner and Yusupov had met at Oxford, where the Russian had lived and studied for three years. If British involvement had come to light, it would have severely damaged Anglo-Russians relations during the First World War – the murder had to be seen as the work of Russians.

The British were alarmed by reports that Rasputin was trying to persuade the tsarina to use her influence to remove Russian troops from the war. The consequences of this would have allowed Germany to transfer 350,000 troops and equipment from the Eastern Front to the Western Front, greatly bolstering its forces against the Western Allies – an alarming prospect for the British and the French.

Rayner, working for the Secret Intelligence Bureau, was present at Yusupov's palace on 29 December, where the prince had lured Rasputin with the promise of women and sex. Rasputin was heavily tortured as his tormentors tried to ascertain what links he had with Germany. His testicles were 'crushed flat'.

Prince Felix Yusupov, 1914.

Yes, Yusupov did try to poison and shoot Rasputin but it was Rayner, it is now believed, that fired the fatal shot. Of the four bullets found in Rasputin's body – one was significantly different, having been fired from a revolver that was standard British issue. This bullet, shot from point blank into the centre of Rasputin's forehead, was the work of a professional killer and would have killed him instantly.

The story is chronicled in a 2010 book by Richard Cullen, *Rasputin: The Role of Britain's Secret Service in his Torture and Murder.*

Demonic

Following his murder in December 1916, the distraught tsarina, Alexandra, had Rasputin buried in the grounds of Tsarskoye Selo, the royal residence, south of Petrograd.

In 1917, after the overthrow of the tsar, a number of Petrograd workers removed Rasputin's corpse and burned it in a nearby forest. Alarmingly for the workers, Rasputin's body sat up in the flames causing them to flee in panic. The men had failed to cut the tendons thereby as the corpse heated, the tendons contracted, making his limbs twist and the torso bend at the waist. The episode may have had a logical reason but of course the workmen were not to know and it cemented Grigory Rasputin's demonic reputation.

During Stalin's rule, the autopsy report into Rasputin's death vanished and Stalin ensured that all those associated with it vanished as well.

Selected Bibliography

Alliluyeva, Svetlana, *Twenty Letters to a Friend*, 1967

Applebaum, Anne, *Iron Curtain: The Crushing of Eastern Europe 1944-56*, 2012

Arnold-Forster, Mark, *The World at War*, 1974

Atwood, Kathryn J, *Women Heroes of World War I: 16 Remarkable Resisters, Soldiers, Spies, and Medics*, 2014

Axell, Albert, *Russia's Heroes 1941-1945*, 2002

Beevor, Antony, *The Second World War*, 2012

Carey, John (Ed.), *The Faber Book of Reportage*, 1996

Evans, Richard J, *The Coming of the Third Reich: How the Nazis Destroyed Democracy and Seized Power in Germany*, 2004

Evans, Richard J, *The Third Reich in Power, 1933 - 1939: How the Nazis Won Over the Hearts and Minds of a Nation*, 2005

Gaddis, John Lewis, *The Cold War*, 2007

Gibson, Edwin and Ward, Kingsley G, *Courage Remembered: The Story Behind the Construction and Maintenance of the Commonwealth's Military Cemeteries*, 1989

Gilbert, Martin, *The Second World War*, 1989

Gilbert, Martin, *The First World War: A Complete History*, 1994

Holmes, Richard (Ed.), *The Oxford Companion to Military History*, 2001

Isaacs, Jeremy and Downing, Taylor, *Cold War: For 45 Years the World Held Its Breath*, 1998

Kershaw, Ian, *The End: Hitler's Germany, 1944-45*, 2011

Laffin, John, *Hitler Warned Us*, 1995

Lewis, Jon E (Ed.), *The Mammoth Book of How it Happened: Eyewitness Accounts of history in the making from 2000 BC to the present*, 2006

Mak, Geert, *In Europe: Travels Through the Twentieth Century*, 2008

Mawdsley, Evan, *Thunder in the East: The Nazi-Soviet War 1941-1945*, 2007

Overy, Richard, *The Dictators: Hitler's Germany, Stalin's Russia*, 2004

Overy, Richard, *Russia's War*, 1998

Prior, Robin and Wilson, Trevor, *The First World War*, 1999

Sebestyen, Victor, *1946: The Making of the Modern World*, 2014

Seligmann, Matthew, *In the Shadow of the Swastika: Life in Germany Under the Nazis 1933-1945*, 2003.

Rayner, Ed and Stapeley, Ron, *Debunking History: 150 Popular Myths Exploded*, 2009

Rees, Laurence, *The Nazis: A Warning from History*, 1997

Roberts, Andrew, *The Storm of War: A New History of the Second World War*, 2009

Schama, Simon, *A History of Britain - Volume 3: The Fate of Empire 1776-2000*, 2002

Service, Robert, *A History of Twentieth-Century Russia*, 1997

Shirer, William L, *The Rise and Fall of the Third Reich: A History of Nazi Germany*, 1964

Sixsmith, Martin, *Russia: A 1,000-Year Chronicle of the Wild East*, 2011

Taylor, AJP, *The First World War*, 1963

Volkogonov, Dmitri, *The Rise and Fall of the Soviet Empire: Political Leaders From Lenin to Gorbachev*, 2010

Walters, Guy and Owen, John (Eds.), *The Voice of War: The Second World War Told by Those Who Fought It*, 2005

Warner, Philip, *World War One: A Chronological Narrative*, 1995

Other Works by Rupert Colley

Fiction

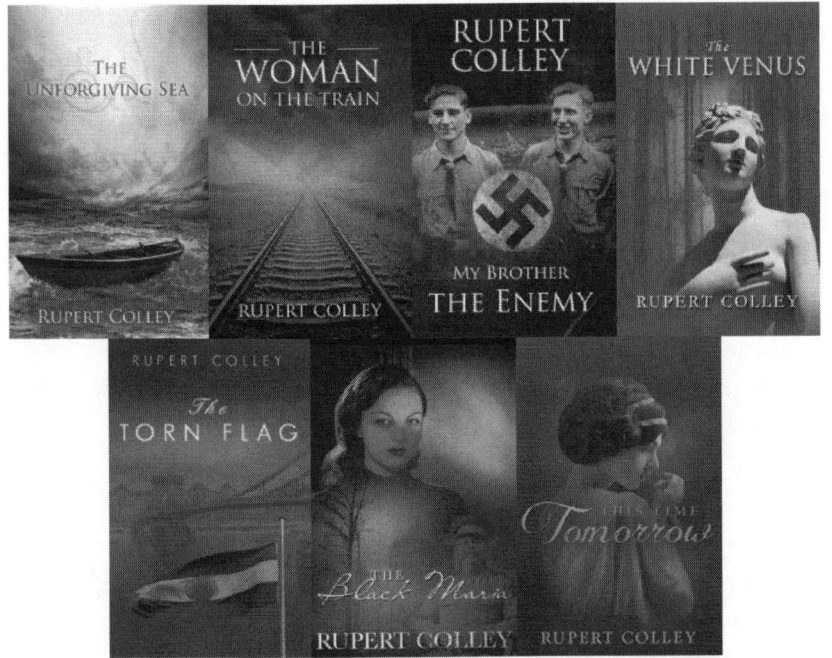

This Time Tomorrow – 'Two brothers. One woman. A nation at war.'
A compelling story of war, brotherly love, passion and betrayal during
World War One.

The Unforgiving Sea – 'Ten men adrift on a lifeboat. Only one will live to
tell the tale.'
A sequel to *This Time Tomorrow*, *The Unforgiving Sea*, set in World War Two,
is, on its surface, a tale of murder, survival and loss, while at its core we find
a story of deep love, loyalty and forgiveness.

The Woman on the Train 'Someone saves your life. How far will you go
to repay the debt?'
A war-time debt threatens to ruin a musician's career and much more.

The White Venus – 'When the ties of loyalty are severed, whom do you trust?'
Set in Nazi-occupied France during World War Two, a coming-of-age tale of divided loyalties, trust and a tragedy never forgotten but never mentioned.

The Black Maria – 'When love becomes your greatest enemy.'
A love story set in 1930s Soviet Union, a novel about fear: fear of each other, fear of being denounced, fear of Stalin's secret police; and, ultimately, the fear of falling in love.

My Brother the Enemy – 'Fear on the streets. Death on every corner. But the real enemy is the brother at his side.'
A story of jealousy, sibling rivalry and betrayal, and a desperate bid for freedom, set against the backdrop of Nazi oppression and war.

The Torn Flag – 'Sometimes the simplest of choices can have the most devastating of consequences.'
Set during the Hungarian Revolution, an epic tale of people caught in the machinations of history, where the choices you make determine your fate.

All seven novels are available as ebooks and paperbacks (http://rupertcolley.com).

History In An Hour series

World War Two: History In An Hour
World War One: History In An Hour
The Cold War: History In An Hour
The Russian Revolution: History In An Hour
Stalin: History In An Hour
Black History: History In An Hour
Nazi Germany: History In An Hour
Hitler: History In An Hour
Mussolini: History In An Hour
1914: History In An Hour
D-Day: History In An Hour
The Afghan Wars: History In An Hour
The Siege of Leningrad: History In An Hour

A History of the World Cup

Images and Disclaimers

The cover shows Adolf Hitler, Joseph Stalin, Malcolm X, and Canadian troops going 'over the top' during the First World War. Although the latter image was, in fact, a contemporary re-enactment for the sake of the cameras.

All the images used in this book are, as far as I can ascertain, in the public domain. If I have mistakenly used an image that is not in the public domain, please let me know at rupert@historyinanhour.com and I shall remove / replace the offending item as soon as I can.

Also, while I have taken great care to ensure every fact and figure is correct, there are a lot of them and I am only human. Therefore, if you spot a mistake, please just let me know without exposing me too publicly, and I will check and amend if necessary. Thank you.

Index

African National Congress, 73, 75

Alexandra, Empress, 254, 291, 292

Algerian War, 253

Alliluyeva, Nadezhda, 71, 265-6

Alliluyeva, Svetlana, 263-267, 280, 281

American Civil War, 259, 260

Arizona, ship, 277, 278

Asquith, Herbert, 15, 270, 271

Auschwitz-Birkenau Death Camp, 173, 174

Bahadur Shah II, 113

Battle of Gettysburg, 259

Battle of Kosovo, 157

Battle of Kursk, 136

Battle of Loos, 15, 79

Battle of Mons, 15

Battle of Plassey, 141-142

Battle of Stalingrad, 31-36, 136, 217

Battle of the Bulge, 40

Battle of the Somme, 16, 166-169, 269

Battle of Verdun, 17, 145, 146, 166, 167, 248

Battle of Ypres, First, 15; Second, 79, 81, 82; Third (Passchendaele), 16-17

Baucq, Philippe, 211

BBC, 19, 204

Beatles, The, 191

Bergen-Belsen Concentration Camp, 170, 174

Beria, Lavrentry, 124, 127, 137, 280-283

Berlin Wall, 187

Bismarck, Otto von, 119, 160, 254

Bismarck, ship, 119, 121

Black Hole of Calcutta, 139-143

Blitz, The, 37, 40, 41

Blomberg, Werner von, 164, 165

Boer War, First, 55-57

Boer War, Second, 15, 57

Braun, Eva, 87, 206, 207

Brezhnev Doctrine, 191

Brezhnev, Leonid, 188-190, 191

Bukharin, Nikolai, 4, 6, 66-72, 193

Butler, Lady Elizabeth, 54

Butler, William Francis, 54, 57

Bystrolyotov, Dmitri, 97-99

Cabrinovic, Nedeljko, 158, 160-161

Cameron, David, 43

Cameron, James, 26

Casor, John, 63-65

Castro, Fidel, 197, 230-231, 234

Cavell, Edith, 149, 210-213

Chamberlain, Neville, 204

Chou En-lai, 77, 78

Churchill, Sir Winston, 41, 116, 121, 128, 145, 146, 168, 248, 249, 250, 251, 252, 254, 257, 268-273, 278, 279

Ciano, Galeazzo, 238

Clive, Robert, 'Clive of India', 141-142

Cold War, 76, 93, 128, 183, 187, 230

Colley, Sir George Pomeroy, 54-57

Cuban Missile Crisis, 230-235

Curzon, Lord George, 142

Czechoslovakia, Soviet invasion of, 188-192

Dachau concentration camp, 60, 162, 203, 246

Dalser, Ida, 236

Davies, Sharron, 185

Davis, Ossie, 44

De Gaulle, Charles, 145, 248-253

De Lisle, Sir Beauvoir, 167

Der Angriff, newspaper, 91

Dettmann, Julius, 173

Dimitrov, Georgi, 61

Djilas, Milovan, 280

Dobrynin, Anatoly, 234

Donitz, Karl, 87

Dresden, bombing of 37-41, 43, 217

Dubcek, Alexander, 188-191

Dunkirk, evacuation from, 145

Dzerzhinsky, Felix 'Iron', 201

Dzhugashvili, Ekaterina, 123-4

Dzhugashvili, Yakov, 36, 265

Dzhugashvili, Vasily, 265

East German athletes, 181-187

East German Uprising, 125-128

East India Company, 109, 112, 142

Eisenhower, Dwight D, 95, 96, 126, 251

Eliasberg, Karl, 178-180

Elser, Johann Georg, 243-247

Enabling Act, 24, 61, 162

Ernst, Karl, 61

Everett, Edward, 259, 260

Ferdinand, Archduke Franz, 156, 157, 158, 159, 256, 289

First World War, 15, 20, 35, 66, 81, 87, 89, 120, 129, 135, 144, 147, 149, 156, 168, 171, 194, 210, 214, 248, 252, 268, 291

First World War Armistice, 144, 147, 248, 256

Flisges, Richard, 89, 90

Foch, Ferdinand, 18, 147, 148

France, German invasion of, 53, 144-149, 257

Frank, Anne, 8, 170-175, 197

Frank, Margot, 170, 173, 174

Frank, Otto, 170, 171, 173, 174-175

Frederick I, 153

French, John, 15, 79

Fuchida, Mitsuo, 276

Gallipoli, 270

Garvey, Marcus, 44

Geipel, Ines, 181, 182

George V, King, 18, 254

Gero, Erno, 225, 226

Gettysburg Address, 259, 260-262

Gettysburg, Battle of, *see Battle of Gettysburg*

Gleiwitz Incident, 203

Goebbels, Joseph, 22, 50, 52, 53, 58, 85, 87, 89-92, 101, 136, 152

Goebbels, Magda, 91

Gorbachev, Mikhail, 117, 297

Goring, Hermann, 34, 58, 61, 114, 147, 164, 214-219

Götz, Falko, 186

Gough, Hugh, 112

Grass, Gunter, 28

Grey, Sir Edward, 160, 255

Groener, Wilhelm, 256

Guevara, Che, 230

Guidi, Rachele, *see Mussolini, Rachele*

Gustloff, Wilhelm, 26, 28

Haber, Fritz, 79, 80, 81, 82, 83

Hague, William, 223

Haig, Dawyck, 18

Haig, Douglas, 15-19, 167, 168, 169, 269

Halder, Franz, 145

Haley, Alex, 48

Hamilton, Duke of, 116

Hardiman, Alfred Frank, 19

Harrach, Franz von, 159

Harris, Arthur 'Bomber', 37, 38, 41, 42

Havel, Vaclav, 189, 191

Hess, Rudolph, 114-118, 147, 204, 209, 218

Heydrich, Reinhard, 203, 217

Himmler, Heinrich, 13, 85, 164, 203, 215, 245, 280

Hindenburg airship disaster, 100-103

Hindenburg, Paul von, 21, 24, 59, 101, 164, 256

Hiroshima, atomic bombing of, 177, 284

Hitler, Adolf, 8, 26, 29, 33, 61, 83, 84, 91, 97, 114, 116, 118, 119, 145, 153, 170, 177, 202, 204, 213, 214, 216, 217, 218, 243, 257, 258, 274, 279, 284; and Geli Raubal, 205-209; and Mein Kampf, 114, 151, 207; and Stalingrad, 33-35; and the First World War, 87, 144; and the Night of the Long Knives, 162-165, 216; and the Reichstag Fire, 58-60, 61; appointed Chancellor, 20-24, 28, 53, 58, 88, 91, 101, 162, 170, 209, 215; assassination attempts on, 33, 243-247; death of, 84-88, 91; declares war on the US, 279; marries, 86-87

Hitler, Alois, 205

Hitler, Patrick, 206

HMS Hood, 119-122

Hoffman, Heinrich, 90, 206, 209

Hola Camp Massacre, 222-223

Holwell, John Zephaniah, 140-141, 142

Honiok, Franz, 202, 203, 204

Horst Wessel song, 22, 50, 53, 148
Hungarian Revolution, 127, 129, 131, 132, 134, 224-229
Huntziger, Charles, 148-149
Husak, Gustav, 190-191

Immerwahr, Clara, 81-82
Indian Mutiny, 109-113

Jevtic, Borivoje, 157
Jews Out Board Game, 12-14
Jodl, Alfred, 147, 148
Johnson, Anthony, 63-65
Joseph, Franz, 156, 157

Kadar, Janos, 132, 134, 229
Kahlo, Frida, 195
Kamenev, Lev, 68, 193, 195, 196
Kaplan, Fanny, 3, 198-201
Kapler, Alexei, 266-267
Keitel, Wilhelm, 147, 148-149
Kennedy, John F, 48, 230-235
Kennedy, Ludovic, 119, 120
Kenya African National Union (KANU), 221
Kenyatta, Jomo, 221, 223
Khrushchev, Nikita, 131, 132, 137, 154, 188, 226, 227, 228, 230, 231, 232, 233, 234, 235, 282-283
King, Martin Luther, 46
Kissinger, Henry, 78
Kitchener, Horatio Herbert, 15, 166, 270
Koltsov, Mikhail, 70
Krieger, Heidi, 185

Kristallnacht, 217, 244
Krupskaya, Nadezhda, 5, 7
Ku Klux Klan, 44, 45
Kun, Bela, 129
Kursk, Battle of, *see Battle of Kursk*

Larina, Anna, 71-72
Lee, Robert E, 259
Lenin, Vladimir, 3, 66, 67, 154, 193, 194, 201, 280; assassination attempt on, 3, 198-201; death of, 3-7, 195; funeral of, 6-7; Testament, 4-5, 67, 195
Lenin Mausoleum, 7
Leningrad, Siege of, 8-10, 136, 177
Leningrad Symphony, 176, 178
Lincoln, Abraham, 259-261
Lindemann, Ernst, 119, 121
Lloyd George, David, 17, 18, 271
Loren, Sophia, 242
Lubbe, Marinus van der, 58-62
Ludendorff, Erich, 23, 256
Lutjens, Gunther, 119

Mafalda, Princess, 107
Maginot Line, 144, 248
Malins, Geoffrey, 166
Mandela, Nelson, 75
Mao Zedong, 76, 77, 78, 93, 228
Marshall, George C, 95
Matteotti, Giacomo, 105
Mau Mau Uprising, 220-223
McCarthy, Joseph, 93-96
Meade, George, 259
Mein Kampf, 114, 151, 202, 207

Mercader, Ramon, 197
Metro-Goldwyn-Mayer, 288
Mindszenty, Cardinal Josef, 131
Mitbauer, Axel, 181
Molotov, Vyacheslav, 135, 153, 154
Montefiore, Simon Sebag, 123
Morrison, Herbert, 101-102
Muhammad, Elijah, 46, 47, 48
Munich Putsch, 22, 23, 114, 214, 244
Mussolini, Alessandra, 241-242
Mussolini, Benito, 104, 105-107, 213, 236-242, 279; brain of, 241-242; death of, 108, 240
Mussolini, Edda, 216, 236, 237, 238, 239, 240, 242
Mussolini, Rachele, 236-242

Nagasaki, atomic bombing of, 177, 284
Nagy, Imre, 129-134, 224-225, 226, 227, 228-229
Napier, Charles, 110
Nation of Islam, 46, 48
Nazi-Soviet Non-Aggression Pact, 29, 152, 202
Nazi Party, 13, 20, 91, 114, 116, 162, 214; Nazi Party in Switzerland, 26, 29
Nicholas II, Tsar, 66, 199, 200, 254, 289, 290, 291
Night of the Long Knives, 23, 162-165, 207, 209, 216
NKVD, The, 70, 97, 135, 193, 196, 197, 280, 281
Nobel Prize, 28, 81

Nuremberg Trials, 10, 36, 61, 116, 117, 118, 218

Olympics, The, 101, 182-183, 185, 186
Operation Barbarossa, 27, 151, 153

Palach, Jan, 192
Pandey, Mangal, 111
Papen, Franz von, 21, 23, 165
Paris Peace Conference, 257, 272
Paulus, Friedrich, 31, 33-36
Pearl Harbor, 274-278, 284, 286
Petacci, Clara, 239, 240
Petain, Henri Philippe, 146, 148, 248, 249, 252
Pfeffer, Fritz, 171, 173-174
Piaf, Edith, 212
Pius XI, Pope, 236
Poland, German invasion of, 145, 150, 202, 204, 271
Pompidou, Georges, 253
Prague Spring, 188, 191
Princip, Gavrilo, 158, 159-160, 161, 256
Pruss, Max, 101

Rakosi, Matyas, 130-131, 224-225
Rasputin, Grigory, 287-293
Raubal, Geli, 87, 205-209
Rayner, Oswald, 291-292
Reichstag Fire, 24, 58-62
Reynaud, Paul, 146, 249
Ribbentrop, Joachim von, 147, 279
Rivera, Diego, 195

Rohm, Ernst, 162, 163-165, 216
Roosevelt, Franklin D, 217, 250, 252, 274, 278
Rosenberg, Julius and Ethel, 95
Royal British Legion, 18
Russia, German invasion of, 27, 29, 151-155
Russian Civil War, 31, 135, 272
Russian Revolution, 66, 98, 129, 194, 195, 199, 272, 280

Savicheva, Tanya, 8-11
Schleicher, Kurt von, 165
Second World War, 8, 19, 26, 31, 37, 95, 106, 114, 128, 130, 135, 136, 202, 204, 216, 220, 224, 238, 273, 295, 296, 297
Sedov, Lev, 196
Sedov, Sergei, 196
Sedova, Natalia, 195, 197
Shabazz, Betty, 48
Shabazz, Malcolm, 48
Sharma, Simon, 139
Sharpeville Massacre, 73-75
Shirer, William, 148
Shostakovich, Dmitry, 176-178, 179
Sievers, Joerg, 186
Silberbauer, Karl Josef, 173
Siraj-ud-Daulah, 139, 141, 142
Sobukwe, Robert, 73
Somme, Battle of the, *see Battle of the Somme*
Speer, Albert, 117
Stalherm, Anka, 90
Stalin, Joseph, 27, 29, 31, 32, 33, 36, 71, 90, 97, 99, 123, 124,

130, 135, 136, 137, 152, 153, 154, 178, 195, 196, 201, 224, 225-226, 252, 264, 265-266, 280, 282, 293; and Bukharin, 66-71; and Lenin, 4-7, 154; and daughter, Svetlana, 263, 266-267; and Trotsky, 193, 195, 197; death of, 125, 127, 130, 137, 266, 282
Stalingrad, Battle of, *see Battle of Stalingrad*
Strasser, Otto, 207
Sverdlov, Yakov, 200

Taylor, A.J.P., 169
Theresienstadt concentration camp, 161
Titanic, film, 26, 29
Titanic, ship, 25, 26, 28, 29, 30
Tojo, Hideki, 275, 284-286
Toscanini, Arturo, 178
Tower of London, 116
Treaty of Brest-Litovsky, 66
Treaty of Versailles, 20
Tripartite Pact, 279, 284
Trotsky, Leon, 4, 7, 31, 66, 68, 71, 193-197; assassination of, 196-197

Ulbricht, Walter, 125, 127, 128
Umberto I, King, 104
Umberto II, King, 108
Uritsky, Moisei, 201

Van Pels, Hermann and Auguste, 171
Van Pels, Peter, 171, 173, 174

Vellore Mutiny, 109

Verdun, Battle of, *see Battle of Verdun*

Victor Emmanuel III, King, 104-108

Victoria Cross, 112, 169

Victoria, Queen, 57, 254

Vogel, Renate, 186

Volkov, Esteban, 196, 197

Vonnegut, Kurt, 40

Vyshinsky, Andrey, 70

Wessel, Horst, 50-53

Weygand, Maxime, 146, 149

Wiener, Alfred, 13

Wiener Library, 12, 13-14

Wilberforce, William, 110

Wilhelm Gustloff, ship, 25-30

Wilhelm II, Kaiser, 81, 104, 212, 254-258

Wilhelmina, Queen, 257

Wilson, Woodrow, 256

Wood, Sir Henry, 178

World Cup, FIFA, 187

World War One, *see First World War*

World War Two, *see Second World War*

X, Malcolm, 44-49

Yalta Conference, 38, 252

Yamamoto, Isoruku, 275-276, 278

Yezhov, Nikolai, 281

Ypres, Battles of, *see Battle of Ypres*

Yusupov, Felix, 287-289, 291-292

Zhdanov, Andrey, 178, 180, 267

Zhukov, Georgy, 32-33, 135-138

Zimmermann, Alfred, 212

Zinoviev, Grigory, 68, 193, 195, 196, 201

Zyklon B, 83

14243834R00189

Printed in Great Britain
by Amazon.co.uk, Ltd.,
Marston Gate.